The Evolution of a Cricket Fan

Samir Chopra

The Evolution of a Cricket Fan

My Shapeshifting Journey

With a Foreword by Mukul Kesavan

TEMPLE UNIVERSITY PRESS
Philadelphia • Rome • Tokyo

TEMPLE UNIVERSITY PRESS
Philadelphia, Pennsylvania 19122
tupress.temple.edu

Library of Congress Cataloging-in-Publication Data

Names: Chopra, Samir, author. | Kesavan, Mukul, foreword.
Title: The evolution of a cricket fan : my shapeshifting journey / Samir
    Chopra ; with a foreword by Mukul Kesavan
Other titles: Sporting (Philadelphia, Pa.)
Description: Philadelphia : Temple University Press, 2021. | Series:
    Sporting | Includes index. | Summary: "This memoir chronicles the
    author's evolving sense of identity as it finds expression in his
    cricket fandom. As he migrates among continents and develops his
    relationship with India's history, nationalism, and diaspora, his
    enthusiasms for teams, players, and the sport itself change"— Provided
    by publisher.
Identifiers: LCCN 2020043372 (print) | LCCN 2020043373 (ebook) | ISBN
    9781439911969 (cloth) | ISBN 9781439911976 (paperback) | ISBN
    9781439911983 (pdf)
Subjects: LCSH: Chopra, Samir. | Cricket fans—Biography. | Cricket—Social
    aspects—India. | East Indians—Foreign countries—Ethnic identity. |
    Nationalism and sports—India.
Classification: LCC GV928.I4 .C56 2021 (print) | LCC GV928.I4 (ebook) |
    DDC 796.3580954—dc23
LC record available at https://lccn.loc.gov/2020043372
LC ebook record available at https://lccn.loc.gov/2020043373

Printed in the United States of America

9 8 7 6 5 4 3 2 1

Dedicated to Ayana, my favorite companion in cricket watching.

Contents

Foreword

IF **SOCIAL MEDIA BIOS ARE** to be believed, the world is dense with cricket "tragics." This self-congratulatory term became common currency after John Howard, then prime minister of Australia, described himself as one. The word itself means nothing, being no more than a way of making a nerdy interest in cricket seem deep and interesting. A cricket tragic is a fan who fancies himself—a spectator on stilts. Unless, of course, he is the author of this book.

If ever there was a person who earned the right to be called a cricket tragic, it is Samir Chopra. His relationship with cricket, as spelled out in this marvelous book, is less a fan's obsession with a game than a witch's relationship with her familiar. In the alternative world that Philip Pullman creates in *His Dark Materials* trilogy, humans, like witches, have familiars—animal manifestations of their inner selves called "daemons."

Cricket is Chopra's daemon. Through childhood, youth, adulthood, and marriage; through his journey from New Delhi to New Jersey; through graduate school; and through the deaths of his parents and the immigrant's rites of passage, cricket is Chopra's hedge against loneliness, his shortcut to solidarity, his online community, his on-field recreation, his petting zoo, and his alter ego.

Eric Hobsbawm, the great British historian, once wrote that what makes "sport uniquely effective as a medium for inculcating national feelings, at all events for males, is the ease with which even the least political or public individual can identify with the nation as symbolised by young persons excelling at something practically every man wants to be good at.

The imagined community of millions seems more real as a team of eleven named people."

Hobsbawm could have been writing a gloss on this book. The great theme of Chopra's memoir is the fraught relationship between national identity and sport. For that sociological archetype—the English-speaking, middle-class, postcolonial Indian—following cricket is both a way of being cosmopolitan and a way of being nationalist.

Well before he acquired a passport or boarded a flight, Chopra's map of the world was a grid of fabled cricket grounds—Old Trafford, Sabina Park, the Gabba and the SCG—not famous cities. His sense of national identity, his reaction to racial prejudice, and his skepticism about a diasporic "South Asian" identity were shaped by his conflicted attitude toward the Indian cricket team.

In Pullman's world, a child's daemon shifts from one animal shape to another till the end of adolescence and the onset of adulthood when it takes on a permanent form. *The Evolution of a Cricket Fan* is Chopra's magical account of the way in which his cricketing loyalties mutate till, as an American citizen, he makes his peace with an Indian identity that now exists only in his mind.

This is not the story of the average cricket fan—thank God for that—but anyone who has been consigned by defeat into day-darkening depression or transported by victory to a hallucinogenic high will read this book grinning or grimacing with recognition. Cricket's literature is rich with magisterial histories; it now has a wonderful, maverick, coming-of-age story that lives and breathes the game.

Mukul Kesavan

Acknowledgments

WITHOUT WHOM, NOT: **MUKUL KESAVAN,** for writerly inspiration and encouragement, and for being the first one to consider reading a draft of this book; Amy Bass, for welcoming my book with open arms; my wife, Noor Alam, for listening to so many of my cricket stories, and as always, for reading manuscript drafts patiently and sympathetically; David Coady, for talking to me about cricket and listening to my rants for all these years; Satadru Sen, John Sutton, Bruce Berglund, and Sree Krishna Kumar, for reading drafts and their kindness; ESPN–Cricinfo, for letting me write for them; John Sutton, for the games we watched at the SCG; my mates at Centrals Cricket Club in Sydney for letting me play with and for them; Willow TV, for bringing cricket into my home; Ashu, Ritu, and Akul for tolerating my cricket obsession on my journeys home; and, of course, the Indian cricket team. Most of all, my father, Papa, for playing cricket, and for turning its stories into invitations to explore the world of cricket and all that lay beyond. My sincere apologies to anyone whose debts I have not acknowledged here.

My deepest debt is, as always, to my wife and best friend, Noor Alam. Thanks for making a home for Ayana and me, and for taking care of us in all the ways you do.

The Evolution of
a Cricket Fan

Introduction

THIS IS AN AUTOBIOGRAPHICAL BOOK by a voluntary exile, an immigrant. My cohort is famously supposed to suffer from dissociative identity disorder, "the presence of two or more distinct identities . . . recurrently taking control of the person's behavior."* Inconsistency and flirtations with incoherence have been an inevitable feature of my being; I carry within me many unresolved tensions. Migrants tell stories of travel, of transformations external and internal; this is mine. It marks and documents changes—political, emotional, and moral too.

I have chosen to tell this tale through cricket. It is a story about that game's presence in my life and how my response to its offerings—sporting, aesthetic, and political—reflected my changing perceptions of myself and of the nations and cultures, those of my birth and those adopted, that I called my own. As I grew and was displaced, spatially and psychically, my understanding of the activities of the men in white changed. I understood their doings differently; I fitted them into alternate templates of understanding. Most broadly then, this book details the transformation in my thoughts about the cricketing world, its cricketers, its fans, and its peoples. To chart these changes is to contribute to a larger history of how those who leave home and live elsewhere devise identities for themselves.

---

* Charles Simic, "What a Beautiful Mess," *New York Review of Books*, 20 February 2014, available at http://www.nybooks.com/articles/archives/2014/feb/20/what -beautiful-mess.

The most elaborate of intellectual systems and doctrinal commitments is a disguised autobiography, a confession. So too, with sporting preferences and hierarchies and fandoms; these serve as reflections of our inner beings, as affect-laden guides to events, people, and inclinations in our lives. To tell a story of lifelong sporting passion is to do no less than provide intimate access to our inner selves. In mine, I found old loyalties to cricket teams disrupted, and new ones built, on the strength of associated personal relations and affiliations, each reflecting inner reconciliations and turmoil. As these changed, so did my ties with cricket.

Why tell such a story of personal change through an autobiographical recounting of the following of a mere game? Because cricket has obsessed and moved me since I was a child; it has remained an invariant, an immovable fixture intersecting with every person and event in my life in some fashion. It thus offers an exceedingly good lens through which to conduct an examination, admittedly and unavoidably partial, of myself. Cricket was not a domain in which I transcended politics, a zone of dispassionate, detached, and impartial contemplation. Rather, it allowed for the vociferous expression of my political—and thus personal—sentiments, whether by something as overt as a written opinion on a blog or as covert as the emotions that surged through me when I saw a scoreboard or a telecast of a game played far away.

So this story is a public, autobiographical accounting of the irrationalities of sporting fandom. I went from being a "misautogenic" Indian—a neologism indicating the archetypal diminished postcolonial who took perverse pleasure in the thrashing of the Indian cricket team by its opponents—to becoming a fan of the Indian team, basking in its reflected glory as it embellished a homeward-bound gaze from my adopted homes and cultures and made its domain one in which I could feel and want to be Indian and, finally, ambiguously, someone with an indeterminate sense of nationality. Such descriptions do not do justice to the complexity of my life's stations. Writing this book clarifies them for myself and possibly for others too.

Like others who attempt to write memoirs, I'm struck by the intractability of recounting a coherent biography for public consumption. Our actions and our pronouncements generate an outwardly directed version of this account; its incompleteness is palpably felt by, and is visible to, its subjects. We are aware that we have kept a great deal, the iceberg's proverbial ninety percent, artfully concealed. Making this story's central character more comprehensible, by greater confessional revelation or forensic investigation, is not straightforward. We have forgotten a great deal; we remember incorrectly; we subject our autobiographies to persistent, ongoing revision; we are good at suppressing and embellishing their details—

where the devil supposedly lurks. (Like all immigrants, I remember the life left behind with more clarity than the new one I constructed on distant shores.) To make more palatable the unvarnished truth, we introduce incoherence; we might construct a too-sanitized picture of ourselves, struck by timidity at the thought of exposure. Our putatively refined exterior surfaces, mask considerably less sophisticated interiors. In writing about the past, I must, as Ernest Hemingway once suggested, keep in mind the distinction between what I felt then and what I feel I *should* have felt then.* We have layers of accreted detail in our selves; a coherent story about ourselves that takes us hundreds of hours to recount on a therapist's couch might not be for the written page. Writing a memoir is a lifetime's labor; it would be tedious and of little interest to anyone. I am not close to solving these challenges.

My relationship with Pakistan—a love affair that went bad—constitutes a prominent and significant thread in this account, offering a personal history of cricketing encounters between India and Pakistan. The game of cricket—often, in naive cricket writing, described as a force unifying nations and peoples and cultures—can also be a divisive factor. It is not just so because politicians "exploit" it. The fans may exploit the game themselves, as they bring their own highly particular agendas to their watching of cricket. The game of cricket is a text, and its fans bring their distinctive prejudices and histories to their reading and interpretation of it. The oft-told tale of modern immigration is that of diasporas bringing together two communities, of revelatory access to the other's cultural productions, and of the Internet facilitating this process. Sometimes it goes the other way, and conventional wisdom is upended. Sometimes distance may have preserved desirable illusion.

Other relationships here changed as well. There were disillusionment and honeymoons that soured. I came to understand the world of Anglo-Australian cricket—which established and represented cricketing ideals, standards of excellence, and cricketing rectitude—as exerting ideological dominion, a mental hierarchy, a hegemonic control of cricketing information and its resultant value systems. Indian cricket changed too, from being a weak outsider begging for scraps and attention and respect at the cricketing table to becoming an arrogant financial dominator of cricket, one that dispensed largesse to those clamoring for it and demanded its pound of flesh in return. Balancing these two perspectives in a stereo-

---

* Geoffrey Wolff Intro, *Best American Essays 1989* (Boston: Ticknor and Fields, 1989), 29.

scopic vision of cricket in my life has often introduced dizziness. Writing about them may induce some much-needed clarity.

My relationship with the Indian cricket team remains a complicated one. Its players carry many burdens. Most heavily of all, they bear the brunt of my frustrations with myself, the anger provoked by others but channeled to them, my need for them to wage battles on my behalf. Even those with whom they do not share nationality—in the official passport-carrying sense—have aspirational claims to make of them, based on their shared provenance. They do double duty for those Indians who live overseas: not only must they win games of cricket; they must also win them in a particular way. The players are thus pawns, unknowingly engaging in disputes pertaining to pride, respect, and the establishment of nationalist credentials. Their treatment by those who are not Indian is no kinder: they are expected to conform to standards selectively applied to them, drawn up and established by strangers from distant lands, caught up in archaic conceptions of them and their cultures. The Indian cricket team might not realize their cricket is a conflict, its parameters established by their fellow citizens and those they joust with—whether on the field or in print or in virtual spaces online. The phrase "proxy war" is bandied about when speaking of sporting contests, and it is an appropriate one, because it speaks of the waging of political and cultural conflict by the medium of sport, for the settling of scores on a field. The Indian cricket team must play its overspecified role in such battles; it is expected to provide healing balms to wounds inflicted by history—an exceedingly onerous task.

It is common in current cricketing literature to make (often amateurish) psychological or sociological claims about the modern Indian fan, but rarely is that fan heard from. This book attempts to remedy that shortcoming. Cricket's greatest modern crisis is a growing rift between the old world and the new world; for this difference to be bridged, fans need to hear from each other, to understand one another better.* My book contributes to this project by providing access to the inner world of the Indian cricket fan and helping the world of cricket understand how its most important demographic might think about and respond to the game's offerings. Most cricketing literature is written by specialists—professional journalists, historians, retired or currently active players—who write from an expert detached perspective, describe the past or present glories of the game, or write biographies of cricketing greats. Autobiographies in

---

* Samir Chopra, *Brave New Pitch: The Evolution of Modern Cricket* (New Delhi: HarperCollins, 2012); Jon Gemmell, *Cricket's Changing Ethos* (London: Palgrave Macmillan, 2018); Gideon Haigh, *Sphere of Influence* (Melbourne: Victory Books, 2010).

cricket literature are mostly written by those who have played the game at the highest level or those who have commented or spoken on it. To inject the emotionally charged narrative of a personal, nonexpert memoir into this discourse is to run the risk of not fitting into an existing normative template of how cricket is to be written about. But this project acquires its relevance from cricketing history in understanding cricket's role in the lives of its fans, a commitment that enables it to rise above the level of being a mere reportage of events and feelings in my life. History is a broad and capacious enough notion to include personal narratives coupled with pointed reflection. This book thus finds its place among the many histories that have emerged from India since its independence, a task unfinished because of the variegated dimensions of the Indian experience. Cricket has played a crucial cultural and political role in this domain; the task of those who write on India and cricket is to adequately explore their relationship to each other. Personal histories such as mine are a tiny fragment of this undertaking.*

My memoir, as a work of history that tracks the transformation of an exile, contributes to histories of the Indian diaspora and to both immigrant and postcolonial literatures by addressing questions that perplexed writers as varied as V. S. Naipaul and Vladimir Nabokov: How does the immigrant view his or her home from afar? What is the curious mixture of shame and pride that the postcolonial immigrant's vision captures? How does the postcolonial immigrant view her or his home from his new home? How does life among the colonizers change the self-perception of the colonized and of that of the new home, now understood through the cognitive and intellectual lenses provided by the colonizer? Nations are not merely physical locations but also ideas; those that immigrants enter-

---

* As Ramachandra Guha writes in *India after Gandhi: The History of the World's Largest Democracy* (New York: HarperCollins, 2007), "The Republic of India is a union of twenty-eight states, some larger than France. Yet not even the bigger or more important of these states have had their histories written. In the 1950s and 60s India pioneered a new approach to foreign policy, and to economic policy and planning as well. Authoritative or even adequate accounts of these experiments remain to be written. India has produced entrepreneurs of great vision and dynamism—but the stories of the institutions they built and the wealth they created are mostly unwritten . . . there are no proper biographies of some of the key figures in our modern history" (p. 13). Guha's analysis here is, sadly enough, almost wholly correct. Guha's own opus, cited above, runs to over eight hundred pages, and yet it is barely more than a sampler, an appetizer, a pointer to the many corners of modern Indian history that remain unexplored. In the face of a historical project as imposing as that of modern India's, even such large works can do little more than gesture at their own insignificance.

tain about their former homes are an important component of nationalist visions that might otherwise be thought to be grounded exclusively in nativism.

In the realm of cricketing literature centered on personal testimonials, works such as *You Must Like Cricket?* by Soumya Bhattacharya and *The Commonwealth of Cricket* by Ramachandra Guha jostle for space with the works of professional cricket writers of the old and new guards—including John Arlott, E. W. Swanton, and Gideon Haigh—who have written personal histories of their relationships to cricket, whether in the playing or the watching. My book sets itself apart self-consciously by being the testimonial of a fan. I do write on cricket, but I do not consider myself a professional journalist or writer on the subject. In what follows, I hope that the fan is visible first and foremost. That presence, along with its supposed irrationality and the unreliability of autobiographical memory, are thought to be the memoir's greatest weakness. However, the considerations I raise above should place this personal work in its proper cultural context and establish its putatively nonacademic nature as its greatest strength. (For even if memory does distort, these distortions are themselves valuable.)

Cricket often brought forth unflattering dimensions of my always-under-construction self. I consider myself politically progressive, but I have been prone to illiberal tendencies and thoughts. In my watching and understanding of cricket, I was often vulnerable to an unvarnished, unreconstructed take, an immediate, visceral response clouded by emotion. I was susceptible to nationalist propaganda, to faux patriotism, to prejudice of every sort. In using these terms to describe my political influences, I am aware I am being more reflective than I ever was, that my writerly self might be considerably removed from my other selves. Cricket was able to bring out both the best and the worst in me; my responses to the game offered me clues to understanding which aspect had come to the fore.

My identity is still not determinate. This book is an attempt to make its outlines a little less blurred.

Prelude

The White Raven

O N 15 MARCH 2001, I worked in my postdoctoral fellow's office at the University of New South Wales in Sydney, Australia. As the clock ticked to 3:00 P.M., I opened a window on the Cricinfo website to check scores in the India-Australia Test, the second of the soon-to-be-epic 2001 series, being played at Kolkata. The day before, I had played hooky, sitting in a pub and watching the Indian batsmen Rahul Dravid and V.V.S. Laxman shock a nation and an entire cricketing order as they transformed the game from a near-certain Australian win—which promised to be that champion side's seventeenth consecutive victory in Test cricket—into first, a face-saving draw for India and then incredibly, to a possible Indian win. Now, as compensation for that afternoon of relentless daydreaming, of attention and passion directed elsewhere, I would have to pretend to do esoteric research in my office-bound distracted state.

My curiosity ran high. I opened a window on the Internet Relay Channel (IRC), where cricket aficionados discussed the events described by the text commentary scrolling by on their screens. It had been years since I had spent time on IRC. I was soon reminded why: irate Australians and Englishmen were berating the Indian captain, Saurav Ganguly, for not trying to force a win by expeditiously declaring the Indian innings closed. Patronizing criticism of Indian Test captains and accusations of Indian timidity and meekness were a dime-a-dozen rite of passage for its Anglo-Australian denizens. I cared little for the opinions of these self-appointed guardians of the world's cricketing morals, who seemed incapable of recognizing the events of the day before, who continued to insist the Indian team conform to their preconceived notions of positive play. I considered such critique my prerogative and resented their constant suggestion that Indian cricketers were too timid, more interested in saving their skins than seeking victory.

The Indian declaration finally came. Australia set off in chase of an improbable 384 for victory. More realistically, the strongest team in the world had to bat for little less than a day to save the Test. I continued to work, keeping the text commentary window open as an avenue for persistent distraction. A doctoral student or postdoctoral fellow occasionally stopped by to discuss the mathematical and philosophical intricacies of nonmonotonic reasoning, modal logic, belief revision, or Test cricket. I idly observed the day wind down. The first Australian wicket fell at 74, the second at 106, and then, to a brief flurry of excitement among the carrels on our floor, the third wicket at 116. But Steve Waugh was still there. Surely Captain Courageous, the perfect man for a cricketing crisis, would save the match and take it to its logical drawn conclusion.

Around seven in the evening, I walked out of campus, toward the bus stand on Anzac Parade. I intended to watch the closing session of the Test at a pub close to my apartment in Surry Hills, as the match would wind down to an honorable no-result outcome, keeping the series alive for the third Test after it had seemed a humiliating innings defeat would wrap up a nice little 2–0 gift for the touring Australians. Buses, as usual, were in short supply, and when they did arrive, they could only move ponderously through Sydney's rush-hour traffic. I patiently rode the number 393 bus to Cleveland Street, disembarked, and decided to make a quick score check at a grocery store before heading for beers and cricket at the Crown Hotel. As I entered the store, a roar went up from the tinny little speakers of a radio playing in a corner. I asked the shopkeeper the score. Bemused, he replied seven wickets had already fallen. That roar—that full-throated emission from a packed Indian crowd at Kolkata—meant *eight* wickets were down. Two more wickets lay between India and one of the greatest Test wins of all time. I left, sprinting down Cleveland Street toward the Crown Hotel, my disbelieving mind awhirl. I had never imagined such a turn of affairs: Victory was possible after suffering the humiliation of following on, after facing almost certain defeat against the world's strongest team, an unbeatable one reckoned among the greatest in cricket's history.

Several beers later that night, I stumbled home and fell into bed, unable to comprehend the scale of the cricketing event that had just transpired. I was shaken. Nothing like this had seemed remotely possible in the years I had watched and followed cricket. I thought of the 1983 World Cup, so long ago—another life, another place, another improbability. This Test was in those same precincts of implausibility. I had never spun out a cricketing fantasy so exotic, so schoolboyish. Never had I dreamed of a comeback so over the top, so back from the edge, so against the wall. Even as a youngster, hopelessly mired in daydreams, I had never, ever, dreamed up something like this. But knowing who I was then, I knew I had been incapable of concocting such a fantasy—with its winners and losers.

IN THE LATE 1970S, my father bought me the Indian sportswriter Partab Ramchand's *Great Moments in Indian Cricket*.* He knew his son was a bookish, nerdish fan of the game and anticipated my grateful acceptance and enjoyment of his gift. He would have been disappointed to find I had been crestfallen on reading Ramchand's book. Of the ten Tests selected by Ramchand—over a period ranging from 1952, when India racked up its first Test win against England at Madras, to 1976, when India chased 403 runs in the fourth innings against the West Indies at Port of Spain—India had won nine. The solitary loss in Ramchand's list came against England at Leeds in 1967. India had lost after following on, staving off an innings defeat, and forcing England into an awkward run chase.

The names associated with these memorable Indian Test victories—and one gallant act of resistance in a losing cause—constituted a veritable pantheon of Indian cricketing greats. But I was not interested in their achievements; I was interested in reading about India's opponents. Reading about India's wins in Test cricket was useful insofar as it granted me access to the feats of the world's cricketers. I had imagined "great moments in Indian cricket" occurred when overseas players—India's opponents—did well against India. And so I pounced with delight on every line by Ramchand that indicated approval of, or pleasure at, an opponent's skills. Those were feats of skill and strength and sporting valor, every one of them.

I read the book again and again, selectively filtering Indian accomplishments—including some of India's most dramatic personal achievements in Test cricket—setting them aside, and suffering little starts of irritation at language that praised Indian players or criticized the opposing team. I thought descriptions of Indian gallantry were guilty of borrowing language better used to describe more valiant players: India's opponents. I thought Ramchand's descriptions of Vinoo Mankad—one of India's greatest all-rounders, an artful left-arm spinner, enticing stodgy

---

* Partab Ramchand, *Great Moments in Indian Cricket* (New Delhi: Vikas, 1977).

English batsmen beyond the sacrosanct Laxman Rekha* of the batting crease so that they could be stumped by the wicketkeeper—were overwrought and hyperbolic. I, so used to, and enamored of, the magisterial tone and baroque prose of English and Australian cricket writers, found this figurative invocation of a classic Indian description of deception incongruous in writing of cricket action. The linguistic frameworks for cricket seemed only to be constructed and informed by Anglo-Australian pens and tastes. I found little charm too, in Ramchand's descriptions of Indian fans bringing an elephant to the Oval on Ganesh Chaturthi Day on 23 August 1971, the day before India would wrap up its first Test and series win in England on one of its most historic grounds. It was an overt display of Indianness that would have made me cringe with embarrassment had I been present at the Oval that day.

I made excuses for India's opponents. I noted that India's thrilling win over Australia at Bombay in 1964 was aided by the injured Norman O'Neill's inability to bat in both innings. The Australians had lost by a narrow margin; surely they would have won had that thunderous strokemaker been fit enough to display his wares. In any case, the Australians had fought hard. They were worthy opponents to be generously acknowledged and applauded. So I understood the concept of being a good loser, but I did not see fit to extend the notion to India in the Leeds Test against England in 1967. India's fight-back in the second innings after following on had sent Ramchand on a tear; his prose seemingly grew several shades of purple. Ramchand made much of the fact that the English batsmen Geoffrey Boycott and Ken Barrington had crawled against the Indian bowlers, scoring runs at a glacial pace. I was uncaring; they were scoring runs against India. I was infuriated that Ramchand mocked Boycott's slow batting, as he wrote with some glee that English newspapers had called for him to be given the "Barrington chop"—to be dropped for slow scoring.† I considered Indian batsmen slowpokes, and frequently accused Sunil Gavaskar, India's greatest batsman, of subjecting me to endless te-

---

* In the great Indian epic *Ramayana*, Laxman, the brother of Rama, is entrusted with the security of his sister-in-law, Sita, while Rama is away. Laxman draws a line—a *rekha*—with magical protective powers around Sita's hut, advising her to not step beyond it to remain safe from the various demons and sprits that inhabit the forest. In Laxman's absence however, Sita is enticed beyond this magical line by the demon ten-headed king Ravana, who cajoles and entreats her to step over it and then when she does, kidnaps her and flees with his misbegotten bounty.

† Martin Williamson, "Geoff Boycott's Indian Bore," ESPNcricinfo, 22 September 2012, available at http://www.espncricinfo.com/magazine/content/story/583298.html, last accessed 26 January 2015.

dium. This criticism by an upstart Indian writer of an English batsman for slow scoring, a sin only committed by Indian batsmen, was entirely unwarranted.

I did not empathize with India; I did not feel its slights the way other Indians did. Ramchand had been angered by Godfrey Evans, the retired English wicketkeeper who, in writing for local papers, had recommended after the first day of the Leeds Test that India not be granted the privilege of playing five-day Tests in England. Ramchand's parting shot, as he wrapped up his glowing descriptions of India's comeback, was, "I wonder what Godfrey Evans had to say in his column later that week." This seemed gratuitous. India had lost; that it had delayed the inevitable seemed inadequate grounding for this smug satisfaction. I remained unconvinced and ungracious.

I took other teams' misfortunes to heart. Reading of the Kanpur Test in 1959, I paid little attention to Ramchand's descriptions of Jasu Patel's mesmerizing off-breaks and instead, with dismay, noted Australia's collapse that gave India its win. Reading of the Delhi Test against Australia in 1969–1970, I glumly resigned myself to India's bowling, as Bishen Singh Bedi and Erapalli Prasanna—with five wickets each—spun India to victory. When I read of the 1976 Port of Spain Test, I was thrilled by descriptions of Viv Richards's powerful stroke play. But despite the comparisons with Don Bradman's 1948 "Invincibles"—the Australian team which on its unbeaten tour of England had made itself the first to score over four hundred runs in the fourth innings of a Test—I failed to register the significance of India's emulation of their feat.

As I read of India's run chase at the Oval in 1971 en route to their victory over our old colonial masters, I found myself hoping the Indian batsmen would not attain the target. But there was no denying them. I was reading of deeds past. I looked at the photographs of the Indian team standing on the balcony at the Oval, waving to their loyal England-resident fans below and tried to summon up pride. But I could not.

EARLY IN 2004, India played the premier events in its cricket calendar: Test tours of Australia and Pakistan. That northern winter and southern summer, I spent my academic break in Melbourne and Sydney, flying back to my old home from New York City, forking out hard-earned money for airfare and tickets to the Tests. Disappointingly, India drew 1–1 with Australia. After winning in Adelaide and holding a strong position in Melbourne but losing, India failed to win the final Test at Sydney. On the last day of the final Test, sitting in the stands at the Sydney Cricket Ground, I was unable to urge the Indian team on to a series-clinching win. I returned to New York City crestfallen, acutely aware I had missed out on a chance to witness the kind of cricketing glory I had grown to dream of.

Back home in New York, I paid a hundred dollars to a bootleg vendor to watch a livestream video feed of India's tour of Pakistan and spent many sleepless nights following India's fortunes till that final moment of glory at Rawalpindi as India romped to a series win. I was jubilant; a long-held dream of beating Pakistan in Pakistan had been realized. Someday we would beat the Australians in Australia too. Beating them at home in India, as in 1998 and 2001, had been satisfying, but nothing would match the sensation of shutting up and shutting out the Australian team—and the crowds that came out to cheer them—in the best manner possible: a Test series win in Australia.* I had lived in Australia for two years and loved the country and its people, but when it came to cricket, the gloves were off.

At some point in the new millennium, I had read Mihir Bose's *A History of Indian Cricket* and Ramachandra Guha's *Corner of a Foreign Field*. I read Indian histories of Indian cricket again. I reread descriptions of the games Ramchand had written about in his book-length tribute so many years ago. Now I gloried in their details and their descriptions of Indian cricketing skill, now occasions to feel a preening pride in the Indian team's wins. I read about much more as well: the early colonial days of Indian cricket on Bombay's crowded maidans, the simultaneously generous and patronizing cricketing education of India and Indians by their English rulers, the English exclusion of Indian players from Bombay's cricket grounds, the struggles of Indian cricketers to command the respect—cricketing and otherwise—of their English counterparts, the failure of touring English players to accept or respect the decisions of Indian umpires, the English players who treated Indian babus as their servants. I read how cricket became not just a cultural and sporting phenomenon with a distinctively Indian flavor, one removed in space and time and style from its English origins, but also a forum for the expression of Indian national sentiments, an avenue along which Indian self-realization could march, a stage on which Indian sporting competence—and thus that of the nation—could be demonstrated.†

---

* A dream that would finally come true in January 2019, as India would win a Test series in Australia for the first time, led ably by their brash and brilliant captain, Virat Kohli. And in 2021, India would win again in Australia, this time with an even more dramatic denouement. See "Postscript."

† Mihir Bose, *A History of Indian Cricket* (London: Andre Deutsch, 1992); Ramachandra Guha, *Corner of a Foreign Field* (New Delhi: Picador, 2002).

The Indian history of cricket was replete with instances of colonial prejudice and servility reinforcing each other. I read with incredulity that Tony Greig was the first reigning captain of England to tour India with an English team; others had simply not bothered to tour, not deigning to grace this tiresome, enervating, dusty land and its grinning, simpering, dusky natives with their regal presence. The Board of Cricket Control in India (BCCI) in its past incarnations—as opposed to its current one of the economic masters and puppeteers of world cricket—seemed fawning and meek, overly eager to please touring teams. I read of the board's refusal to treat the Indian team on par with visitors from foreign lands: cricket teams from overseas traveled through India by train on air-conditioned coach, the Indian team in ordinary first-class. Indian cricket had catered to the whims and prejudiced sensibilities of touring teams; it had reinforced their diminished assessment of India and all things Indian.

In my newfound sense of postcolonial identity, after reading of the lack of solidarity shown by the Caribbean's black people to their East Indian compatriots during the Indian team's tours, I found the West Indies just a little less admirable. My childhood heroes' home crowds seemed less friendly, less festive. I looked for, and read of, diaspora pride, of how the East Indian Caribbean community in Trinidad and Guyana had proudly welcomed the 1953 Indian team and how Indian fielding had impressed Caribbean crowds. I knew just how they had felt.

I eagerly looked for evidence of Indian assertion in cricket but found little. When I read of Wesley Hall and Roy Gilchrist bouncing India into submission in the 1958–1959 series, I wondered whether Indian umpires, who did not rebuke the West Indies' excessively intimidatory bowling, were infected with the BCCI's kowtowing sensibilities. I wondered too, about the Indian lack of resistance in the face of fast bowling. Why did our batsman not hook and pull more, launching a fierce counterattack against the hostility that sought to cow them? Why did they instead back away, from both fast bowling and cricketing fortitude?

I had once been a clone of those hankering for Anglo-Saxon approval in the 1930s and 1940s and later. Those men, Ranjitsinhji and Duleepsinhji, whose playing for England had once seemed like such an honor, whose stories I had lapped up with delight in the Neville Cardus books I had once so loved, now seemed considerably less heroic to me. They appeared as little more than "brown sahibs," the original "coconuts"—brown on the outside, white on the inside. I had once thought like one myself. How had things come to be that my conception of cricket and thus myself—or was it the other way around—had changed so much?

Part I

Genesis and Misautogeny

An Australian friend once described my interest in cricket as "neutral." Our conversation had centered on my obsessive following of cricket: I watched Tests all day, from the first to the last ball; I read cricket books by the dozen; I rattled off cricketing statistics at will; I speculated about the cricketing fortunes of countries other than my own. My friend was, like me, interested in the history of the game. He too was fascinated by the statistical markers and feats it had thrown up over the years. But his primary interest, nevertheless, was Australian cricket. He followed those Tests and one-day internationals Australia played; cricket was another game Australia was good at, one more venue in which he could assert his being Australian. Despite talk of "cultural cringe"—that particularly Australian manifestation of postcolonial insecurity and diminishment*—my Australian friend seemed to possess an unambiguous national identity, a zone of comfortable security. I had several such identities, and very often, none to my liking. And I was never neutral in my following or understanding of cricket.

I was born in Maihar, in the state of Madhya Pradesh in Central India, home to the Maihar *gharana* (school) of Indian classical music and the sarod and sitar maestros Baba Ala-ud-din Khan, Ali Akbar Khan, and Ravi Shankar. My hometown had its plebian side: in 1930, shortly after finish-

---

* Arthur Angel Phillips, *A. A. Phillips on the Cultural Cringe* (Melbourne: Melbourne University Publishing, 2006).

ing his studies at Lahore's Government College, my grandfather moved there to manage limestone mines owned by his in-laws. He left his ancestral home in the Punjab behind; it is now part of Pakistan. Every generation after his was displaced. His three sons, one of them my father, grew up elsewhere. As did their children; Maihar was never home for me.

My father, after schooling at New Delhi's Modern School and St. Stephens College, then ranked among the postcolonial new Indian middle-class' elite educational institutions, declined to join the family business and became an Indian Air Force pilot instead. He had been away at a "nonfamily" air force base when my mother, then staying with her in-laws, my grandparents, had given birth to me. My mother had been born in Batala in the Indian Punjab. She was married to my father after stubbornly resisting—for five years—my grandfather's demands that she marry one of the many well-qualified suitors he had lined up for her. It is an enduring legend about my mother that this resistance was enacted so that she could complete the education she desired for herself. My grandfather had first attempted to marry my mother off after she finished high school. Then she had indicated she wanted to attend university and study English literature. My grandmother was suitably and energetically supportive. Later, after my mother finished her first degree, my grandmother again supported her as she rejected another suitor, claiming she wanted to earn a postgraduate degree. She did so, taking an especial interest in American fiction and literary criticism. Only then did she agree to her father's suggestions that she meet a dashing air force pilot who seemed like a good match for her. That young aviator—looking for an urban Anglophone Anglophile like himself—had to be content with a small-town Anglophone instead. My mother liked her potential groom, even though she thought he was a little stuck-up and distant. He, for his part, expecting a small-town woman to be considerably unsophisticated, was pleasantly surprised by her keen and cosmopolitan interest in his flying and his European travels.

Once they were married, my father introduced my mother to air force life with its secluded, poorly equipped bases; the frequent unrelieved loneliness; the glamorous though often dangerous flying of fighter jets; the mixed-sex gatherings that served meat and alcohol late into the night, where women sipped on rum and Cokes and danced the twist and the foxtrot with men who were not their husbands; and the adventurous travel to remote parts of India, sometimes by road, sometimes by train. There was adventure and camaraderie too on those airbases and a sense of community often found elusive in civilian life.

My elder brother and I were military brats. Our father was our hero and idol; we were fascinated by fighter jets and the men who flew them. We were enamored of the happy-go-lucky life that seemed to be the life of the serviceman. We knew little of its challenges. My parents kept my brother and I well insulated from the low salaries and the inadequate housing; we were surrounded by bounties of other kinds. My father told us nothing of his career destroying clashes with obdurate, cruel, and incompetent senior officers or of the crippling military bureaucracy that drove grown men to distraction and made the cockpit the safest place to be for a pilot.

I loved and admired my father. He was a fighter pilot, a man who had fought in two wars, capable of feats of valor and skill that boggled my juvenile mind. He was impossibly charismatic. How could he not be, when he could pull off tricks like telling me one bright morning as he headed for work, stomping out the door in his flying overalls and boots, "Watch the sky to the right of the house at five; I'll be in the second jet that comes over," and then sure enough, showing up as promised, at the right time, in the right place. His Hawker Hunter appeared like a wraith on the horizon, silent and lithe, skimming improbably low over a grove of eucalyptus trees, and then suddenly, quickly, it was flying past our house as I heard its Rolls-Royce engine ear-shatteringly announce its awesome presence. I could not see my father in the cockpit. He had become identical with the sleek and powerful jet he flew.

My father flew fighter jets—French Mystère IV As and Russian Sukhoi-7s—with distinction in the 1965 and 1971 wars against Pakistan, earning a gallantry medal for his efforts in the former conflict. But he said little about his wartime experiences. I would often ask for stories of his wartime service, his medal, and his exploits in combat. My father's measured response was that he was "doing his job." He described war as an overly exalted combination of the tedious and the terrifying, as "ninety percent boredom and ten percent confusion." A more determined deglamorizer of war would be hard to find.

I grew up in an air force pilot's home, supposedly the abode of a militaristic patriot, a veritable den of unvarnished patriotism. But my father did not—despite his large, eclectic book collection that included American, Russian, English, and French masters of philosophy and literature and his combat experience in two of India's post-Independence wars—own many books on Indian military history. Instead, I read books by English and French pilots like Neville Duke, Pierre Clostermann, and Johnnie Johnson. I read books about the legendary and legless ace Douglas Bader, one of the Royal Air Force's many heroes of the epic Battle for Britain. I read of aerial and land and naval combats in the First and Second World Wars, as the Allies took on the Axis. And I read of air battles in Korea and Vietnam, of the exploits of those who flew Sabres and Phantoms.

But of Indian military history, I knew little. My wartime heroes were not Indian; they were from elsewhere. The only descriptions of Indian heroism I read were in a little booklet that accompanied my father's medal investiture ceremony, which described briefly the exploits of those being awarded honors on that day, and a few purplish blurbs in Indian newsmagazines. My father would not talk about his own heroism; nor did he talk of Indian military exploits before or after Independence. He seemingly did not read books about Indian wars. Or if he did or had—as he must have when attending the Indian Defense Services Staff College—he did not talk about them with me.* He did not instruct me to instill Indian heroism in my mind, to make it my lodestar.

My father might have fought for his country, but his admiration was often directed elsewhere. He had not joined the Indian Air Force to defend his country, to lay down his life for his nation. More than anything else, he had wanted to fly. It was the adventurous thing to do, the logical next step after his sporting adventures in college playing cricket, boxing, and hiking in the Himalayas. In 1960, as a young pilot, he had traveled through Europe, fulfilling a long-held dream, one he had saved and scrimped for. That journey—travel to a distant, inaccessible land of unimaginable promise and accomplishment—had acquired mythical status in my mind. My father spoke glowingly of Europe's literary, cultural, and artistic achievements and of its rich and storied history. Elsewhere, not here, was the place to be. Others, not Indians, were the ones to emulate.

But even when my father pointed me to India, I looked away. My father's vinyl record collection—the music I grew up with and that served to acculturate my sonic senses—was played on a turntable, piped through a Philips amplifier, and emitted through a pair of custom-made speakers. It was eclectic and diverse, ranging from Amir Khusrow ghazals and *qawwalis* to Bill Haley and the Comets to Benny Goodman to Ella Fitzgerald to Louis Armstrong to K. L. Saigal to Noor Jehan to Polish jazz to Cuban salsa to Bollywood soundtracks to Manu Dibango to Tchaikovsky to Bach. From this diverse buffet of offerings, I mostly selected and listened to the non-Indian music. Despite my father's suggestions that I sample the pleasures of Indian classical instrumental and vocal music, despite being born

---

* In my father's defense, as the Indian military analyst Arjun Subramaniam—among others—has noted, Indian military history has been notoriously poorly studied. Arjun Subramaniam, "Military History as Adjunct of Political Strategy," *The Hindu*, 5 November 2014, available at http://www.thehindu.com/opinion/op-ed/military-history-as-adjunct-of-political-strategy/article6564499.ece, last accessed 26 January 2015.

in the town that had been the birthplace of some of India's greatest classical musicians, in a family whose members counted those men as de facto uncles, in a house that sometimes staged their informal concerts, I could not. It was incongruous with my life and its configuring parameters.

I lived in an India that had only recently—in 1947, twenty years before I was born—become independent of English rule. Growing up in this India, a nation unsure of its self-worth after so many years of systematic—and for many Indians, shamefully easily maintained—subjugation, meant my Indian identity was up for contestation. I was not satisfied with the one I had by birth and citizenship; I was implicitly—and sometimes explicitly—instructed not to be happy with it by all that surrounded me, by a lexicon in which the synonym for *heaven* was *abroad* and the synonym for *good* was *imported* or *foreign*, and where contact with a relative returned from abroad was a brush with fame. A late-night trip to Delhi's Palam International Airport to pick up or drop off relatives or friends was always occasion for melancholy. Others traveled to distant lands; I did not. They brought back shopping bags stuffed with markers and mementos of their travels: chocolates and electronic goods wrapped in packaging never seen in India. When I viewed Hollywood movies, my gaze was directed not just at the actors on the screen. I looked around the edges, at the landscapes, the mode of living, the objects and detritus that surrounded them.

I was often told tales of Indian history, of how glorious our past was, how accomplished and prescient our sages and ancient science, how rich and varied our culture, how wise our philosophical systems and scriptures, how India was the Golden Bird, despoiled by uncultured and cruel invaders of all stripes. But this momentous and distinguished past was of little interest to me when I lived in a considerably more humdrum and undistinguished present. The rich and varied culture that was supposed to be mine belonged instead to another India, one I was cut off from by time and space and language.

I was most distant from Indian culture in terms of language, for Indian languages were not ones in which I expressed myself the most fluently. They were not languages that did justice to my bookish self, and which, no matter how many government-sponsored television programs I was exposed to, simply failed to tickle my sensibilities. I grew up in a mixed-language household in which my parents spoke a mixture of English and Hindi. My father spoke predominantly in English, with some Hindi, with my mother, brother, and myself. My mother spoke in both English and Hindi with us, but the former often took precedence. The language of the streets outside our home was a potpourri of Hindi-Urdu-Hindustani—my experience of air force bases was restricted to those in

North India, and my civilian life was spent in New Delhi—but our social milieu, made up of air force officers drawn from all over polyglot India, relied on English. The movies we watched in theaters were in English; the weekly Sunday television movie was in Hindi-Urdu-Hindustani. The former was first-class, the real thing; the latter, a plebian substitute to be watched with the hoi polloi. The language of instruction in the schools I attended was English; we learned Hindi as a language in a separate class. My grades in Hindi were poor; when I studied Sanskrit for three years, I did even worse, reaching my nadir in the eighth grade, when I scored precisely sixteen marks out of one hundred. These Indian languages were alien, foreign languages to me. My reading skills in them were poor, my writing only a notch or two above chicken scratches in the dust.

So I grew up bilingual, but the combinatorial explosion of words and concepts that takes place in a child learning a language occurred for me in English, because it was the language of instruction in school, the language in which I was introduced to bookish knowledge, and as such, the language in which I began to read outside school. It became the language in which I dreamed, fantasized, speculated, wondered, and schemed. I spoke Hindi with some family members and English with yet others; I spoke Hindi with some friends and English with others. But when I was by myself and my books, which was a great deal of the time, I thought and imagined in English. It became, very quickly, my first language. It was the language of those whose works I read, who wrote on India, and of Indians too, writing about themselves. It was the language with which I constructed my visions of India, my nation, and myself.

I suspect one of the reasons I respected and admired my father so was that he seemed distinctively not-Indian. He did things most Indians did not: he flew jets and he did things those men in the war comics and books I read did. Somehow, by virtue of fighting in wars and achieving victory, a most un-Indian thing it seemed, he had been not-Indian. My father's elder brother might have been a distinguished and accomplished choreographer of Indian classical dance, but those bodily movements, which to a trained interpreter transmitted rich poetic and cultural messages, indeed an entire aesthetic and philosophy, were utterly incomprehensible to my sensibilities. I had been born in a town host to India's most distinguished school of classical music, but those chords found little resonance with my aural apparatus. I was living in India, growing up a stranger in a strange land.

India was on the margins, a place where little of consequence or quality happened or was made so. We possessed the world's most productive movie industry, but the movies I wanted to see came from elsewhere, and they came years late to our shores. We might have had the world's most prolific playback singers, but the music I wanted to listen to was not made in India, and again, it came to India years after it was released. Things happened first somewhere else; we were sent the remainders once the world had vetted them. We were diminished versions of those that lived elsewhere; we were pale copies, aspirants, wannabes. We strove to catch up; we were never there. I wanted therefore, to be someone and somewhere else.

I found some imagined lives to supply me with clues. Besides superheroes inspired by DC and Marvel comics, I found human heroes in the Second World War comics and books my brother and I read. When I played war games, I cast myself as a U.S. marine storming a Pacific beach, earning glory at Saipan, Tarawa, or Iwo Jima, or as a U.S. navy pilot, flying Grumman F6F Hellcats or Vought F4U Corsairs off an aircraft carrier or land airstrip, shooting down Japanese Zeros. My brother wanted to be a rugged Russian army soldier, driving the Wehrmacht back from Leningrad and Stalingrad. Somehow, we did not cast ourselves in the role of an Indian Air Force pilot waging war against Pakistan.

Other childhood fantasies were engendered by street and courtyard games of cricket. My imagined cricketing life—enacted solo in our backyard by my whirling a wooden log over and about my head, much to the embarrassment of my mother—revolved around an Australian cricketer. He scored centuries on debut, scored double centuries in quick time, opened the bowling, and batted at number three. I gave him a long and distinguished career of twenty years. I gave him a name: Clive Hayes. He was from South Australia, home of Don Bradman, David Hookes, and Ian Chappell. He was unbeaten as captain and led Australia to a 5–0 win over England in England. I was a boy living in India, who had never seen Australia play live, spinning fantasies about being an Australian player. I concocted every cricketing fantasy a schoolboy could. Except for one about India winning a Test against the reigning world champions after India had followed on, facing a possible humiliating defeat.

I have few memories of cricket from those air force days. I do not remember India winning in England and the West Indies in 1971—though I do remember, quite clearly, the blackouts during the war against Pakistan in December of that same year—and only have dim recollections of Tony Lewis's English team visiting in 1972–1973. The West Indies came and went in 1974–1975; Andy Roberts, Viv Richards, and Clive Lloyd became household names. I knew and understood little about cricket. On being told that Andy Roberts bowled at one hundred miles an hour, I asked, "Why doesn't he run in the Olympics?" My first companions in watching cricket were my mother's cricket-crazy brothers, my uncles;

some of their fandom must have rubbed off on me. They did the things cricket tragics did. They stayed up all night for radio commentary, copied out scorecards from newspapers, and were distraught or overjoyed by cricketing catastrophe or good fortune. I was suitably impressed when they were able to predict what would happen next on a highlights tape—such as Bhagwat Chandrashekhar, the Indian bowler and notoriously poor batsman, being bowled first ball for a duck.

In 1972, shortly after the conclusion of the Liberation War for Bangladesh, my family moved to New Delhi. My father was posted to air headquarters. He would be posted out of Delhi again, but then we stayed put. He had decided our schooling in New Delhi's public schools was more important than accompanying him on his movements over the country. In 1976, disgruntled and irate, passed over for promotion and humiliatingly superseded by an academy classmate, my father left the Indian Air Force, breaking my heart forever. His flying days were over; he did not want to direct flying operations from a desk. He had never seen himself as a garden-variety patriot, and enough was enough. But I did not want to be a civilian living in the big city. I wanted to continue living the sheltered life on an air base, in the company of other air force kids, using the swimming pool and the club and playing games on the spacious lawns at the air force officers' mess. But the die was cast.

We moved toward a mundane civilian life, staying on the same street in New Delhi where we had first moved to in 1972. Now we moved from a two-bedroom apartment into a one-bedroom one. My brother and I slept on folding cots in the living room; come morning, they were folded and put away. My father started a business, an incongruous turn of affairs for a former war hero. My mother taught in a humble vocational college. We had come down to ground.

From then on, cricket would begin to provide me heroes and material with which to construct dreamscapes.

Enter Cricket

I WAS BORN in the cricketing sense, as a cricket fan, during the 1976–1977 Indian cricket season. My childhood amnesia effaces memories of the famous 1976 Port of Spain Test; I cannot remember India's chase of 403 to beat the West Indies. I wonder how my cricketing life would have turned out differently had I been aware of that historic win and allowed myself to be caught up in the euphoria it generated among Indian cricket fans.

My sporting consciousness had emerged just a little earlier, in the summer of 1976—before the cricket season began—during the Montreal

Olympics. In that primordial, bringing-to-life-a-sporting-sensibility event, India did not win a single medal. The space on the victors' podium was reserved for athletes from elsewhere. The Indian hockey team, once world champions and multiple gold-medal winners in the Olympics, finished in seventh place. They lost, brutally, 1–7 to Australia. Shivnath Singh came in eleventh in the marathon; a man reckoned India's greatest long-distance runner did not even place in the top ten finishers. Sri Ram Singh came in seventh in the eight hundred meters, bringing up the rear, a spot reserved for Indians. The Indian nation was content praising Indian athletes' qualification for the finals, never mind their finishing in the top three. India, it turned out, was a nation of sporting also-rans and failures. Newspapers and magazines wrote about India's humiliation, its failure to produce a medal from a population of 800 million. India had sent twenty athletes to three sports: hockey, track and field, and boxing. That was the extent of the Indian sporting footprint. We were pathetically incapable of performing on a sporting field; we did not belong there. Our boxers were knocked out early; that physical dismissal, that lack of masculinity—that was Indian sport. We entered the ring and then bowed out; we made others look good. Sport was a zone of Indian failure and incompetence; others—strapping symbols of non-Indian virility, strength, skill, and Olympic heroism, upholders of Olympic traditions—belonged here. It was a world of American swimmers, Cuban boxers, and Greek weightlifters, but not Indians. Black and white were the colors of sporting skill, not brown. The languages it spoke were not Indian ones.

Getting Used to an Idea

IN THE WINTER OF 1976, I was a fifth-grade student at New Delhi's Bal Bharti Air Force School. My classmates and I were a shell-shocked bunch, terrified of the corporal punishment—the furious slaps and canings—our teacher dished out. But soon, thanks to her changing responsibilities and eventual transfer, we wallowed in the kindness and attention of her replacement. Rita Ummat rescued us, making us considerably more cheerful about our weekday existence in the schoolyard and classroom. And besides her solicitous care, there was cricket.

The English cricket team—or the Marylebone Cricket Club (MCC) as it was known then—had arrived in India to play five Tests.* Tony Greig,

---

* "Marylebone Cricket Club," available at http://en.wikipedia.org/wiki/Marylebone _Cricket_Club, last accessed 26 January 2015.

the six foot seven English captain, was literally and figuratively a giant. His reputation in India—as an imposing, skilled showman on the field—had been securely established by the 1972–1973 tour. I associated a peculiar invincibility with him; someone so tall was well out of reach of all thrown his way. On the first day of the first Test at Delhi, England won the toss and elected to bat. At school I eagerly awaited the start of play, and finally at recess time, jam sandwich in hand, I walked over to some boys listening to the ubiquitous transistor radios that dotted the Indian landscape in the cricket season. When I asked how many runs Greig had made, I was informed he had been dismissed for twenty-five. I was shocked: pygmies had brought down a giant. (Finding out cricket scores during school hours was facilitated by a straightforward strategy; you excused yourself from the classroom for a bathroom break and went looking for a radio. Invariably, a school staff member would oblige. If you had a radio yourself, you could duck into a quiet corner and tune in.)

England rolled on. It was the first Test I had ever paid serious attention to, and India lost by an innings in response to an English first innings total of 381. The Test was played in the Indian capital, which once again became the venue for demonstrations of English power. It was played and concluded in glorious sunshine, but the sun only shone on English feats. (In signs of innocent times, long before the troubles in the Punjab that would so afflict the Indian polity in the eighties, young Sikhs went running out to the middle of the Ferozeshah Kotla, New Delhi's cricketing ground, to garland Sunil Gavaskar with marigolds as he reached a thousand runs in a calendar year.)

England's victories in the first three Tests—one after another—drew a simple picture of cricketing reality: India played cricket, and India lost. The team's business was to lose, and to provide entertainment by letting other teams do well against them. (The "Vaseline incident" in the third Test, the suggestion by the Indian captain Bishen Bedi that the English swing bowler John Lever had doctored the cricket ball to change its movement through the air, barely made an impression.* I dismissed it as Indian carping, sour grapes in response to a well-deserved loss.) I scarcely noticed Indian performances, not that there were any in the first three Tests worthy of remembrance. I was thus set up to be shocked at India's win in the fourth Test. Bhagwat Chandrasekhar, India's quirky leg spinner, capable of brilliance and mediocrity in the same spell of play, ran through England

---

* Martin Williamson, "The Vaseline Affair," ESPNcricinfo, 30 November 2012, available at http://www.espncricinfo.com/magazine/content/story/594464.html, last accessed 26 January 2015.

and became the destroyer of my dreams, the ones that centered on batsmen scoring heavily against India.

When I first became aware of cricket and its workings, my immature, impressionable mind had formed the rough and ready conception that the established order was that of Indian defeats. I never thought to question it on any basis, either sporting or patriotic. It was just the way things were. India and the Indian team played cricket, but the rest of the world's cricket teams and players were the true luminaries of the game. Sunil Gavaskar, the biggest name in Indian cricket, did not have the effect on me that cricketers of other nations did. Indeed, I disliked Gavaskar and cared little for his statistical feats; his batting seemed colorless and defensive. The Indian spinners, the giants of world cricket in the turn department, did not evoke my admiration as players from overseas did. They certainly were not as admirable, glamorous, and virile as the fast bowlers and stylish batsmen other teams packed their rosters with. I did not regard the Indian team as "my team" or "our team"; I felt little bound me to the Indian team. My heroes were drawn from elsewhere. The English, for instance. They were not colonial rulers; they were the folks that won the Second World War, heroes of the *Commando* and *Battle Picture Library* comics and war books I consumed by the dozen, authors of the books I liked to read, winners of Test matches.

I regarded sporting competence as the domain of other nations and their representatives. And I enjoyed sporting feats at India's expense. It was perverse, and even then, as a not-quite-ten-year-old, I was aware of it. It was not just enough that India lose; it felt better when India lost heavily. On a bathroom break during the third Test, I learned of India's stunning 60–6 score as it collapsed to an eventual 83 all out. It was a statistical rarity, the first time I had seen it happen in a Test. I was enthused on seeing India fall for less than 100. You could describe my reactions as masochism, but that would be wrong. The masochist finds pleasure in pain; I felt no pain when India lost, only pleasure. Perhaps I sought to guard myself against the disappointment of Indian defeats, but I cannot remember experiencing any such emotion. India's sporting record, the genial contempt with which Indians talked about their teams' performances in international sporting competition underwrote my diminished assessments of Indian sports teams, but it does not fully explain why I *wanted* Indian teams to lose. This peculiar sporting pathology demands greater explanation.

Many Indians like me thought little of their culture, were ashamed by our colonial past, and looked to the West for moral and intellectual edification. We were apologetic about our histories and cringed at the litanies of subjugation and servility they contained. But we had internalized them too; they made themselves manifest in our sporting inclinations. Years later, when I made Australian friends and read about Australian explorations of identity and their "cultural cringe," their reckonings of themselves as transplanted Britons, cut off from the mother country, doomed to play cultural and intellectual catch-up, I empathized, even as I realized the difference in our insecurities in magnitude and visceral sensation.

Mine might have been a unique pathology. A black American in Jim Crow United States might have had a diminished sense of self, and even a self-hatred of sorts, but surely he or she never cheered for Max Schmeling or Rocky Marciano—white men both, and symbols of a political system that had conspired to ensure their subjugation—to beat Joe Louis. Perhaps there were American blacks who cheered as Rocky Marciano knocked out Joe Louis. Having internalized white notions of "uppity blacks," they might have thought Louis was one and wanted him to get his ass whipped. It's not flattering to think I might have entertained similar notions. My analogy does not work precisely, because Joe Louis was often considered a "model black man" by both black and white America. A better example might be Muhammad Ali who, at his loudest, and who, during the early days of his allegiance to the Nation of Islam, invited much derisive commentary from some African Americans too. They might have supported the many Great White Hopes who went up against The Greatest, hoping to silence him and quieten his fists.

There was another dimension to my self-flagellation: Indian wins in cricket seemed disappointingly tame, a "good boy" occurrence at best. There was something far more edgy and exciting in their losses to more glamorous players from overseas. Indian players were staid, domestic, and familiar. My symbols of glamour were air force pilots; compared to them, Indian cricket players were not exciting or stylish enough. Besides, those pilots seemed to have little to do with matters Indian. Often, they were like my father, Anglicized, urbane, dressed in white slacks and shirts, suavely smoking cigarettes while listening to jazz and rock and roll at their alcohol-fueled parties. Overseas players were symbols of glamour transported from elsewhere; their wins were part of the natural order in even the aesthetic dimension. A win for India felt like a victory for the conventional and depressingly familiar. A win for an overseas team was a flirtation with the adventurous and the edgy, a pleasing and thrilling vindication of the sporting good.

Treachery: India in Pakistan

ON THE DAY MY FATHER RETURNED FROM THE 1971 Bangladesh Liberation War against West Pakistan, he stood in the doorway of our kitchen wearing his sweat-stained flying overalls and dashing aviator sunglasses, eating a hearty breakfast of scrambled eggs, toast, and coffee, and said with cheerful and blunt dismissiveness, "We gave the Pakistanis a good thrashing." That day, standing in the courtyard of our home, he was glad to be back with my mother—his beautiful wife—and his admiring sons, eating home-cooked food on a sunny winter day in North India. He was smiling, relieved and happy to see us again, back from war and the losses of his comrades. He had given us a little sound bite, something that would convey the essence of what had happened—and yet filter out its terrible details—on battlefields that were not so distant. He knew we would understand what he meant: someone had misbehaved, and my father had taught them a lesson, handing out a disciplining they clearly needed. He did not call his opponents—the Pakistani armed forces—murderers or rapists. He might well have, given what was known about the Pakistani army's behavior in Bangladesh: thousands of women raped and hundreds of thousands of Bengalis slaughtered before the Indian army showed up and forced surrender in Dhaka. His description made them irksome schoolchildren who needed chastisement.

Pakistan was a part of my parents' lives. They were both children of the Partition, British colonialism's brutally accurate parting shot, the violent sundering of the Indian subcontinent into India and Pakistan, two nations supposedly divided by religion. As murderous riots and population transfers began in 1947, my mother was a seven-year-old girl in Amritsar in the soon-to-be-Indian Punjab. My grandparents must have told her who was responsible and to blame for the carnage she could see around her. (My father was already in Delhi, sent away from home at age seven to attend boarding school. His father's family had been displaced from their village, Dilawar Cheema, now in Pakistan's Gujranwala District.) My mother remembered Amritsar in the year of the Partition vividly. In the right audience, I can still recount with some relish and embellishment, her heart-pounding stories of going to the rooftop of her brick-walled home with her little sister to sleep on its cooled surface, seeking relief from the heat of the interiors below, and then, lying on her back, watching tracer bullets light up the sky as they sang and whistled overhead. She told me of mass funeral pyres burning late into the night, of terror-stricken cries of "the Baluchis are coming!," of trains filled with dead bodies rolling across the border and into Indian railway stations, and of naked, dead girls with "Long Live Pakistan" bloodily carved into their chests. As these tales were told, I did not think of Pakistanis as Muslims. I thought of them as Pakistanis, a world and sensibility apart.

I knew little else about Pakistan other than a potted history of the partition of India, some mention of the divisive and secessionist perfidy of its founder, Mohammed Ali Jinnah, and caustic references to the incompetence of its armed forces in the wars we had fought and won against them. Stories of its military defeats and surrenders filled my ears and made them inferior enemies. I had seen photos of the Pakistani army's surrender in Dhaka, those long lines of soldiers with their arms lying on the ground, humbled by the Indians, forced into POW camps. In some manner of contact that spoke of contagion, by their very association with us, by being part of our history and stories, all things Pakistani were dull and prosaic. Pakistan was provincial, dusty, sidetracked. How could it not be, when it had been carved out from India?

Pakistan did not register on my cricketing map; I had no Pakistani cricket heroes. But I knew Pakistan played cricket. In the 1970s, the Indian sports magazine *Sportsweek* often produced special issues devoted to cricket. In one such issue of *The World of Cricket*, I chanced upon a statistics column listing the highest individual scores in Test cricket. The doyen of Indian cricket statisticians, B. B. Mama, had picked a score of 270 as the cutoff point for inclusion in his list. In that column lay a name, Zaheer Abbas, which I had never seen before. Abbas had scored 274 against England in a Test in 1971. I filed this statistic away, intrigued by the existence of a Pakistani name in the list of Test cricket's greatest achievements. (Thanks to the lack of an accompanying photograph, another name, Hanif Mohammed, did not register in quite the same way.) That was the extent of my cricketing knowledge of Pakistan.

In 1978, seven years after the end of the Liberation War for Bangladesh, when the resumption of Indian cricketing ties with Pakistan was announced, I was only mildly intrigued. Though I had never seen a live telecast of a sports event, the news that the three Tests of the series were to be broadcast live had little effect on me. This was India playing against a neighbor—a little too close to home, a little too domestic and parochial. (During the series— thanks to photographs of Sikhs crossing the international border, traveling to Lahore to see the Test and visit Sikh pilgrimage sites stranded in Pakistan—I would realize just how close Pakistan's cities were to Indian ones.)

On the opening day of the first Test, I was at a friend's house, visiting for lunch. The television was on, and Pakistan was batting. I paid scant attention; there was little excitement in the air. Faisalabad's ground was shabby and nondescript. After the excitement of the previous year's cricket against Bobby Simpson's Australian team—a series India had obligingly lost 2–3 and that I had witnessed on the Australian Broadcasting Corporation's high-quality television highlights—this was a humdrum affair at best. Later in the afternoon after I had returned home, overcome by curiosity, I switched on the television again.

It was 16 October 1978, a little less than seven years since the Pakistani army had surrendered to the Indian army at Dhaka. I was eleven years old. My father joined me, back home after a day at the leather goods manufacturing unit that incongruously enough was now his workplace. What a fall. From flying fighter jets to managing the manufacture and export of leather belts, wallets, and handbags; from glamour to grind in a few easy steps. My father—once wicketkeeper and hard-hitting opening batsman for Delhi's strongest college team, St. Stephens—had never lost his interest in cricket. He stopped to watch the Test, thoughts of changing and settling down for the evening momentarily put on hold. A Pakistani batsman—Zaheer Abbas—was approaching his century. Together, we watched Zaheer flay the Indian bowlers as he progressed from 91 to 107 with four boundaries, each garnished with power and style. Zaheer wore a white Panama hat and tied a kerchief around his neck. His batting and his appearance went together. I had never seen anything so striking, so elegant, and so revealing of the beauty hidden behind every ball bowled in a game of cricket. I was primed, ready to be awed. Zaheer stepped up and did it. As we watched, my father spoke, his voice full of admiration, "This guy is going to give the Indians a thrashing."

From that simple remark, I learned cricket appreciation spanned boundaries in a manner unlike mine, for there was no doubt my father supported the Indian team. But I learned too, that my father, a man who had battled them and almost certainly caused the deaths of some, did not demonize Pakistanis. I did not hear a derogatory word for the Pakistanis from my father during that series as we watched, stunned and disbelieving, the Pakistanis demonstrate attacking cricket at its best. My mother also admired Zaheer Abbas; she said he looked like a "film star," the highest praise an Indian woman could bestow on a man. As the series progressed, there were other heroes to be found: the slim, dapper Asif Iqbal; the elegant, Panama hat–wearing Majid Khan; the loping, wily, Mephistophelean Sarfraz Nawaz, with flowing hair and mustache; the lean, feisty, and mustachioed Javed Miandad.

The Lahore Test began dramatically; Pakistan won the toss and put India in. I had never heard of such a thing. Winning the toss had always meant batting first. On asking my father why Pakistan had chosen to bowl, he replied briefly, "The pitch must favor the bowlers." Thus was I introduced to the idea that bowling first could be an attacking move. The Test began with a batting collapse, with India's fall triggered by an unconventional Pakistani tactic.

On the second and third days of the Test, as Zaheer scored an awe-inspiring 235, I spent hours glued to the television, watching the distant cricketing action with my parents and brother. The Dussehra holidays were on; a lovely autumn in Delhi provided an appropriately salubrious backdrop as we watched the cricket. Around noon on the second day, our doorbell rang. I ran out. A young man, a young woman, and an elderly woman stood at our door. The elderly woman, Pasha, hailed from a Muslim family in Maihar, a family friend of ours from time seemingly immemorial. My father's *muh-boli bahen*, a de facto sister, she tied a *rakhi*, the thread that marks sibling ties between brother and sister, on my father's wrist every year. Now she was in Delhi to marry her daughter off to a police officer named Mansur Ali Khan. (I instantly nicknamed the putative groom "Pataudi," a glib homage to India's legendary captain of the 1960s and 1970s.) The young man, her son, watched the cricket with me. We both spoke admiringly of Zaheer's batting and clucked over the carnage visited on the Indian bowlers. As tea and snacks were served, a Muslim and Hindu Indian pair of cricket fans watched a Pakistani batsman score runs at will, cheering on his strokes, his devastation of Indian hopes.

India needed to bat for more than two days to save the game. They almost made it, batting till tea on the fifth day. Gavaskar and Chetan Chauhan provided ample hope to Indian fans with an opening stand of 192, inspiring Indian newspapers to proclaim, "India keeps the lights burning at Lahore." I failed to appreciate the magnitude of the Indian openers' feat and did not join in the dismay at their dismissals to umpiring decisions reported as dubious. My primary concern was that Pakistan win; I had been converted by the Pakistani team.

On the last day of the Lahore Test, India fought on as Pakistan pressed for the kill. As Indian wickets fell, my excitement grew. My uncles grew progressively crestfallen as we listened to the radio commentary at my grandparents' home. (Thanks to a power failure, there was no live telecast.) When at last India was bowled out and Pakistan was set a not-impossible victory target that required them to score quickly, the electricity supply miraculously resumed. We ran to my grandparents' bedroom and—as was standard practice among cricket enthusiasts because television commentary was thought to be boring—switched on the television, turned down its volume, and turned up the radio. Pakistan took off on a flyer. As Kapil Dev bowled a line well wide of the stumps, ostensibly designed to contain and frustrate the Pakistani batsmen, Majid Khan pulled a stump out of the ground and pointed to where he thought Kapil should bowl. I was delighted by this cheeky gesture, one completely in keeping with the Pakistani spirit on ample display.

Fittingly, Zaheer scored the winning runs as Pakistan cantered home, scoring six runs an over. I wonder if I cheered loudly in the presence of my uncles as the Pakistanis won. Perhaps I did and they forgave me, for I was only eleven. Both teams deserved accolades, but for me there was only one worthy recipient. Later, I was stunned as I watched Mushtaq Mohammed the Pakistani captain, say in a post-match interview on television that Pakistan's win was one Muslims the world over had prayed for. I did not want to think the Pakistani cricket team was doing battle for Muslims against India, tying itself up in complicated ways with India's past and present. I wanted them to continue belonging to a world apart, one easier to admire and revere. (In response to Mushtaq's thanksgivings, an Indian columnist wrote in severely dry prose, "At these words of Mushtaq's, one's mind turned to thoughts of Bedouins in North Africa falling to their knees as Zaheer scored the winning runs.")

On the final day of the Karachi Test, bored by the Indian defense to save the game, I went to see *The Taking of Pelham 123*. Escapist fare from Hollywood could pull me away from cricket, especially if it did not look like India's opponents would win. The match was headed for a draw; it was safe to take the afternoon off and spend it at the movies. On my return, I walked into our makeshift dining room and asked my father for news on the result. With a huge smile on his face, he replied, "The Pakistanis won!" After India had been dismissed in its second innings, Pakistan had needed to score at seven an over to win. Asif Iqbal and Javed Miandad, with some incredible running between the wickets, had made the chase possible. They stayed close but still fell marginally behind the asking run rate. Then fatefully, Bishen Bedi the Indian captain, brought himself on to bowl. Imran Khan hit him for seventeen runs in the over. The Indian team lost the Test, and Bedi lost the Indian captaincy.

My father's cheerful approval of the result and of the skill and bravado of the Pakistani batsmen in scoring the runs needed for victory further indicated to me approval for the Pakistani team—ostensibly enemies of ours—was kosher. This was all that was required to transcend the barriers of prejudice or nationalist sentiment at my impressionable age: a signal from one whose approval I sought that deviation from the norm was acceptable.

While many around me admired Pakistani cricketers, there was little doubt most wanted to see them fail. Some Indian fans might have wanted a Pakistani cricketer to do well as India won. I might have been the only one who crossed the line and wanted Pakistani players to do well at the expense of the Indian team. In an environment of total support for the Indian team against their most hated rivals, I contrived to not just be a supporter of the individual feats of the enemy but to also wish for a contrary result for the Indian team. It was not enough for Pakistani batsmen to score centuries while Pakistan lost; I wanted them to score centuries and for India to lose. My treachery ran deep.

I shrugged off Indian complaints about Pakistani umpiring as sour grapes; I shrugged off Indian media, my friends, and my cricket-crazy uncles. They were unhappy and disappointed at the result of the series. I was not. Indian cricketers too, were not kindly disposed toward Pakistan. Sunil Gavaskar pointed out that he had been out in both innings of the Karachi Test without scoring—before he went on to score centuries in each innings—but had refused to walk because he was playing in Pakistan. I was flabbergasted by this admission of blatant dishonesty, this acknowledgment by Gavaskar that his innings had been counterfeit.

In this admiration and protectiveness of Pakistan, I was isolated outside the confines of my home. I cared little. I was a solitary artist; my cricketing pleasures were drawn in isolation. The question of whether others agreed with my cricketing views did not arise. I cared little for the opinions of those—like my playmates in the neighborhood park—who showed scant tolerance for my cricketing incompetence and were not shy about heaping loud scorn and ridicule on my attempts to score runs or take wickets. A pox on their houses; I was better off daydreaming about these cricketers. I knew who my heroes were and who I wanted to see winning Test matches.

Had my love for cricket been truly impartial I would have been indifferent to the victor's identity, but I was not. I wanted Pakistan to win; I wanted India to lose. There was an active rejection here, an active distancing, and mysteriously enough I had not sought refuge in some white-skinned enclave but in one considerably closer, in neighbors for whom I had only heard contempt thus far. I can only surmise my father's admiration for the Pakistanis had granted me the freedom to transfer to them my cricketing allegiances, ones already disinclined to be directed toward the Indian cricket team.

Forty-two years later, as a middle-aged man looking back at his teen years, I still consider the 1978 Tests at Lahore and Karachi paradigmatic examples of how cricket should be played. And the format of those two wins—bowling out the opposition on the first day or shortly thereafter, batting second, building a lead, grittily bowling out the opposition, chasing a small target in limited time in the dying hours of a Test match—was for long, in my scales of cricket appreciation, the supreme variant of a Test match. My normative vision of cricket was shaped thus by the Pakistani team. For years, the failures of the Indian team to win a Test match of that type, in that fashion—as long ago as at Melbourne in 1986 and as recently as in Dominica in 2011—rankled deeply. The refusal to pick up the thrown gauntlet was galling, indicative of a lack of cricketing moral fiber and competence.

Those autumn days of 1978, when we watched Pakistan play Test cricket on our black-and-white television, which my father had bought with much difficulty on our limited budget and that never worked for any extended length of time, was the first and last time my family spent leisure time watching cricket together. Less than a year later, early on the morning of 30 April 1979, it was all over; my father passed away suddenly from a heart attack, changing our lives forever. Our home became desolate in the years following his death. My mother—still reeling from the devastating suddenness of that blow, from the loss of her partner of sixteen years—took over the family business and plunged into the difficult task of bringing up two boys by herself. We—two boys aged fourteen and twelve, just starting out on our difficult journeys of adolescence—were only partially cooperative, giving my mother ample opportunity for parental anxiety.

I had cricket and the Pakistani team to console me. I followed its progress with an intensity unmatched by any other cricketing devotion of mine. I dug up Pakistani cricketing history. I read avidly about the 1971 and 1974 tours of England and about Pakistan's first win over England on their very first tour. I discovered Zaheer's 240 at the Oval in 1974 and was gratified to learn Zaheer had scored centuries in both innings of a first-class match on eight separate occasions, that he was on target for a hundred first-class hundreds and would be the only Asian to reach that exalted landmark. My interest in Zaheer Abbas rivaled my interest in Don Bradman; he was my first brown cricketing hero alongside the black and white ones I already acknowledged.

Sarfraz Nawaz's miraculous feats in the first Test of Pakistan's tour of Australia in 1979 were confirmation Pakistan was capable of cricketing magic. The bare facts of the Australian collapse bear repeating decades after I first read of it in a newspaper one morning in New Delhi. The Australians, chasing 381 to win, were 305/3. They then lost seven wickets for five runs; Sarfraz took them all for one run. But the next Test was marred by a series of ill-mannered and unsportsmanlike incidents. Tempers flared, and accusations of impropriety flew in both directions. Pakistan's bad-tempered behavior directed at Australia—the other contenders for my cricketing heart, thanks to the legends of the Ashes and Don Bradman, about whom I had become alarmingly well-read all too quickly—was disillusioning, the first blemish on their otherwise spotless reputation.

All this while I steadfastly ignored Indian cricketing history. I was adopting a distinctive blinkered approach—with a palpable hostility at its heart—to Indian cricket. But there was a curious shortcoming in my admiration of Pakistan. I, like other young boys my age, made up imaginary players—like Clive Hayes—and lived out their careers. The closest I ever came to wanting to be Pakistani was in some backyard games with my cousins. I would pretend I was Majid Khan or Zaheer Abbas taking apart an unspecified attack with a devil-may-care attitude, driving the tennis ball with abandon far over the distant flowerpots next to the neem trees. But I could not act out the mental fantasy of the life of a Pakistani cricketer the way I had for my Australian hero. I could not imagine myself with a Pakistani name; I could not imagine a Pakistani's school or college background. A Pakistani cricketer never became my imagined self. Some of the mist swirling around Pakistan had seeped into my subterranean self. The subconscious connotations of that word and the history it evoked had led to an acute failure of imagination. I found it easier to imagine being an Australian than a Pakistani. I knew that much of the difference between us.

Places in the Mind

HERE IS A NONDESCRIPT DECIMAL NUMBER: 796.358. In my relationship with cricket, no other number has had as much significance; it anchored me to cricket's history.* It ensured an entrenched set of memories, images, and romantic associations with the game and was the key to an education in cricket, creating prejudices and inclinations that shaped a worldview long impervious to change.

According to the Dewey Decimal System, 796.358 is the library classification code for cricket; it ensures cricket-related books are placed together on library shelves. I am not enough of a librarian to know how 796.358 points to cricket, how three and five and eight add up to bat and ball, to willow and leather, to pitch and pavilion. But these numbers worked as a set of navigational coordinates in any library I visited—whether in school, college, or elsewhere. They were the numbers visible on paperback and hardcover spines, through the plastic sheath, typed in black ink. They were the GPS coordinates of their time.

Most significantly, I used 796.358 in the British Council Library. That venerable institution, then located at the All India Fine Arts Council building in New Delhi, was a weekend destination for our family for many years. On each trip I ran up the stairs, entered through a set of massive wooden doors, briskly walked past the curious librarians, and headed straight for the 796.358 shelves. The books were covered by plastic dust jackets, they featured scorecards and indexes chockablock with legendary

---

* This section borrows from my essay titled "The Significance of 796.358," in *Eye on Cricket: Reflections on the Great Game* (New Delhi: HarperCollins, 2015).

names, and their pages were filled with tales of adventures in distant lands. This was a schoolboy's delight. I was a walking cliché: a public school–educated Anglophone middle-class Indian spending my weekends at and borrowing four books at a time from the British Council Library.

I was not alone in seeking treasures in The Land of 796.358; other library patrons engaged in similar explorations. We were in India, land of the cricket tragic, and this was the British Council Library, regarded as the storehouse and fount of cricketing wisdom. All too often, bewildered and irate, I would find many objects of desire missing from the shelves, perennially out on loan. It was infuriating to be reminded that my attraction for cricket was not a solitary pleasure. But library reservations, the hold, and the recall came to the rescue. I would diligently fill out a card listing the title and the call number, asking to be notified when a book had been returned and kept on hold. When the books came in, I made a trip to the library and would return home beaming, a new stash to be devoured and savored.

Over in the reference section, copies of *Wisden*, Bill Frindall's statistics almanac, and the *John Player Yearbook* were permanent, immovable residents. Laying hands on them was a simple matter of temporal competition; I merely had to be among the library's first visitors. The library opened at 10:00 A.M. After some careful calculations of travel time on a Delhi Transport Corporation bus, I would set off, arriving early and waiting outside the door for the librarians to open the barricades.

The residents of the precincts of Area Code 796.358 included the usual suspects, members of the pantheon of English cricket writers—Neville Cardus, E. W. Swanton, Alan Ross, John Arlott, Ian Peebles, David Frith, Pelham Warner, R. C. Robertson-Glasgow—and of course, many a retired and sometimes long passed away, English Test cricketer. There were no Indian writers here, though token Australians—such as Ray Robinson, Jack Fingleton, and Arthur Mailey—were featured. My mind became attuned to a very particular history with its preferred narratives, locales, heroes, and legends. From its texts I read off an entire sporting order along with its yardsticks and frameworks for assessing cricketing performance and quality.

For many years in my cricketing youth, the most significant dates in my reckonings of cricket history had little to do with India. The year 1932—when India first played Test cricket—did not suggest itself as a significant date to me. Neither did 1971—the year of historic twin triumphs, away in England and the West Indies. This ignorance was especially curious because I was brought up by a father who had told me stories of watching, with great pleasure, those grand old gentlemen of Indian cricket, C. K. Nayudu, Mushtaq Ali, and Vijay Merchant. In cricket at least, my father had had Indian heroes. He also told me stories about the Australian Services team, of a memorable encounter between C. K. Nayudu and Keith Miller,* and of running into Frank Worrell's 1960 West Indies team, heading to Australia for their legendary tour that southern summer on an ocean liner,† but these stories never crowded out Indian cricket history. Perhaps I was only susceptible to his commentary when it confirmed my prejudices. My father might have wondered why his son was not as fascinated by Mushtaq and Merchant as he was by McCabe and McCartney. In my mind, Indian cricketing achievements remained marginalized and diminished.

As an ideology-promulgating institution, the British Council Library was wildly successful. I grew up with a very particular cricketing mythology—the Ashes, Anglo-Australian cricket, county cricket, bucolic English grounds, the Yorkshire-Lancashire rivalry, the storied Lord's, the Oval, Trent Bridge, Headingley, and Old Trafford were all central to my conceptions of the game. The key to the colonization of the mind can be found in reams of postcolonial scholarship but also in the simple pleasures of reading cricket books written by representatives of empire.

One afternoon while browsing in the British Council Library, I chanced upon an essay on an innings Zaheer Abbas had played for Gloucestershire in the county championship. The writer described the cold day in May, the small crowds, the loneliness of the ground, but above all, elevating the humdrum proceedings of an obscure county game to real drama, he wrote of Zaheer. I savored the descriptions of Zaheer moving into top gear, spreading runs and shots over the ground. As I read, I added images of fans sipping tea from flasks, sitting on wooden benches with sweaters and scarves, rubbing their hands to keep warm, shouting encouragement at their overseas professional. Somehow, I knew how uncompromisingly damp and cold—and unfriendly to cricket—the early part of the English summer could be. I knew that later in the summer, English grounds would become browner, their pitches drier and friendlier to spinners. I knew less about seasonal variations in Indian cricket locations. At the time, I had never been to England and to this day have spent a total of ten days in that land,

---

* Samir Chopra, "Memories Faithful and Unfaithful," ESPNcricinfo, 3 February 2010, available at http://www.espncricinfo.com/blogs/content/story/617044.html. A rewritten version can be found in Chopra, *Eye on Cricket.*

† Samir Chopra, "Cricket On The High Seas With Sobers and Co," ESPNcricinfo, 5 August 2015, available at https://www.espncricinfo.com/story/_/id/20599856/cricket-high-seas-sobers-co.

all of them in London or close to it. But England felt intimately familiar, its landscapes conjured up effortlessly in my mind. Like the protagonist of Amitav Ghosh's *Shadow Lines*, I was armed with descriptions of an England I had never visited; it was a common Indian experience of an almost wholly imagined land.* English county cricket spoke of lands far away, places we yearned to visit, places we made ours despite the intervening black waters. They were the staging grounds of the world's parades; our lands were merely the backwaters, marginal venues for sideshows and diversions and irrelevancies.

Cricketing literature ensured many places on the map became real for me in a way they never would have if physical contact had been the sole guarantor of familiarity with them. I knew Lord's and the Oval were in London, the former adorned by the figure of Father Time, the latter by its famous gasholder at the Vauxhall end. Headingley was in Leeds, Edgbaston in Birmingham, Trent Bridge in Nottingham, and Old Trafford in Manchester. I knew the nature of the pitches at each ground. Headingley—forever for me Bradman's happy hunting ground—was a dodgy pitch often soaked by the hostile Leeds weather. Trent Bridge and Edgbaston were featherbeds. Lord's famous slope needed to be mastered by the quicks who bowled there, and Old Trafford was a "quickie's wicket." I knew where Caribbean grounds were: Bridgetown in Barbados with its Kensington—not Kennington—Oval, Sabina Park at Kingston in Jamaica, and the Bourda at Georgetown in Guyana. I knew the first two were bouncy, fast tracks, fast bowler's paradises; I knew the third was a batsman's dream. And so for Australian locales: Melbourne, home to the world's most capacious cricket stadium, home ground to canny, phlegmatic Victorians; Sydney, breeding ground for innumerable blue-capped New South Welshmen, future Australian stars, its beautiful scoreboard so admired by Don Bradman, its "Hill" the roosting spot for the legendary Australian barracker Yabba, his most pungent lines instantly committed to memory by me; Adelaide with its beautiful cathedral and short square boundaries that created hookers and pullers, home to Don Bradman; and Brisbane, venue for the most famous Test of all, the epic Tied Test between Australia and the West Indies. Few English or Australian fans knew then, or know now, the states or provinces where Indian Test grounds are located. Very few know anything about Indian grounds other than that they favor spinners or are good to make big scores on. They do not need to. They are not bewitched by Indian cricket, promised a land not available to them.

---

* Amitav Ghosh, *Shadow Lines* (New Delhi: Ravi Dayal, 1988).

I would run through this list of hallowed cricket grounds in my mind, ensuring I had it in place, locked away for secure access. I associated images with each, often unaided by photographs or television. I would not leave India in my childhood; indeed, I would not board a jet aircraft till I was twenty years old, heading to the United States. But I had traveled the cricketing world, thanks to the books I read. These cricketing venues were not just places on the map. They were places in the mind.

Later, when I would live in Australia, I was often disappointed to hear suave Eastern Suburbs Sydney-siders speak disparagingly of Brisbane, Adelaide, and Perth, referring to them as overgrown provincial towns. I resisted these remarks; I wanted my personal fiction of them as momentous venues to be preserved. This vision had already created a peculiar relationship with travel guidebooks. When I looked up an entry for a city with an international cricket ground, a terrible disappointment would steal over me as I would find only a small note on that venue. This made eminent sense; it was only one of the many attractions in the city. But I had been made to realize the cricket ground was not the city; it was merely the place where the cricket was played. The Adelaide Cricket Oval had become simply "Adelaide" in my mind. I had let the ground expand and fill the entire space of the city.

Indian grounds did not acquire this aura. I did not think of Bombay's Wankhede or Calcutta's Eden Gardens as I did of Lord's and the Oval. I did not hanker to visit those grounds in the way I dreamed of going to Lord's or the Sydney Cricket Ground or Sabina Park. The latter appeared as worthy destinations for pilgrimages; the former were humdrum stations of the ordinary. Test matches took place in my own city, my home, New Delhi, but I did not think of attending them. I first attended a Test match at the Ferozeshah Kotla at the age of sixteen, despite having several opportunities to do so before. The "real" cricket happened somewhere else; here was only imitation and unsuccessful aspiration.

The British Council Library was not the only zone of escape. Shortly before my teen years commenced, my parents arranged a membership for me at the American Library in New Delhi. The library was administered by the United States Information Service. Its membership rules only allowed adults as members, but my parents spoke to the librarians, convincing them I could handle the books on its shelves, signed up for two library cards, and handed them over to me. But I was too callow to be more than an uncritical consumer of the library's offerings.

The American Library was an ideal location for the concoction of elaborate fantasies about leaving India and heading straight for America's shining shores. It quickly became another venue for learning another nation's history, for processing its narratives about itself, all the while not noticing the absence of an Indian one. The American Library carried no books about cricket on its shelves, a fact that placed it one rank lower than the British Council Library in my mental pegging. It did, however, feature—among many other collections—elaborate histories of the Second World War and the American Revolution; tales of the American West; and miles of American literature, essays, and popular science, all of which I avidly consumed. (The American Library also featured an extensive video archive and showed a weekly capsule of the American Broadcasting Corporation's news broadcasts.)

I spent many hours in the American Library's confines, reading books on U.S. history and culture, watching videos that made me privy to the details of American life in glorious color, and looking through American periodicals for a glimpse of the present-day United States. The United States Information Service could not have hoped for a more ideal purveyor of the information it hawked. During my reveries in the library's spaces, I dreamed of a life elsewhere, on a sylvan campus, in a manicured suburb, well away from India and its untamable dysfunction.

Nothing quite set you up for that indoctrination experience like walking into the American Library's cool, air-conditioned interiors after a hot and sweaty ride through Delhi's crowded buses. That change, as I walked in from Delhi's loud bustle to the pristine silence of the library's shelved spaces was a blessed relief; it gestured at the change that would presumably be introduced in my life once I left India and moved to the United States. Outside was searing heat and cacophonous noise, the bedlam of the street, the sounds of street vendors and honking traffic, and then, as the library's doors were pushed and swung open, came the first blast of air-conditioned air, settling on perspiring skin and feverish brow, cooling and calming. You walked on, flashing your identification—the treasured library card—and then upstairs to the brightly lit main level, with its neatly arrayed shelves, its glass-top tables, its soothing tranquility. This did not feel antiseptic and colorless; this atmosphere was a balm, easing a soul made restless and agitated, and eventually inert in all the wrong ways, by the furnace outside. Ideology promulgation takes many forms; sometimes it appears as a set of functioning air-conditioners, symbols of efficiency, power, and relief from the world's troublesome afflictions.

I was particularly susceptible to this promulgation now that our home was denuded of its central figure, now that my family had run aground and helplessly beached itself. Escapism was the most perspicuous strategy of all. I was twelve years old, I was "a connoisseur of the unavailable,"* keen to make it mine, to be in a land of promise and energy, where my raw daydreams would be magically transformed into the manifest and tangible.

Doing Well Abroad

THOSE PLACES ELSEWHERE THAT AUTOMATICALLY sanctified cricketing feats led me to develop a revealing obsession with Sunil Gavaskar when he played for Somerset in the 1980 English cricket season. I had been rather unenthusiastic about Gavaskar's cricketing prowess; his exalted status in the minds of those around me was not matched by his placement in my pecking order. But in 1980, Gavaskar was playing abroad. He was not playing for India and had a foreign employer, Somerset, an English county. Now his performance mattered. I was conscious of the stage and the audience, though I had not cared when India had played in Pakistan. Pakistan was not "abroad" enough. While I had not wanted Gavaskar's success in Test cricket, against India's international rivals, I did want to see him score runs in county cricket, of whose matches and settings Cardus had written so glowingly. For Cardus had convinced me that county cricket was the proving ground for heroes of all sorts. Those lovely, green, idyllic English grounds, sites of the beloved village game, sometimes featuring majestic cathedrals in the background, were more appropriate venues for cricket and cricketing heroism than India's crowded, dusty, and pockmarked maidans, perennially ringed by urban bedlam or rural grime. On these near-mythical grounds, even an Indian's efforts could be redeemed, made to shine just a little brighter, and somehow slotted into cricket's central narratives. The thought ran through my statistics-obsessed mind that an Indian might score a hundred first-class hundreds and join an esteemed gaggle of Anglo-Australian cricketers to have done so. The only way to do that was to play county cricket, the enabler of staggering cricketing feats, the stuff of cricketing legends.

It mattered then, whose gaze was trained on Indian cricketers. While playing county cricket, Gavaskar would be written about in an English publication, and I would soak up the reflected glory. Praise from those quarters would be gratifying. I had been flattered to read Ian Botham, the superstar English all-rounder, had wanted Gavaskar to play for Somerset

---

* Mukul Kesavan, "Remembrance of Things Past," *The Telegraph*, available at http://www.telegraphindia.com/1120506/jsp/opinion/story_15457508.jsp, last accessed 26 January 2015.

as a replacement for Viv Richards, the West Indies master batsman. An English player speaking highly of an Indian one—now that meant something. It certainly meant much more than the overexcitable, boringly nationalist hyperbolic praise that was the Hindi commentator's trademark, the Indian cricket reporter's stylistic distinction.

My days that Delhi summer followed a regular pattern: wake up, trudge out to our apartment's narrow balcony, pick up the morning newspaper, and turn eagerly to the sports page. Cricket updates from England were only partially available in the morning paper; county matches ended at 11:00 P.M. or later the previous night, and newspapers did not get the full scores by then. To beat the heat of the summer, my mother would make me—as a morning pick-me-up—rather than the customary tea, a glass of cold, sweet lemonade. It was a lovely treat to start the day, and I would wait till the lemonade was at hand before I turned to the sports page. I was often disappointed. Sometimes Somerset's scores were missing; sometimes I had miscalculated and thought there was a match on, when in fact there was not. But most disappointing of all was looking at a partial Somerset scorecard and realizing Gavaskar had not done well enough to have his name included in the short list of selected performers.

As the season went on, as Gavaskar's star briefly shone and then faded, my disappointment grew. At one stage, he had scored the most sixes in the John Player Sunday League but not so by the end of the season. I wondered if Gavaskar would score a thousand runs in the summer; Zaheer had scored two thousand runs in an English season many times. The write-ups in the English press on Gavaskar were disappointing: he had not performed to expectations; he had not enjoyed the grind; he had not adjusted to the amount of one-day cricket played; he was not an adequate replacement for Viv Richards. He failed to leave a distinctive mark. He came and went. There were no stories of friends he might have made in Somerset. No illuminating, edifying anecdotes emerged from his stay. He finished his season and came back quietly.

My disappointment ran deep. An Indian batsman had an exalted public stage available, and he had not seized the opportunity. Gavaskar's failure in England meant an Indian batsman—one I was only too glad to see fail when performing for Indian crowds and commentators—had let me down by not performing in the right place, at the right time. I wanted to read glowing reports about Indian cricketers written in the English press and desperately sought English writers' approval of Indian players; those words counted for something in my mental hierarchies of cricketing excellence.

In another dimension, Gavaskar had begun tearing down the edifice of the monuments I had erected to the world's cricketing order.

Shine a Light on Me: Reading *Sunny Days*

IN READING GAVASKAR'S AUTOBIOGRAPHY *Sunny Days*,* I heard an Indian cricketer "speak" for the first time. I was used to hearing them praised, criticized, and analyzed; I had heard them speak in clichés in television interviews. This was different; it was unvarnished in all the wrong and right ways.

Gavaskar was severely critical of many who crossed his path. His writing—most distinctively characterized by painfully long run-on sentences—was often intemperate and vitriolic; it is a matter of some astonishment he retained any friends after *Sunny Days*. That he did spoke volumes about the stature of the man and the short memory of his associates. Many a sacred cow was skewered: the Indian spinners on the 1974 tour of England, fellow Indian players, the Indian consulate in England, his batting partners, the Board for Cricket Control in India, but most importantly, the cricketing world "outside."

Gavaskar was unawed by the cricketing world I idolized. He punctured the English cricketing balloon with its pretensions to be the perennial standard-bearer and did not unquestioningly accept the status granted to it. Unimpressed by English tradition and cricketing hagiography, he dismissed the supposed "home of cricket," Lord's, as a boring ground, staffed and populated by the stuffy. His descriptions of the discomforts of touring overseas suggested these mythical lands had rough edges too: bad weather, inedible food, uncooperative and unfriendly hosts, and small, uncomfortable grounds. He spoke sharply and critically—in both sporting and personal dimensions—about English, West Indies, and Australian idols, sweeping them off the pedestals on which I had placed them. He was alarmingly irreverent, an incorrigible iconoclast. An outsider to the Anglo-Australian tradition and its sporting and evaluative nexus, he had dared to pass judgment on the cricket world. We had only been the lowly subjects of such exalted pronouncements before.

Gavaskar's book induced an acute discomfort in me. Though I felt little affection for Gavaskar, I found many of his critiques irresistible. It was the first suggestion that "abroad" was not as desirable a venue or destination as I understood it. It was the first intimation my idols might have the proverbial feet of clay, that they were not as perfect as I might have imagined. Gavaskar suggested my admiration and aspirations were misdirected: "abroad" could be the subject of aspersion too.

---

* Sunil Gavaskar, *Sunny Days* (New Delhi: Rupa, 1976).

My misautogenic sensibility was also buffeted by the pride Gavaskar took in Indian cricketing achievements. He was capable of favorably assessing the cricketing world without abnegating Indian cricket achievements. I had not acknowledged this catholic attitude in Ramchand's book; reading it in Gavaskar's made a difference. While Gavaskar was often lavish in his praise of the cricketing abilities of overseas players, he proffered the same generosity to Indian players who had been his teammates, mentors, and companions. He humanized them, introducing me to their personalities, their humor, their foibles and quirks. It was my first intimate contact with them.

Gavaskar was ready to go to bat for these mates of his. I had mentally crucified the opening batsman Sudhir Naik for being a shoplifter—a national disgrace!—when he had been accosted as one after a visit to the English departmental store Marks and Spencer during the 1974 tour. It had been considered the final humiliation of that blighted summer, one in which India had gone down 0–3 to England, losing heavily in each Test. But Gavaskar provided a straightforward recounting of the incident that cast Naik in considerably more innocent light, and which indicted instead the apologetic attitude of the Indian managers on the tour, who refused to accept their player's version of events. It was a simple expression of playerly solidarity that I had not understood before in the Indian context.

I had never had such an internal perspective on the Indian team and cricket. I found it easier to accept praise of India when it came couched in a critical package. I had acquired a facile suspicion of, and skepticism about, nationalist discourse, the purplish versions of which I was all too often subjected to while living in the Indian capital, the stage for tedious, interminable Republic Day parades and incomprehensible Independence Day speeches ponderously delivered from the ramparts of the Red Fort. I was a curiously incoherent mix—ready to reject over-the-top affirmations of the nation, thus showing my critical side, but too uncritically accepting of self-abnegation.

One notorious section of *Sunny Days* is still evoked in modern readings of Gavaskar's book: his description of the infamous fourth Test at Kingston against the West Indies in 1976, an Indian defeat in which India was bounced into submission by a West Indies pace attack led by Michael Holding and commanded by a Clive Lloyd still irate at India's epochal feats in the Port of Spain Test.* Gavaskar insisted the West Indies intended to injure and maim, to adopt unbridled intimidation as a cricketing tactic. I

---

* See, for instance, Gideon Haigh, "Gavaskar's Double Role," ESPNcricinfo, 15 January 2008, available at http://www.espncricinfo.com/magazine/content/story /331054.html, last accessed 26 January 2015.

struggled to reconcile his descriptions of the "bloodthirsty" Jamaican spectators egging on West Indies pace bowlers to inflict injury on Indian batsmen with images of the jovial, postvictory crowds on the West Indies tours of England in 1973 and 1976 as West Indies captains opened bottles of bubbly on pavilion balconies and sent their contents cascading down on the festive throngs below. The West Indies and the crowds that came out to cheer them were supposed to be happy-go-lucky calypso types; it was a facile stereotype that obscured their susceptibility to being animated by a xenophobic nationalism. I had imagined an easy solidarity with the West Indies, but it was a more elusive quality than I imagined.

Gavaskar insisted Indian batsmen had fought hard and batted courageously at Kingston; they had not run away from the field of battle. There, India had declared in the first innings with batsmen injured and unable to bat. It was established gospel Bedi, the Indian captain, had declared the second innings as well, effectively conceding the Test with only five Indian wickets down. I had thought this reluctance to offer resistance a badge of shame, a glaring pointer to Indian cowardice. But the official scorecard indicates the innings was officially completed and Gavaskar, for his part, insisted the rest of the Indian batting lineup was hurt and could not come out to bat. The Indian response then, was as brave as it could have been without the modern protections of helmets, armguards, and restrictions on the number of bouncers in an over. And even if the Indian batsmen were not injured, I wonder now, in light of the Australian batsman Phillip Hughes's tragic death to a bouncer-inflicted injury in 2014, whether Bedi's decision to not expose unprotected, incompetent batsmen to deliberately intimidatory bowling was, in a more comprehensive reckoning, ultimately the correct one.

Cricket on the Sidelines:
The Packer Years

AFTER INDIA'S RETURN FROM PAKISTAN, the West Indies, led by Alvin Kallicharran, alighted on Indian shores. The West Indies' stars were missing, away playing in Australia for a man I despised, Kerry Packer. He had eviscerated the nation-based game I loved by starting his own league, World Series Cricket (WSC), which would furnish cricketing content to his television channel, Channel Nine, and thus compete with the official cricket staged by the Australian Cricket Board.* The West Indies team featured

---

* Gideon Haigh, *Cricket War: The Inside Story of Kerry Packer's World Series* (Melbourne: Melbourne University Press, 2007).

promising new players such as Sylvester Clarke, Faoud Bacchus, Sew Shivnarine, Basil Williams, and Malcolm Marshall; indeed, the new crop of West Indies players had produced an exciting series against the Australians a little earlier. Still, I reasoned, if they were any good, they should not have been playing India. The best players were playing in Packer's WSC.

To host official teams while World Series Cricket went on Down Under was to be a cricketing reject, a discard, a marginalized entity. I was acutely conscious that Packer's circus, the WSC, was underway while India was hosting second-string teams. While WSC's contests were not official, its theft of the world's top players made it clear a party was going on that India was not invited to, one that had the players and stars I considered heroes. Pakistani players were playing in WSC and had been even before the 1978 Indian tour; they had been recalled to do justice to the importance of the series against India. I knew only one Indian player—Gavaskar—had been seriously considered a WSC candidate. I would have been happier had the Indian team been gutted. We would have been as welcome as other nations at this great cricketing feast, a most desirable validation. We had been dealt a double blow: our cricketers were not good enough to play with the best, and Indian fans were to be handed discards from other teams. We were second-class citizens of the world cricketing fraternity. Ironies abounded; I considered Indian players not good enough when they played international cricket, but I felt shamed by their exclusion from a global cricketing carnival. This was confirmation of my low opinion of them, but that was scant comfort. My views were, uncomfortably enough, reflected in the gaze of those whose appreciation I desired.

There was some chatter in the Indian press about how Gavaskar—supposedly offered a contract by Packer—would be a traitor if he signed up with the WSC. In response, Gavaskar's wife Marshneil defended his serious consideration of the offer. Her argument deployed a familiar rhetorical pitch, customarily employed in the defense of Indians going abroad to make their fortunes: Surely Gavaskar should follow the path of his fortunes and go where his talents were properly showcased. I agreed. His acceptance would also have had the salutary effect of affording me some much-desired reflected glory.

Back in India, I had no such fond feelings for Gavaskar. I feared this would be a long season; my least favorite batsman would score heavily against a blunt attack on slow pitches. I took solace as usual in the opposition. In the second Test, in India's first innings, Gavaskar was out first ball—caught by Sew Shivnarine at gully off Clarke. His summary dismissal was exhilarating. Irritatingly, in the third Test, Gavaskar scored centuries in both innings. Years later, I watched a highlights newsreel of that

Test. One shot stood out: Gavaskar square-driving Sylvester Clarke with impeccable power and timing. I would not have had the eyes to appreciate the shot had I seen it live. India wheeled away on the final day, trying to dismiss the West Indies, but fell a wicket short as Sew Shivnarine held out. Multiple unsuccessful light appeals by Shivnarine did not endear him to the crowd, but for my part, I was convinced there was conspiracy afoot: Indian umpires were in contemptible cahoots with the Indian team to hustle a weak West Indies team to defeat. But in the end, it was all a little too murky for play to continue and the players had to troop off, denied a result.

The West Indies' luck ran out at Madras, ironically enough the fastest and bounciest wicket in India. There, I was treated to the astonishing sight of a West Indies fielder running up to a bowler to pat him on the back after an Indian batsman had been felled by a bouncer. I uneasily thought back to Kingston 1976. The West Indies were not joyful, carefree cricketers after all. My dissonance was sparked too, by the sight of the Indian batsman brought to his knees. For the first time, I felt protective of an Indian cricketer and saw the rest of the cricket world as an Other opposed to India, one that did not feel benign.

The Test series concluded with a pair of high-scoring draws that confirmed cricket in India was a domain of boredom and staidness. Cricket that winter was frustrating and disappointing, all too often inconclusive, and always suffering by contrast with the cricket being played in Australia by the world's best players. During the Packer years, it became abundantly clear India was not even capable of convincingly beating the WSC-weakened teams sent to its shores.

We were the scum of the earth. We were not invited to the WSC; we could not crush weak teams at home. I was right to promulgate my slogan: Anyone but India.

Lowest of the Low

INDIAN INCOMPETENCE EXTENDED to cricket of all varieties. In the 1979 Prudential World Cup in England, India bowed out quickly, beaten by all and sundry: the West Indies, Sri Lanka, and New Zealand. The crowning humiliation—for some—was the loss to Sri Lanka—associate members of the International Cricket Council (ICC), not even a Test-playing nation. I sensed it was the appropriate outcome. We were hopeless at this exotic species of cricket and unlikely to get better.

I had other interests in the World Cup. One match became the focal point for me: the semifinal between Pakistan and the West Indies. My favorite uncle—my *chota mama*—and I settled down with a radio to follow the commentary. He was twenty-four years old and I was twelve, but in an important dimension, cricket, I was his peer, and he never talked down to me. While possessing no great fondness for the Pakistani team, he wanted to see by way of an abstract, inchoate subcontinental solidarity, a Pakistan win. Pakistan's first wicket fell at ten as they chased the West Indies' formidable 292, but Majid and Zaheer came together and began to take Pakistan toward an improbable victory.

My heroes were going to pull it off. They would beat the mighty West Indies and go on to the final. The score reached 176 before the second wicket fell. It was bad enough that the wicket to fall was Zaheer's, but things got worse. Majid fell at 187. I still hoped; Javed was there. But Javed was out first ball. It went downhill rapidly, in undignified fashion. Pakistan's collapse, its fall from the glories of the Majid-Zaheer partnership, was precipitous: 176–1 to 250 all out. It was a brutal blow, unmitigated by the generous assessment that Pakistan had fought hard and lost honorably. But I did not need another team of good fighters and good losers. I already had the Indian team for that.

My uncle and I followed the match late into the night, sitting in the air-conditioned comfort of my grandfather's bedroom, the Philips transistor radio next to us, as the BBC commentary swooped and plummeted, the shortwave static crackling in the night. It was a brutal June in New Delhi and outside, the summer pressed against the windows of our home. When I occasionally took a break and went to the bathroom, the heat drove me out again quickly. That summer I had lost my father. A few months after his death, I was happy again, made so by two Pakistani batsmen who promised to transport me to the days when my family was together, when there were four of us, and we had watched Zaheer score those runs against India. Majid and Zaheer were doing much more than playing a game of cricket. For a couple of magic hours, they took me to an earlier, happier, time in my life.

The 1979 World Cup was edificatory in another dimension. Cricket was a different game when the World Cup final's highlights were viewed on BBC: all the way from the opening music score—years later, as a long-haired, pot-smoking, wannabe hippie dancing at the Squaw Valley music festival in Northern California, I learned the theme was Booker T. and the MGs' "Soul Limbo"—to the beautiful clarity of the slow-motion replays. As I watched Derek Randall field, as he raced in and slid in to the boundary ropes to save a certain four, as I watched Collis King and Viv Richards take apart the English attack, as I saw the magnificent, proud, body language of the West Indies, cricket's possibilities were redefined. My sense of watching cricket beyond India's capabilities grew. This was real cricket, not the watered-down, unathletic version the Indian team provided. I felt—acutely, again—India was a trap. We had been kept apart from the rest and the best of the world for fear of contaminating them with our mediocrity.

The Great Miss

ON THE DAY INDIA'S 1979 Test series against England began, I was visiting the American Library. On most days as the library closed, with great reluctance I would leave to patiently wait my turn for the 401 bus at Connaught Place's crowded bus stops. But on the first day of the first Test, I left early. Only one thing could make me abandon the American Library: I wanted to return home and turn my attention to Test cricket. As I rode home, the radio commentary began at 3:55 P.M., heralding the beginning of the end of the hot Delhi afternoon and the start of an evening occupied by cricket. The roar and crackle of the feedback from hundreds of transistors amplifying each other filled buses and streets. It was the sound of a broad cultural engagement, an absorption in a game played thousands of miles away. I did not need to carry my own radio with me; I could hear the commentary quite distinctly from those that were being played in the bus.

Finally, away from India and the weakened teams that toured it, this was the full-strength English team; there was to be no pussyfooting around. This was the real thing. And unsurprisingly, far away from the safety of their shores, from the Packer-denuded sides they had hustled to unconvincing defeats, Indian bowlers were put to the sword. By the end of the first day, England had reached 318 for three; on the second day, England put on 315 runs in four and a half hours. (The English innings belonged to David Gower, who made a double century. I had only dimly heard of Gower; I knew this slim, graceful left-hander with blond hair had scored a four off the first ball he had faced in Test cricket, en route to a century on debut against Pakistan. Those sparse descriptions were enough fodder to construct a vision of a new hero come to lay India's attack to waste.) As the commentary went on late into the night, I thought this was the kind of cricket I liked best: a cascade of runs scored off India. England's declaration seemed like an unnecessary halt to the slaughter. The gigantic scores of Bradman's days, which I used to read about in the books I borrowed from the British Council Library, were being attained—why throw a spanner in the works? I wanted nothing more than transportation to those fields of dreams—even if, or especially if, at India's cost.

That season, Indian listeners struck gold in All India Radio's commentary team: Sushil Doshi, Dicky Rutnagur, and Ashish Ray. I was not above recognizing quality in Indian commentators, and Ray quickly became a favorite—for the measured quality of his commentary, for his encyclopedic knowledge of cricket statistics, and for his provision of a balanced picture of the game, including the stellar quality of not getting hysterical when India did well. I associated Hindi commentary with the more partisan—and hence personally irritating—members of the commentary box, but I enjoyed Sushil Dosh's work immensely. There was snobbery in my usual rejection of Hindi commentary; it was evocative of the India I distanced myself from as an Anglophone. But there was that old unfamiliarity and aesthetic preference too: I just understood cricket better in English.

A few days after the conclusion of the first Test, an innings defeat for India, Doordarshan broadcast a bundle of its television highlights. We no longer had a functional television; our long-suffering model had given up its struggles with functional competency. The only way to watch the highlights would be at my grandmother's home. Through the years we had not owned a television, it had been the venue for the Sunday evening movie. Now with our television out of order, she would have to provide succor again. I waited eagerly for my mother to return from her bruising workday in Delhi's industrial outskirts. She would have to provide transport—and timely too—if I was going to get to my grandmother's in time. As she drove into our narrow lane and parked, I ran down and apprised her of the situation. My mother wearily agreed to get back in the car and drive; her maternal love easily overrode the mental and physical exhaustion she frequently struggled with in this new life of hers.

We walked into my grandmother's home just as the first session of highlights ended. They would resume after a short break for the news, and I would be able to watch most of Gower's innings. I waited impatiently for the news to end. As the closing credits flashed up, I leaned forward in anticipation. But as the opening credits for the cricket began, my grandmother stood up and spoke, "Everyone out of the room" (or words to that effect, since she only spoke Punjabi.) She was not going to sleep; she was not going to watch an alternative program—there were no other channels; this was the India of the 1970s. She simply did not want to be bothered by company. I protested to no avail. I asked my *chota mama* why we could not watch the cricket. I was staggered by his unquestioning acceptance of patent injustice: "If your grandmother doesn't want to have the TV on, there's nothing we can do about it." My grandmother's selfishness colored my relationship with her; her unreasonableness became a prime example of ungrandmotherly behavior, of her lack of love for my brother, my mother—her daughter—and me. She could not indulge her grandchildren in their simple pleasures; she would deny them a rare sporting confection.

The last Test of the series, at the Oval, became famous for Gavaskar's epic 221 and India's brave but disorganized chase of a winning total of 438. India blew its chance to score the highest fourth-innings total ever, losing the plot and sliding to 429–8 despite being 301–1.* The 1979 Oval Test was deemed a "brave fightback," a "glorious draw" by an admiring English and Indian press. India earned the platitudes it specialized in accumulating, but a familiar loss of tactical and psychological nerve ensured the greatest of cricketing glories slipped from its grasp.

By drawing the Oval Test, India missed out on the greatest run-chase of all time, in England, with an English press contingent watching. Had India won, Gavaskar's innings would have been reckoned the greatest of all time; the anointment would have been swift. There was no doubting the identity of those who controlled the cricketing world's information order and formulated its paradigms of excellence. A game witnessed by an English journalist was understood differently in the game's pecking order. If a tree fell in the cricketing forest and an English journalist did not hear it, it never happened; excellence in cricket's marginal spaces was destined to not be recognized appropriately by its keepers. An Indian batsman scoring a double century in England, taking India to a win, squaring a Test series by heroic feats on the last day at one of England's most storied grounds? The descriptions of Gavaskar's feat would have been colorful and overwrought. English cricket writers would have followed the maxim of those who wrote that nation's military history: the glory of our foes redounds to us.

On that night, I only felt relief as India stumbled at the last hurdle. I could not bear to accept the glory being thrust into my hands and willed its rejection. I could not, and did not want to, believe this victory could be Indian.

No Voyagers

Though I was amazed to read Gavaskar predict in a magazine article that Pakistan would "beat India to pulp" on its 1979–1980 tour, I was all for it.† Six Tests of Pakistani mayhem lay ahead, of Zaheer, Asif,

---

* This paragraph and the next two draw upon the essay "India's Great Misses: The Oval 1979," in Chopra, *Eye on Cricket.*

† Devendra Prabhudesai, *SMG: A Biography of Sunil Manohar Gavaskar* (New Delhi: Rupa, 2009).

Majid, and Javed scoring thousands of runs, decimating Indian bowlers as their own quick men blew away the Indian batsmen. A photograph of Bishen Bedi, the now retired Indian captain, greeting Asif Iqbal the new Pakistan captain, at Delhi's international airport made front-page news; reviews and statistical trivia filled the newspapers; and radio commentary was provided for even lowly tour games. I tuned in to Pakistan's first match against Central Zone at Jaipur. Javed scored a century, Zaheer a fifty, and on the third day of the game, Pakistan scored 100 runs in an hour. It would be the last time I would find comfort during the series.

On the first day of the first Test, I was attending a school sports meet in Delhi's National Stadium, waiting for the games to begin, both there and elsewhere. I moved from schoolboy to schoolboy—each one with a transistor glued to his ear—asking for the score again and again as Pakistan finally batted after a delayed start. Zaheer made a paltry forty, a score that terrified me with its intimations of mortality. I consoled myself riches waited in the Tests to follow.

During the Delhi Test, on the third day, I was at school, impatiently waiting to go home to watch the live telecast. Zaheer was batting. In the school bus on the way home, I kept my ear cocked at an angle, turning it into an antenna for the radio commentary around me that informed me of Zaheer's progress. As I alighted at my bus stop, Zaheer got to fifty. I sighed with relief. I would walk home, settle down to watch television with the meal my mother would have provided, and watch him rampage on to a hundred. Zaheer walked out after tea. Roger Binny bowled the first ball after the break; Zaheer edged it to Kirmani. I sat stunned, disbelieving. Life was bitterly ironic. I had restrained my impatience all day to see my hero bat in the beautiful Delhi winter sunshine, the stage had been set perfectly, and the one ball I saw him play dismissed him. Only a conspiracy, some benighted twist of fate, could have made such a turn of events possible.

The disappointments came thick and fast that winter: Gavaskar scored heavily, Kapil Dev turned in stellar all-round performances, and Roger Binny, seemingly a friendly trundler, took bagfuls of Pakistani wickets. India won the series 2–0. Amid this carnage I found new Pakistani heroes: Azeem Hafiz, the pace bowler with the withered left arm, an immediate poster child for overcoming adversity,* and Wasim Raja, Pakistan's mellow, bearded, elegant left-handed batsman, who looked as if at any mo-

---

* Samir Chopra, "The Story of Azeem Hafeez," ESPNcricinfo, 18 July 2011, available at http://www.espncricinfo.com/blogs/content/story/619908.html, last accessed 9 April 2015.

ment he'd start quoting Urdu poems while sipping on wine, looking like those figures in the drawings that accompanied Omar Khayyam ditties. His narrow failures to attain the century mark—twice in the series—engendered an acute heartbreak.

In the last Test at Calcutta, with typical Pakistani attacking flair, Asif declared with Pakistan behind in the first innings and daringly set out to salvage a win—akin to those memorable ones at Lahore and Karachi, which had so ignited my passion for the Pakistani cricket team. But Pakistan did not deliver. Set 265 runs on the last day its batsmen puttered around aimlessly as they scored merely 179 for the loss of six wickets in sixty-five overs. To cap the irony of it all, a player whose stodginess I despised—Dilip Doshi—ran out Asif in his last Test innings. The Karachi Scrambler, that fleet-footed runner, had gone down in a heap. The cruelty was complete.

My heroes had let me down. They had given credence to those who said they could not perform their magic outside Pakistan. The worst disappointment though, lay in Pakistani complaints about the Indian umpiring; my heroes' failure to accept their defeats with a steely graciousness was distasteful. Their behavior approximated that of the carping Indian fans I had distanced myself from. I did not want to believe umpires cheated—even Indian ones—and I resented Pakistani attempts to force this cynical interpretation of cricketing results on me. I was disappointed by Pakistani nonperformance, but I was not ready to believe they were victims of an Indian conspiracy. I was bemused too, to read Majid Khan suggest Indian umpires should wear bangles. I failed to discern a causal or even correlative relation between a lack of manhood and a proclivity for cheating or incompetence at umpiring. My heroes were not perfect, in the sporting or moral sense.

When Australia toured Pakistan in 1979–1980, I found myself conflicted again. I was a proud fan of the Australians and a rabid fan of Kim Hughes, the most irrepressible strokeplayer of that era. Once the Tests began, my support for Pakistan easily swamped that for Australia. My approach to the cricket was uncritical: I found Pakistan's run-scoring thrilling even if it only resulted in high-scoring draws, the kind I had condemned in India. But a mystery emerged: the reported dislike the Australians had for Pakistan. I trusted Australian reactions more than I did Indian ones, and these complaints set up a jangling dissonance. A little later, when the West Indies toured Pakistan in 1980, I was surprised to hear their beating Pakistan in Pakistan was a singular feat. This was the first indication that beating anyone at all was difficult for the West Indies. I wondered whether there was truth to Indian fans' claims that beating

Pakistan at home was impossible because of the Pakistani umpires. The West Indies too, did not seem comfortable in Pakistan. The ugly incident involving Sylvester Clarke, who had thrown a brick back at Pakistani spectators, had conjured up images of hostiles pressing at the fences.* While I idealized and idolized the Pakistani cricket team, the cricketing world had considerably less affection for its land and peoples. I did not stop to ponder the acute similarity between these complaints and those made about touring India.

Topsy-Turvy Down Under

IN 1980, I left home. Rather, I was sent away. Not that I minded. The year following my father's passing away had seen me increasingly distracted. Schoolwork no longer attracted my diligent attentions, I had barely made it into the eighth grade, and I had started partaking of the pleasures of tobacco. My mother thought the watchful eye of my father's old college friend, rector at a boarding school in India's northeast, would help. She acted expeditiously on this belief and packed me off. I was delighted to leave New Delhi and my melancholic home behind. The prospect of nine months a year spent away from my mother and brother did not deter me. Dormitory life, attending school in natty blazers and ties—it was all more glamorous than the dispirited, gloomy home and humdrum existence that was my lot in Delhi.

On my return to Delhi after my first session in boarding school, India's Test series against a full-strength Australia began. As it did, I was away in Maihar, on a brief vacation to my grandfather's home. There, I would rise early to the sounds of radio commentary. Outside, close to my bedroom window, sat my grandfather, tuning into cricket on his portable transistor set. I would stagger out, bleary-eyed, to join him. The glorious sunlight of those cold winter mornings, the hot, sweet tea served by our faithful cook, and the commentary, listened to while bundled up in sweaters and prickly woolen shawls, entailed a perfect start to the day: cricket before full waking consciousness had been attained.

Cricket sustained my seventy-three-year-old grandfather much as it would sustain me years later in the United States. Six years before, he had been a sprightly sixty-seven. I delighted in telling stories of him com-

---

* Martin Williamson, "When Sylvester Clarke Bricked It," ESPNcricinfo, 13 May 2006, available at http://www.espncricinfo.com/magazine/content/story/246963 .html, last accessed 26 January 2015.

mencing his weekly swimming sessions by diving off trees that overhung the river Tamas that ran close to Maihar. Then he suffered a stroke, which paralyzed his left side. Remarkably, he recovered the use of his limbs and regained the ability to walk, albeit with a cane and a drag in his left foot as he pulled it forward to keep balance. Two items never associated with him now became so: a transistor radio and a cane. On the radio he traversed the landscapes denied to his physical form. He found news, plays, and classical music recitals, which entertained him as he parked himself on a chair at a chosen point of repose. His love for cricket was nascent; he became a bigger fan of the game once forced to take refuge in his radio. When Test cricket was on, the sound of the commentary emanating from his beloved radio marked his location in our home and became its confluent point for the day.

Before the series, Indian newspapers suggested a mere Indian pretender—Sunil Gavaskar—would one day overhaul the mighty Don Bradman's world tally of twenty-nine Test centuries. The start of the series was thus perfect: in the first over of the Sydney Test, the scoreboard read "Gavaskar c Marsh b Lillee 0" as a usurper was emphatically shown his rightful place. India collapsed; Sandeep Patil batted bravely, but his dismissal, felled by a Len Pascoe bouncer, was an appropriate symbol of India's inability to withstand the might of Australia. In 1979, India might have harassed the weak, Packer-decimated Australian team, but now, up against the full-strength team—including Greg Chappell, who made a double hundred—there was little resistance. It confirmed my impression of the Packer years: we had been playing second-class cricket. This was not a hypothesis that needed the exhaustive empirical support I sent its way, but I could not, and would not, cease and desist.

Shortly after the Test finished, I laid my hands on an Australian sporting magazine that suggested India "shape up or ship out." I thought this language appropriately directed at the slackers who called themselves the Indian team and repeated it with gusto to my brother. He responded with distaste, "That magazine you're reading is a bit too patriotic." It was a remarkably restrained comment. I could understand dimly what my brother was getting at but resisted the temptation to think further about the implications of his remark. I was particularly sensitive to jingoism or unbalanced nationalism in local sports writing but not so when it came to the productions of other countries.

As my vacation progressed, my mother, worried about my loneliness at home and my inability to concentrate and finish my holiday homework, suggested I spend a couple of weeks with my aunt. I could work on my homework during the day, and at night, seek my uncle's help with math problems. My aunt could feed me the home-cooked, piping-hot breakfasts, lunches, and dinners my guilt-stricken mother was incapable of providing as she worked twelve-hour workdays at the business that was now her increasingly onerous responsibility.

My aunt did not mind me listening to cricket commentary in lieu of doing homework. As the Adelaide Test began, I woke early and stayed transfixed by the radio. The second day was sublime. It was a beautiful winter, as all Delhi winters are, and I basked in the bright sunshine coming through the doors that opened to our backyard. As Kim Hughes made a double century, as his score blossomed and grew, I was ecstatic. A hero was coming good at a ground I loved—it was the home of Don Bradman and David Hookes—against India. When I saw the television highlights of the Adelaide Test, Hughes's innings struck me speechless. The power and beauty of his shots in slow motion stunned me. Cricket was truly a different game when watching a batsman of such high quality, his feats suitably enshrined by crystal-clear television coverage. The next day, in India's response, Sandeep Patil pulled the proverbial chestnuts out of the fire. As Patil launched into his thundering cover drives off Dennis Lillee and Len Pascoe, there was no mistaking his poise and authority. But I would only fully appreciate Patil's batting in this match much later. Now, all it did was block an Australian win, one I wanted.

For the third and final Test at Melbourne, All India Radio's commentators were supplied with a television set in their broadcasting box. As Viswanath was dismissed in India's first innings, Narottam Puri reported the decision was "dubious" and urged listeners to wait for his description based on the television coverage: "Let's wait for the replay to see what happened. Yes, not out; it did not hit his bat." My immediate reaction was irritation, the kind an Australian would have felt on hearing the archetypal Pommy whinge about Australian umpiring. In India's second innings came the Gavaskar-Lillee incident: Gavaskar was declared leg before wicket (LBW), protested, got into a verbal tangle with Lillee, the bowler—who called him a "cunt"—and angrily threatened to leave the ground and concede the game. I was perplexed. Though I reflexively disagreed with anything Gavaskar said or did (but not wrote), I wondered how bad things were, umpiring and Australian players included, that matters had come to such a pass.

After India set Australia a modest target in the fourth innings, I prepared for a preening session. Surely, Australia could not lose from here. Early the next morning, I listened in stunned silence as Australia collapsed to defeat. I wonder if those Australians who personally disliked Greg Chappell—I had heard there were many—were as upset as I was when he was bowled first ball by Karsan Ghavri. In a performance for the ages, Kapil Dev bowled with a bad knee to take five wickets and bowl India to a win and a drawn series. Looking for scapegoats, I settled on the uneven Melbourne Cricket Ground (MCG) pitch, disregarding its sameness for both teams. I did not realize, possibly because Indian press reports made little of it, that the Indian team had been visibly belligerent as they defended the small target they had set. A summer's worth of resentment at Australian sledging—in the press and on the ground—and umpiring had finally bubbled over. Most notably, Alan Border received an angry verbal send-off from Kapil Dev and Yashpal Sharma. It remains the only overt gesture of aggression from Indian players from that era; it took something extreme to push them over the edge. But I did not see it; I had skipped the highlights.

The Great Bore: England in India and Vice Versa

A YEAR LATER, my honeymoon with my boarding school was over. I loved the views of Kanchenjunga's triple massif and its surrounding huge mountain ranges from my dormitory; I loved the tennis courts that looked down on green hill slopes; I loved the views from our cricket field; I loved the collection of cricket books in our library. But even the staggering natural and architectural beauty of that hilltop campus, its steeping in a classical cricketing culture, complete with school colors and an old-fashioned pavilion, could not make me stay there any longer. Boys' boarding schools—young adolescent men cooped up together with harsh discipline enforced via a sadistic team of prefects—were a surefire recipe for disaster. That school year's events—a series of violent encounters between juniors and seniors—proved it to be so. I had had enough. I was shell-shocked, I had failed to live up to the standards of masculinity required in a boy's boarding school, and I wanted out. I was scared, nauseated by fear. I had been slapped around and made to perform physically exhausting punishment drills one too many times by prefects. Home felt like a much safer place.

On the last day of school, I left Darjeeling with some classmates, traveling by jeep and car, heading for Siliguri to catch the nighttime Tinsukia Express. I did not know it then, but it was the last time I would ever see those lads. We left school in high spirits and enjoyed, first, a glorious lunch in the sunshine at my friend's tea estate and then a scenic drive down to the plains. Once left in Siliguri to our own devices, we indulged in those silly adventures only schoolboys released from a strictly regimented boarding school can. Then finally late at night, the Tinsukia Express rumbled into New Jalpaiguri station. We hopped on and headed back home to meet our families, who had been denied our company for nine long months. I have often wondered what date all that occurred on—a day marked by sparkling sunshine, the lush verdant hillsides of West Bengal tea estates, and finally, the unbridled glee of schoolboys released from headmasterly and prefectorial control.

There was a simple way to find out: the scoreboard. It all happened on 1 December 1981. That was the day England collapsed in Bombay while chasing a target of 241 in the first Test of the 1981–1982 series. As we left the school premises, England's chase had started. By the time we arrived at my friend's tea estate, England had lost its opening batsmen. There were no televisions at hand, so we sat in the glittering sunshine and cool breeze, drinking tea, polishing off an assortment of baked goods, all the while listening to the sonorous tones of the commentary crew. Later, as we careened down one curved hilly road after another, the radio remained on as England stumbled quickly to 102 all out. A Test win over the English was in the bag. We were free, an extended, adventurous train ride awaited. What more could a schoolboy want? One wanted an English win.

My hills school session had ended in December 1981; I would not start school—back in the plains—before July 1982. I would be off from school for seven months. With England touring, Botham and Gower included, the pleasurable opportunities for watching live cricket seemed endless. For anyone who endured that winter's cricket of five consecutive turgid draws after the first Test, that hope is a grim joke. My potentially dreamlike vacation at home—no school, five Tests telecast live—turned into a series of boring, lonely, mornings and afternoons. My mother was at work, my brother was at school. Our house was denuded; my father's absence was still palpable. Cricket would have provided a respite, but none was forthcoming. Elsewhere in the world, exciting cricket continued to be played—the West Indies had played a riveting series in Australia that southern summer—but in India we were confined to a diet of dull draws. The world watched Hollywood; we watched Films Division documentaries. There was ample opportunity here for self-flagellation.

When India toured England in 1982, during the drawn second Test, I saw an Indian batsman do something I had not seen a Pakistani batsman do: Sandeep Patil smashed the English pace bowler Bob Willis for six fours—including five consecutively—in a seven-ball over. While statistical feats requiring merely dogged application had always seemed within Indian players' reach, I did not think they could excel in aggressive, attacking cricket. I liked Indian cricketers more when they played the way I imagined Pakistanis always played. As I watched Patil's batting on a highlights reel, I realized yet again that I preferred India playing abroad, on international television, lapping up praise from overseas commentators. It was the second time Patil had assaulted fast bowlers from distant lands on their home turf, and I sensed a warming to his brand of cricket, and thus to the Indian team.

I grew sensitive, for the first time, to the condescension I could hear dripping from English match reports and television commentary; some previously insensitive antennae had started picking up signals. My immediate conjecture for this increased sensitivity was that for the first time, I had read English responses to the West Indies fast bowling attack on the 1976 and 1980 tours and realized a previously sacrosanct bastion of cricketing rectitude was not above its own petty biases. The endless complaints about short-pitched bowling and glacial over rates and the skepticism about Clive Lloyd's captaincy skills, which did not recognize Lloyd's man management of an eclectic team of players drawn from diverse and disparate regions, were indicators that underneath the cool, distant, erudite sophistication of the English journalist lay plebian emotions that underwrote jaundiced assessments of glowing self-worth and other unworthiness. There seemed little generosity directed at the West Indies' brilliant cricket; instead, there was a bitter, carping resentment. An acute dissonance had been set up in my older self's admiration of all things English in all matters cricketing.

Captain Courageous:
Imran at the Helm

I FOLLOWED PAKISTAN'S fortunes as it toured Australia in 1981–1982 and went down without a fight. My disappointment ran deep; the Pakistani cricketers were indeed not capable of playing well away from home. Besides, the Pakistani players' strike, mounted against Miandad's appointment as captain, was jarring. I had never heard of a players' strike, never heard of such deep discord in a band of brothers. And then there was the infamous Lillee-Miandad incident in the Perth Test, when the two had almost come to blows, aiming kicks and cricket bats at each other. I could dimly make out that both had been at fault, and my distaste ran high.* I preferred my heroes to be gentlemen; the combative street-

---

* Martin Williamson, "One of the Most Undignified Events in Test History," ESPNcricinfo, 12 November 2010, available at http://www.espncricinfo.com/magazine/content/story/486739.html, last accessed 26 January 2015.

fighter was not then my model for a sporting hero. It would only become so later.

The players' strike had an immediate effect on Pakistani cricket. Imran became captain for the tour of England in the summer of 1982. Frustratingly, Pakistan lost the series, but they did win the second Test against time, with Miandad—sent up to open—and Mohsin Khan scoring seventy-seven runs in thirteen overs even as rain closed in. It was precisely the way I wanted them to win. The World Cricket Digest made immediate note of Mohsin falling to his knees in prayer as the winning runs were hit, an exoticizing description that provoked some indignation on my part. As the tour progressed, I felt more stirrings of unease at the language often used by the English press to describe the Pakistani cricketers—"over-excitable"—and Pakistani crowds—"shrill." This did not amuse me; I felt defensive and protective about the Pakistanis. These English descriptions of all things Pakistani were a little too reliant on stereotypes, not above the snobbery and prejudice I had been told had often underwritten English colonial rule in my neck of the woods. I had begun to detect a pattern in the English descriptions of Caribbean, Indian, and Pakistani cricketers and their fans: they were always excitable, undisciplined, and unruly, not quite in conformance with cricketing traditions defined by English journalists and ex-cricketers. They were the pickpockets and the touts of the cricket world, hustling and devious, offering cut-rate deals for dubious goods. That language resonated with that deployed by English sahibs against their native bearers and cooks and *babus* and *sepoys* when they had ruled the subcontinent. Those subjects qualified for the same lexicon of patronizing adjectives; they too, had needed encouraging pats on the back and firm chastisement when they overstepped the bounds of decorum drawn up by others. Subcontinental cricketers were natives in whites, admitted to the gymkhana if they promised to behave, their every move scrutinized for the failure to conform that would see them expelled again.

But public displays of religiosity bothered me, and this overt exhibition of private faith by a Pakistani player made me uneasy. Earlier that year, the Pakistani hockey captain Akhtar Rasool had begun an interview with the press after the 1982 World Cup final with "*Yeh sab Allah-Tara ki meherbani hai*" (This is all by God's grace), which triggered a similar response in me. There was no inconsistency here; I knew an Indian cricketer thanking Bhagawan or an English or Australian cricketer thanking his Savior, Christ, after a Test win would have bothered me as much. These pronouncements, these reminders of difference, triggered an unease more primeval, a holdover of those tales of partition and perfidy I had been told in my childhood. I wanted Pakistanis to keep their otherness at bay somehow, to not assert their religious difference so overtly. But from whom? There were millions of Indians after all, who were Muslims just like the Pakistanis were.

That summer, Pakistan set more attacking fields, used a leg spinner, and were the more attractive team to watch. Yet they lost. I was an unabashed apologist for their failure. As I read about umpiring decisions that went against Pakistan, I could barely contain my frustration and anger at the English umpire, David Constant, who had committed one howler after another.* English umpires, it turned out, were not perfect; they were capable of incompetence and of being infected with the same prejudices that had infected their compatriots in the press box. The claims of the pristine professionalism, the quiet, effective competence that was supposedly the easily acquired hallmark of the English umpire, appeared overblown, a ludicrously inflated self-aggrandizing assessment. Pakistan and Imran felt conspired against; I felt the same way. I found English complaints about Pakistani overappealing ludicrous; loud speech was required when speaking to those who feigned deafness.

Pakistan did better once they returned home. Australia did not stand a chance as it toured Pakistan late in 1982. The Pakistanis won all three Tests handsomely, but I felt little elation. My doubts about Pakistan flared up when I looked back on the series in England. Qadir—for all his supposedly mysterious talents—had failed to be a match winner in England. His metamorphosis into an unplayable demon at home had been rapid. A photograph of a scruffy and unwashed Alan Border shouldering arms to Qadir summed up the Australia tour: a refusal to engage in a contest. Australia was not fighting; Pakistan had dispirited the Australians. Australia did not want to be there; they did not mind losing in Pakistan. They wanted to go home—uncaring of their loss to Pakistan and convinced of their inability to win.

Why would any cricket team—especially one like Australia's—want to give up? What was it about Pakistan that corroded their spirits so? In some distant corner of my mind, the answer had less to do with Australian inability to engage in competitive cricket in an unfamiliar environment, Australian failure to be flexible in the kind of cricket they played, and Australian in-fighting than with a particular brand of hostility experienced in Pakistan. Old prejudices stirred; Pakistan was a very distinctive

---

* Martin Williamson, "India's Constant Problem," ESPNcricinfo, 29 August 2014, available at http://www.espncricinfo.com/magazine/content/story/775503.html, last accessed 26 January 2015.

Other. Its menace was on display in its team's internecine conflict, its players' contentious personalities, its hostile crowds, and its umpiring. This menace, which I was not willing to accept as bogeyman when noticed by Indians, was believable when Australia complained. I was ready to disregard Indian prejudices about Pakistan, because they were Indian ones. But not so the Australian ones; they were trustworthy witnesses. Their complaints fell on fertile ground as I played host to a self-infection by all I had heard about Pakistan from those near and dear to me. The Australians were not a neutral party; they could not have been. But in this mental dispute, they were.

Imran Ascendant, India Descendant

DURING INDIA'S 1982–1983 TOUR OF PAKISTAN, I found for the first time, Indian cricketing heroes. They were of a very particular ilk.

In the first Test, Mohinder Amarnath, the Delhi batsman—making a comeback after suffering head injuries inflicted by various fast bowlers over the years—held the Indian innings together in response to a huge Pakistani first innings score. Mohinder's penchant for hooking bouncers had earned him—besides painful blows to his cranium—the ire of many critics, but I found his defiance and aggressive response to fast bowling admirable. And a cricketing child prodigy, Maninder Singh, another Delhi player, made his debut in the second Test. Maninder had played for my old air force school; he had come up through the ranks to Delhi's Ranji Trophy team and from there into the Indian team for the Pakistani tour, a quick and dramatic rise to the top. Reading the names of my former schoolteachers and hearing the references to the school's mighty cricket team induced an emotion more properly experienced in those older than me: nostalgia. It was possible to fantasize too, about a similar career track for oneself; my cricketing idol was not a distant, inaccessible ideal, but a rather more proximal aspiration.

I had started to acquire a Delhi identity. I had not identified as a Delhiite before attending boarding school in Darjeeling. There, during my first time away from home, I was relentlessly reminded I was one. Calcutta boys, the Biharis, the Bengalis, the Marwaris, the Sindhis, the Parsees, the Sikkimese, the Nepalis—everyone had a tag. I was a Punjabi and a Delhiite. Much to my astonishment, there were derogatory nicknames reserved for my clan, my ethnic demographic, and the fellow dwellers of my city. For the first time, an awareness of my ethnic identity was forced on me. I was made aware that within the capacious nation that was supposedly my home, I had been assigned a very particular location.

On the cricketing front Delhi's wins in the Ranji Trophy, India's domestic championship, against Bombay had aroused a local pride. A local winner was easy to back and use as a basis for identity formation. (Delhi won the Ranji Trophy in 1979 and 1980, lost in the final in 1981, and then won again in 1982.) I had been glad to see the hated Bombay team—they were Gavaskar's team, after all—taken down a peg or two. This local allegiance marked, though I did not realize it then, the beginnings of a translation into a broader national allegiance. It was an unexpected sequence for someone who—thanks to his father's military service—might have been expected to have been steeped in nationalist alliances from the very beginning.

An abstract identification with all things Indian did not come easily to me. The Indian nation that claimed my allegiance, whose history and culture I did not understand, was too diffuse to command sentiments of loyalty and fealty. A common nationality and citizenship had not been of much use to me in my encounters with my mates in boarding school. Our national history was impossibly distant; India's antiquity, rather than serving as a source of pride, placed it in remoteness, indifferent to present concerns, irrelevant to the construction of contemporary relationships. Our cultural and linguistic diversity—the one covered up by a veneer of Westernization on air force bases and middle-class urban communities—was bewildering and disorienting. I found pleasure instead in identification with the local, with Delhi—the site of my home and its street and the boys I played cricket with, my adventures with my parents and brother, and the venue for festivals and holidays with family.

To cheer for Maninder and Mohinder was only one step above cheering for those who played in local parks and schools in familiar venues and locales. The Indian team, by dint of the hero worship that was directed at them from elsewhere, was rendered more abstract. They played on distant grounds in distant cities I had never traveled to. (I have never been to Kolkata or Chennai and have spent a grand total of seven days in Mumbai and Bangalore.) They were supposed to be the closest thing to Bollywood superstars, but those were remote fantasy figures, not the kind you identified with. A Delhi star was from "around here." Indian players *looked* like me, but Delhi players could have *been* me.

On the first day of the second Test at Karachi, India batted first as Gundappa Viswanath sparkled briefly against Abdul Qadir. Bishen Singh Bedi—commentating on Pakistan Television—was busy pointing out Qadir's faults as a leg spinner: Qadir did not have enough of a pivot when he bowled; there was no googly to be found. I was mystified by this ungracious response to a spinner whose talents had been praised by the English press and who had so comprehensively blown away the Australians. It was vintage Indian crabbiness, the over-the-top converse of the Indian cringe. It was a pompous proclamation of the superiority of all things Indian, evident often in claims of a glorious intellectual past, a vibrant culture, a superior moral sense, and a tolerant, philosophically sophisticated syncretic religion. These qualities lacked enduring efficacy, though. They had been unable to prevent colonization or equip us with cricketing competence. But like Bedi, Viswanath was similarly unawed, effortlessly picking Qadir's googly and dispatching it for four. I was vindicated when Qadir struck, dismissing Viswanath caught behind. There were suggestions in the Indian press that Viswanath had been given out wrongly. But this was just sour grapes, a mean-spirited refusal to acknowledge spinners capable of dismissing Indian batsmen, supposedly the best players of those who turned the ball.

On the second day, I hoped to transcend an acute social discomfort for the sake of cricket. Since I had stopped attending air force schools, I had been out of my element: first at St. Paul's in Darjeeling and now at the Modern School, an institution attended by a disproportionate number of sons and daughters of New Delhi's nouveau riche. Some of my new schoolmates were driven to school in cars; others sported haircuts costing fifty pounds, acquired on their latest vacation to London; some owned videocassette recorders and talked glibly about the latest not-yet-available-in-India movie; and yet others talked about the record albums their cousins had brought back from the United States. Their homes were containers for objects I had only seen in the pages of glossy magazines. Invitations to parties were made by printed cards; I never received any. This was another India, inside Delhi, and I did not feel part of it.

But I had good reason to push my incongruent class identity away during cricket season: some of my classmates owned giant, large-screen color televisions, including the elusive Sony Trinitron, ideal for watching cricket. We did not own a color television, and I was desperate to watch Zaheer and Miandad in the full splendor of a color telecast. So I walked over to a friend's house—one who I knew owned a large-screen Trinitron—and joined a group of my schoolmates for the day. Sitting in my friend's spacious, luxuriously furnished living room, I watched as the Pakistani batsmen—including Zaheer—got to work on the Indian bowling. All that I had wanted in the 1980 series was now coming true; the tables had been turned conclusively. My favorites were now scoring heavily and freely, riding roughshod over this puny bowling attack ranged against them. Just as some calculation was needed on whether Zaheer would get his double century before stumps, he was trapped LBW by Kapil Dev. There, I thought, that should take care of those who thought Pakistani umpires were cheats.

It is possible to precisely date the start of the Imran Khan legend in the Indian fan's mind: Christmas Day 1982, the third day of the second Test, as India began its second innings facing a staggering Pakistani lead. The first wicket fell early, but Gavaskar and Dilip Vengsarkar came together and went on to 102. That evening, I was preparing for a twin celebration. A friend was throwing a birthday party, and then we were going to a rock concert; there were such things in New Delhi in the 1980s. As I left my home and our television and walked out on the street, a roar told me another wicket had fallen. I walked on quickly, hearing more roars along the way. On arrival at the party, I was greeted with the news India had slumped to 114–7. The rout was complete: six wickets had fallen for twelve runs. Imran had taken five of them, all bowled or LBW, with fast off-cutters or in-swingers moving a prodigious distance from outside off-stump back on to leg or middle. As I stuffed *golgappas* into my mouth and looked around for seconds of the sundry treats on offer, the conversation surrounding me described in increasingly rude terms just what Imran had done to the Indian team: "*gaand maar dee*" (we've been fucked), "*India ki toh fatli*" (India is screwed). We then forgot about the scenes of cricketing devastation, got drunk, piled into a car—this was before the days people worried much about drinking and driving—and drove off to see an old, famous band from Delhi—Electric Plant—ply their wares. That crisp Delhi Christmas Day, Muhammad Ali Jinnah's birthday—as the Pakistani commentators on television reminded us again and again—Imran's pyrotechnics provided a gift-wrapped offering of five Indian scalps to the Qaid-e-Azam.

A day later, the Test was over. For a supposed fan of the Pakistani cricket team, that win in a largely empty stadium, against a team not able to resist, filled me with a curious unease. I had gotten what I wanted: a century from Zaheer and defeat for India. But I knew my approval meant little to the Pakistani team. My heroes could survive without my adulation. This was a Pakistani moment; Indian fans were not invited. And the suddenness with which the Test had ended meant a denial of almost two whole days of Test cricket, a disastrous deprival in the winter break.

My brother and I were now latchkey kids. We ate lunches left for us, somehow miraculously cooked by my mother in the mornings before she scrambled to drive an hour away to work. That winter, my daily routine was cast in stone. I would return from school and pick up the house keys from our neighbors—where my mother would have left them. My timing was down pat; a brisk walk from the bus station brought me back almost exactly at 3:00 P.M. Then, armed with my warmed-up lunch, I would watch the post-tea session at home. During the third Test, on the second day, as it was at Delhi on Pakistan's tour in 1979–1980, the scene was set for me to watch Zaheer at leisure as he had just walked into bat. Zaheer now scored his third century in as many innings in that series. Pakistani commentator Iftikhar Ahmed waxed purple, "From now on, Zaheer will not be compared to other batsmen; other batsmen will be compared to Zaheer." But something was gratingly suspicious about Zaheer's proficiency here at home and not in England when those big hundreds would have won Pakistan the series. The Pakistani team could only bat in Bradmanesque fashion against the Indians, whom I did not think much of anyway. Whence then, the glory of their feats? I had run into an old problem with denigrating those whose you wage battle against; go too far, and you denigrate your own triumphs.

The next day the massacre continued as Miandad, Saleem Malik, and Imran scored centuries. Listening to the battery-powered radio commentary rather than watching the television since Delhi's power supply had decided to play truant yet again, I gloried in the slaughter of the Indian bowling, urging Imran and Malik on to score centuries so I could aurally witness an innings in which four centuries had been scored. Pakistan obligingly delighted the statistician in me; Pakistan would do what India was unable or unwilling to do.

But it's not like I wanted India to excel statistically in cricket. I did not want Gavaskar to break Bradman's record of twenty-nine centuries in Test cricket; I winced every time he made a century after his twentieth. This was not garden-variety protectiveness of a world record; most fans wanted to see a sporting record broken by their countryman. But in my reckonings, these records would be sullied if an Indian were to possess them; a world record would not be one if an Indian could possess it. Gavaskar's quest for Bradman's record was not mine; I did not see him as my representative. Not only was abroad the chosen venue of excellence; sporting feats were only distinguished if performed by those who lived there. The diminishment, the negation of all things Indian was complete. (Even Pakistan's feats were infected by this diminution of the non-Anglo-Australian. During Miandad and Mudassar Nazar's gigantic partnership in the fourth Test, my loyalties were severely tested. My mental hierarchy of preferences set the Anglo-Australian, and especially Don Bradman, above all else. I was not sure I wanted Pakistani batsmen to break Bradman and Jack Fingleton's third wicket record. As the pair crept closer, I agonized. The Don was inviolate. I had zealously defended him from Gavaskar's assault on his record. The problem was solved in the most Solomonesque of ways: Mudassar was out with the partnership equaled.)

On the last day of the Test, as India slowly slid to defeat, Gavaskar battled away, resisting my desire he not score another century. My dislike for Gavaskar would not reach through the television set and affect his concentration. Gavaskar carried his bat—staying not out as all ten wickets fell at the other end—but I did not understand the magnitude of his feat. I was only able to appreciate such feats when Mudassar Nazar emulated Gavaskar in the fourth Test. (Mudassar's run scoring considerably exercised Indian cricket fans, who suggested the world's weakest bowling attack—the Indian one—had resurrected his career and let him fatten his run balance. I resisted the truth of this claim; an acknowledgment of Indian incompetence would diminish the Pakistanis.)

In the fourth Test, thanks to another Imran-triggered collapse, India lost six wickets for twenty-eight runs; complete and utter devastation. Out on the ground, a lone bugler could be heard heralding the Pakistani charge. The sunlight in Hyderabad was fierce, casting a brutal glare; it was bleaching Indian bones out on the pitch. In their second innings, following on, India collapsed once more, clusters of wickets falling as it subsided to an innings defeat. Sarfraz Nawaz bowled Kapil Dev, knocking over all three stumps—an apt symbol of India's failure to resist.

The last two Tests were dreadful bores, foreshadowing the several India-Pakistan series to follow. Six Tests was too much of a good thing. By series end, I was sick of seeing the Pakistanis and the Indians. India-Pakistan cricket had become associated with a grimness that would not be dispelled. I was growing as a cricket fan; while I enjoyed displays of power by my favorite team, I enjoyed close contests much more.

A singular cricket event lay around the corner, one that would change my orientation toward, and understanding of, Indian cricket and cricketers forever.

Part II

The World Is Ours

O N THE FIRST DAY of the first Test of the 1983 India–West Indies
series, there was bad news: there would be no radio commentary.
All India Radio had been unable to make the necessary technical
arrangements. I cast about in disappointment, venturing out for a desul-
tory walk in the evening and only returning when it was dark. A commen-
tary-free night stretched out emptily ahead of me. But my mother had
better news on my return: my uncle—the one with whom I had listened
to the World Cup semifinal commentary in 1979—had called to let me
know a relay of Caribbean radio stations been arranged. I started up the
radio as Michael Holding began the Test by bowling to Gavaskar. This was
the first encounter with the post-Packer West Indies; we were finally playing the genuine item.

Years later I would write in the ESPNcricinfo collection of the best
matches ever* that India versus West Indies at Kingston, 23–28 February
1983 was one of the greatest Tests of all time. Enough time was lost to rain
over the five days that it looked like the match would be drawn. Then, suddenly and fatally on the last day, India slumped, setting a victory target for
the West Indies of 172 off 25 overs at almost seven an over. Greenidge,
Haynes, and Richards got them off to a flyer; the loss of their wickets kept

* ESPNcricinfo Staff, "100 Great Matches of the Century: The Ones We Missed,"
ESPNcricinfo, available at http://static.espncricinfo.com/db/INTERACTIVE/MILLEN
NIUM/READERS_EXTRAS.html, last accessed April 2015.

matters interesting. Finally, Mohinder Amarnath bowled the last over of the day with the Windies needing six to win; Dujon hit a six off the second delivery. It was an incredible finish, made all the better by the West Indies winning. For matches played in the West Indies, All India Radio would relay commentary live from 10:00 P.M. till two in the morning, record the post-tea session and then play it back starting at five in the morning. That dramatic last morning I woke up fiendishly early and moved the radio closer to my ear, trusting the commentary had started again. The familiar, friendly crackle of the radio heralded India's collapse. I knew I was listening to prerecorded commentary, but the excitement of the West Indies' run chase did not diminish. Surprisingly, my schoolmates did not share my exultation at the West Indies win. This desire for a boring draw was inexplicable when the honor of an exciting loss to the mighty West Indies was possible.

Later in the series, India obligingly subsided at Bridgetown, losing by ten wickets. Amid this defeat, I was able to appreciate Indian performances by a Delhi player. Despite being struck in the face by a Michael Holding delivery and suffering an injury that required stitches, Mohinder made ninety-one and eighty—a pair of innings that included a series of fierce hooks and pulls, some of which went for six—and cemented his place in my pantheon of cricketing heroes. His lone resistance was magnificent; a batsman aggressively taking on fast bowling with the hook was worthy of admiration. My cricketing sensibilities had become sufficiently sensitive to dispense appreciation with an unprejudiced eye in some domains. Besides, Amarnath's feats had not interfered with a West Indies win. My appreciation of Amarnath's batting was akin to Neville Cardus's appreciation of the Australian great Victor Trumper: do well, but may your team lose.

One result on that tour should have been paid more attention by all concerned: India beat the West Indies in a one-day international at Berbice, Guyana. But one-day cricket still felt ersatz, only one notch above benefit matches, which were invariably one-day games. I applied the converse formulation and regarded all one-days as benefit matches, fringe entertainments on the sidelines of the real business, Test cricket. Indeed, the very fact that India had managed to beat the West Indies in this form of cricket indicated so. My thesis of Indian cricketing mediocrity was not easily disconfirmed.

The 1983 World Cup began on the day Margaret Thatcher would be voted back into power in the United Kingdom, changing the face of that land forever. I had little anticipation of, or emotional investment in, the World Cup: I expected the full-strength West Indies to win as they had in 1975 and 1979. I expected India to lose heavily, to continue its displays of incompetence in the World Cup and limited overs cricket.

On the first day of the tournament, I was intrigued by India's respectable score in its rain-interrupted opening match against the West Indies. Scoring at four runs an over in a sixty overs game, against the mighty West Indies in England, was an unlikely accomplishment by those supposedly inept in one-day cricket. Still, I did not expect the Indian total to trouble the West Indies. The main interest for me lay elsewhere, in Pakistan's progress, who hammered the Sri Lankans for 338 with 72 scored in the last five overs. India could never pull off something like that.

The next day, I read the stunning news that after resumption, India had beaten the West Indies, that great outfit's first loss ever in the World Cup. Surely this was a freak occurrence, unlikely to be repeated; the West Indies were too intimidating, and India would roll over and die for the rest of the tournament. But by beating Zimbabwe next, India became a contender for the semi-finals; suddenly, calculations were afoot about the points needed to qualify.

Successive losses to Australia and the West Indies convinced me anew the first Indian win had been a fluke. But India's improbable run was not yet over, and so, I tuned in to the game against Zimbabwe; a loss here would end it all. India batted first and collapsed to 17–5. But Kapil Dev turned things around, taking the score to 266–8 with his incredible 175 off 138 deliveries leading the charge. As the score steadily mounted, as Kapil relentlessly assaulted the Zimbabwean bowlers—ones capable of giant-killing, as Zimbabwe's shock victory over Australia had shown—I stared at the radio in disbelief. This could not be India. India had never shown signs of fighting adversity with aggression, of fighting back from the brink—not because their opponents had allowed it but because they had commandeered it. Most surprisingly of all, I found myself cheering for the Indian team with other Indian cricket fans, urging them on over the ridge to the Promised Land that lay ahead.

A mysterious new emotion had found form and expression in me: a desire that the Indian team succeed in transcending a once insuperable barrier. Some of this new feeling was grounded in an older sentiment: I was conscious of the stage India occupied. As India was playing overseas in England, I was aware of the gaze of the rest of the world, of the gathering of the world's players on the English stage; the sentiments on display when Gavaskar had played in county cricket had found an opportunity to recur. Perhaps I cared for India's success because these were one-day games and not Test cricket, not the "real thing." Perhaps my support for Mohinder Amarnath and Maninder Singh had induced, as a side effect, a more affectionate view of their companions on the Indian team. My adoption of a Delhi identity had led me to consider a national one.

Most importantly, there was out on the streets a communal feeling I was swept up in, one that I had never allowed to infect me before: the passion of the Indian cricket fan. I experienced what a tourist might experience on traveling to strange lands when partaking of an unfamiliar festival. As the tourist is carried about, pushed hither and thither in the celebrating throngs, he feels himself infected by the emotions of the crowd. As he participates in the external observances of this novel ritual, he finds himself summoning up, and overcome by, its requisite inner sensations. An atheist too, might fall to her knees if surrounded by the passionate and kneeling devout in a house of worship. Some emotional or psychological barrier had broken down; I had let myself become susceptible to the pull of being an Indian cricket fan, of wanting a share in Indian glory, of identifying with the men in white who donned national colors on our behalf. The "let myself" component is crucial; I was primed for the changes I was playing host to. That perennial cognitive dissonance within me, the discordance of cheering for those not supported by those around me, had finally induced conformity.

It might have been the first time I had felt Indian; it took cricket to bring about this change. It was more effective than tales of military victories and long-fallen empires that stretched from coast to coast, of emperors who embodied and promulgated moral and intellectual virtues, more effective than paeans to the famed Indian tolerance and syncretism and the glorious culture that had to be relentlessly promoted by national television in order to get anyone to pay attention to it. Cricket, the company of other fans, the participation in its rites of passage, was more effective in inducing nationalist sentiment in me. It had been the zone, the domain, within which my diminished sense of Indianness had found its most virulent expression, and it was within those same confines that I first found a sense of national belonging. I had found companionship with my cohort. I was cheering India on. I had been converted.

The Indian team now had the wind behind them, and their next opponent—Australia—was destined to be blown away, as they were. I was incredulous; India had made it to the semifinal of the World Cup. The Indian team would be on live television, on the most exalted stage of all, because Doordarshan, our staid national channel, had decided to telecast the game—an acknowledgment of the game's importance. When the telecast began, I was further converted to the Indian cause. The sight of that BBC telecast, in color, live in our dressing rooms, and those plummy English voices and accents converted me all over again, but in a wholly different manner. I wanted the Indian team to win against the English in England, to beat the team the English press wanted anointed as winners. It was the first time I had desired such a result. I wanted the English press to acknowledge Indian cricketing virtues—not just in a losing cause but in a winning one. Against their own team.

As England's openers blossomed, I was crushed. The Indian team would come this far and fall on this exalted stage. But India choked the English lineup. I cheered as Gower was caught down the leg side, and I cheered as Ian Botham was run out. I was cheering for the dismissal of my former heroes—by Indians. An Indian fan, even if a fair-weather one, was being born, all of sixteen years old.

India's batting bogged down in its reply, but dramatically and power-fully, the Indians lifted themselves. That six that Yashpal Sharma hit off Bob Willis—the one every Indian schoolboy of that era remembers—was symbolic of more than the half dozen runs it added to the Indian score. Willis represented the last gasp of English power; Sharma dispatched him summarily. The dismissive confidence of the Indian players was new to me. *We*—I had never used that term before—used to cowering in England, in front of the world, our incompetence painfully on display, had sud-denly stood up and demanded to be counted.

In the end as India ran out victors, Indian fans mounted the pitch in-vasion I associated with jubilant West Indies fans celebrating another win over England. The Indian team came out on the players' balcony to ac-knowledge the cheering Indian fans below—something I had only seen the lithe, powerful, beautifully black West Indies do. Here in England, Indians could do the same pavilion balcony victory strut I had seen the West Indies perform—in England, stage for those glorious feats I had read and fantasized about so often. This was Old Trafford, Manchester, in Lan-cashire, Yorkshire's archrival, a ground Cardus had written about so often, and it was India's. Yashpal Sharma came out and flexed his muscles; it was a gesture of, dare I say it, non-Indian power and arrogance. We had ar-rived, the stage was ours. (Away in the other semifinal, the West Indies disposed of Pakistan. I cared little, because my cricketing priorities had suddenly changed. Indeed, I did not want India to play Pakistan in the final; I wanted them to play the world champions. I did not want a "local" final; playing against Pakistan—our neighbors—would not be interna-tional enough. Validation for the Indian team lay elsewhere, in a contest against those who had been crowned world champions twice before.)

On the day of the final, my mother, my uncles, and I watched the game on the novelty of color television. I would be watching the game in the company of those whose fandom had nurtured mine. The atmosphere in the opening overs was electric; the full-strength West Indies team was on display. Reared on a diet of black-and-white photographs in magazines, I had dreamed of seeing them live. Now gloriously in full color, here they were. Clive Lloyd, Viv Richards, and Gordon Greenidge were in the slips, in their distinctive, alert, crouching stances that indicated an unshakeable confidence an edge would soon be headed their way. On the screen were Andy Roberts and Joel Garner and Michael Holding, the West Indian fast bowling greats. I had never seen them bowl live before. This was real cricket. We were not on the sidelines anymore. India was facing up to the world's deadliest attack with gumption and aggression. The insults of the Packer years rolled away; India was no outsider now, no ghost at the banquet.

When Kris Srikkanth and Amarnath opened out, the tide turned. India had the batsmen to take the bowling by the scruff of the neck. Srikkanth played an electrifying cover drive; every Indian schoolboy alive back then knows which one. But soon, the always dangerous Malcolm Marshall trapped him LBW. I was stunned; I was a fool for expecting too much. A little later, Holding came bounding into bowl to Amarnath. For a fraction of a second, I lost sight of the ball. Then, as I heard the roar of the crowd, I saw a stump cartwheeling away. As the Indian batting slumped to a paltry 183, my heart sank. The Indian dream was over.

When the West Indies innings began, I was startled to see Sandhu bowl Greenidge as he shouldered arms. My momentarily resuscitated hopes were rapidly snuffed out as Richards walked out and imperiously began thrashing the Indian bowlers. Soon after, the satellite connection for the live telecast was lost; it would be a while before coverage would resume. I left my aunt's house and sauntering aimlessly on the streets, decided to console myself with an illicit cigarette. The Indian team had promised much; they had converted me to their cause, and now they were going down with nary a fight. The roar from the radio as I approached the *paan* shop to buy my palliation told me drama was afoot. Before I could inquire into its cause, the *paanwallah* informed his customers: Richards was out. I turned and quickly walked back home. There was still no satellite connection, so I turned on the radio. As the score came on, I was informed two more wickets—those of Larry Gomes and Clive Lloyd—had fallen. The West Indies could have been rescued by that pair of calm gentlemen ticking off one single after another. And then another wicket—Bacchus—went down. The telecast now resumed; the drama of the West Indies collapse had taken place away from Indian eyes. The Jeff Dujon–Malcolm Marshall partnership that followed almost convinced Indian fans we had dared dream too much. But India was not to be denied. Mohinder's little dibbly-dobblers did the trick, dismissing both Dujon and Marshall. India won, and Indian spectators came pouring across the field.

There were West Indies fans in that crowd, but they were now the vanquished. Their color, their spirit, their exuberance were all possessed by Indian fans. The Indian team posed and flexed again, this time on the hallowed Lord's pavilion. We were world champions.

The next day, when I awoke, I was living elsewhere. The headlines in the Indian newspapers read "The World Is Ours." I had never thought or spoken of myself as an Indian before the World Cup. Now I did. A win in a cricket tournament, in the right place, against the right opponents, had given me a nationality and an identity.

No Love for Sunny

I MIGHT HAVE BECOME INDIAN, but it was an unstable and fragile sense of belonging, as I found out when the West Indies met India again later that year.

The scoreboard for the first one-day international played at Srinagar cryptically informs the reader the West Indies won by attaining their "revised target." Their target had been so altered because the match was disrupted several times, not by rain but by Kashmiri spectators running out onto the ground to celebrate the loss of Indian wickets. It was 1983, the year of the great Kashmiri scandal when the Congress (I) fixed the state assembly elections to make sure the local National Conference would not win in the Kashmir Valley. Those spectators, "antinationals," unconvinced of the blessings of the Indian nation and their Indian nationality, were demonstrating an inner sentiment whose components I had often entertained.

The Indian team, back in India, was back to its bad old Indian ways. The high-performing capability visible in the English summer, on English grounds, in the friendly, high-resolution gaze of the BBC cameras, had quickly evaporated in the bright, clear Srinagar sunshine. The Indian bowlers were back to serving up mediocre bowling that touring batsmen could feast on. In the dull black-and-white Indian telecast, the glamour of the world-beating, world-pleasing Indian team was gone. Now that India was back playing on Indian grounds, on Indian television, being described by Indian commentators, I felt some of my World Cup–generated support for them fade.

The most vivid indicator of this sentiment was my reaction to Gavaskar during that series, as he approached Bradman's mark of twenty-nine centuries. By the end of the second day of the first Test, the Indian batting had crumbled to Malcolm Marshall, inspiring Indian newspapers to proclaim, "Marshall Law at Kanpur." Gavaskar was out second ball. A duck for the great pretender to Bradman's inviolate title of the greatest ever. (During the third Test, the West Indies' captain Clive Lloyd went on a rampage against Indian umpires in the press. His outburst did much to lower my opinion of him, for in these matters, my hero worship of overseas stars was not to be found. My morality in matters cricketing followed a conventional path: I disliked dissent with umpires, and I disdained sledging and boorish behavior. But there was also a new defensiveness stirred up in this new identity of mine.) Later, I cheered for Gavaskar's dismissal for ninety, now held up, after his attacking century at Delhi in the second Test, in his inexorable march toward the Don's world record. At Calcutta, Gavaskar was dismissed off the first ball of the Test, caught behind off Marshall. It was his second duck of the series, and once again, I was glad to see him go. Somehow, perversely, I possessed an irrational dislike for the only Indian batsman in that series to show resilience against the West Indies' attack. (By way of bizarre contrast, Mohinder Amarnath, in poor form and suffering from various mysterious physical ailments, produced a string of scores that read 0, 0, 0, 1, 0, 0.) It might have helped if Gavaskar had not been a contender for Bradman's throne, a sacrosanct zone not to be populated by pretenders from India. India obligingly collapsed in the second innings at Calcutta. A petulant crowd rained debris on the Indian players, and Gavaskar swore never to play in Calcutta again. Somehow, amid my Gavaskar-dislike haze, I found admiration for his bloody-minded response to the Calcutta crowd's ungracious reaction to Indian defeat.

Finally, my worst fears came true at Madras as Gavaskar scored his thirtieth century. I had expected the blow for a while; its harshness was one I had lived through and anticipated for so long that its eventual occurrence was an anticlimax. Gavaskar made many Indian schoolboys' dreams come true by breaking Bradman's record, but they were not mine. Gavaskar would become retrospectively, in an act of great mental revisionism, among my most respected Indian players. That winter, there was no one else I wanted more to fail.

During the Tests' telecast, we were often treated to the dulcet tones of the Guyanese commentator Joseph "Reds" Perreira—then doing duty for a Caribbean television station—as he stopped in at the Indian television commentary box. Reds would often bring news of the Pakistan-Australia Test series in Australia. The eagerness with which I anticipated his relaying those games' scores was an indicator of an old sensation: cricket being played somewhere else was the real thing, not this Test match in India, even one that pitted the mightiest cricketing team in the world against my country. I had experienced a similar sensation during the second Test as it petered out into a draw after—to my great disappointment—the West Indies made no attempt to chase down the fourth-innings target set for them by India. Something about being in India did that to teams; India was only a venue for uninspiring cricket. The West Indies could not be bothered showing off its best wares in this land.

Azadi at Nehru Stadium

IN BETWEEN THE FIRST AND SECOND Tests of Pakistan's 1983–1984 tour of India, a seemingly inconsequential one-day match had been scheduled in New Delhi. It was a day-night game played under floodlights, the first of its kind in India. A common error Indian fans would make in later years was to consider this game an official one-day international. But it was an unofficial benefit match, classified a "festival tie," whose proceeds would go to the Indian Prime Minister's Relief Fund. Its psychic and cultural importance would be greater than that of many official one-day internationals to follow.

On the day of the match, some friends and I finished hockey practice at school and then, wearing our uniforms thrown quickly over our still sweaty sports gear, our nosebleed tickets burning holes in our pockets, caught a bus to the giant Jawaharlal Nehru Stadium. This was my first time inside its cavernous confines. I had not attended a single event at the previous year's Asian Games, dismissing them as hopelessly provincial, a pale substitute for the Olympics. Indeed, during the Asian Games, I had exiled myself from Delhi and visited my grandfather for my annual winter vacation. There I had followed the commentary of the hockey final between India and Pakistan as, in a catastrophic defeat, India went down 1–7 at New Delhi's National Stadium to their arch-rivals. Later, quite inevitably, I heard a family friend remark that Zafar Iqbal, the dazzling right flanker and Muslim captain of the Indian hockey team, "must have taken money to lose the game." I had groaned. Yet another reason to support Pakistan: idiotic accusations that Indian Muslims were fifth columnists, supporting Pakistan in hockey and cricket. I wonder what our friend would have made of an Indian Hindu cheering for Pakistan in cricket.

When play began, Pakistan's batting was shackled as the Indian bowlers pegged them back to 197 off fifty overs. The visual effect of a match played with white ball and colored clothes though, was unforgettable. The high visibility of the white cricket ball had one salutary effect: I could track its flight against the background of the crowd. It was to play a crucial part in my reaction to what followed.

India's chase quickly ran aground. Wickets fell; World Cup heroes—Srikkanth, Patil, Sharma, and Amarnath—came and went. Soon India was 101–8. The crowd began heading for the exits. A father and son sitting next to us groaned at India's failures. As the irate and disappointed father kept up a steady stream of disgruntled commentary, the son shook his head frequently as if to excuse himself. Finally, they had had enough of the incompetence on display. Fearing a crush for the exits and unwilling to watch India lose to Pakistan, the man stood up, gestured to his son, and waved him out. We watched them go, fearing the worst.

Now, Kirti Azad and Madan Lal—a pair of Delhi stalwarts—came together. I had a soft spot for "Maddi," a big-hearted, perennially striving all-rounder hero of Delhi's Ranji Trophy wins in the 1980s. Azad, who had made his name as a big hitter on the Delhi University circuit, had played as an off-spinning all-rounder in the World Cup but remained nondescript. I invested some local pride in this pair, but I did not expect them to win the game.

That India won the game was surprising; the way it did so was astonishing, for Azad and Maddi did it in style, with fierce hitting and electric running. Most memorable of all were Azad's four sixes, for they blotted out everything else. In my mind's eye, there they are: the bowler running in, the batsman swinging, and then abruptly, beautifully, the white ball rising, rising, toward the crowd, the entire mass rising behind the ball, around me, in front of me, all over the stadium, as the ball soared and soared, thousands of eyes tracking the arc of its flight. It seemed the ball would never come down. A common fiction in the legends this game spawned was that those sixes were hit into the upper tiers of the stadium's stands. None were, but it was not the distance, it was the occasion and manner that made those sixes legendary. Those spectacular sixes, hit boldly with eight wickets down, spoke of a refreshing new Indian aggression. The Delhi pair added eighty-six runs and took India to 187 before Zaheer, bringing himself on, dismissed Madan Lal. There was a little flutter, a few palpitations. Nine wickets were down. But there was no denying India. India had fought back in style against the odds, and against Pakistan.

I had been surrounded by my Indian friends and an Indian crowd. In that zone, something happened to my understanding of Indian cricket and the Indian cricket fan—it took me beyond the station I had reached during the 1983 World Cup. An Indian cricket crowd was a living thing, and I was in the belly of the beast. It spoke and chattered and laughed; it made me laugh, grimace, and groan. The crowd shook, pulsed, clapped, cheered, shouted, and danced. We were up in the terraces, up in the nosebleeds, high above the action, above the garishly lit green ground. Up there it was a different world. We were under the giant floodlights, and I could see the moths gathering over their glare. The air was humid; a steamy, sweaty miasma hung over us. As one young man behind us took off his shirt and began to dance, I felt a giddy recklessness come over me. I experienced a mingling, a commonality, a desire to participate in whatever would make this crowd happy. It was a big night out, at the top of this giant stadium, this emblem of the reconstructed Delhi, the capital of the new India that had hosted the Asian Games a year before. The horrors of 1984's political assassinations and vicious pogroms were still a year away. I wanted to be part of this; I wanted this crowd to win; I wanted this crowd to move on to the next level of the collective insanity that was building up and spreading through the stadium. The stadium felt like a living, breathing thing, an entity whose parts—the colors of the crowd and the uniforms of the players, the white cricket ball, the black sight screens, the silvery light of the floodlights beating down on the players and the umpires—were available to see and inspect and pull apart momentarily but responded as one.

After the match was over, the garrulous crowd poured out of the stadium. I was tired, hoarse, and sweaty; I was borne along on the euphoria those sixes had engendered. Outside the stadium a poor vendor's cart was ransacked by hooligans expressing their exultation at India's win in the most sordid fashion. We walked slowly to the bus services set up to transport the crowds back home. I said goodbye to my friends and patiently stood in line for a bus. This was tedium; I was exhausted and hungry and yet sustained by memories of the match. The bus was packed, pervaded with a composite odor of cigarette smoke, roasted peanuts, noxious petrol fumes, old oil encrusted on the engine's grimy hood, and the day's accumulated sweat on the bus's inhabitants. It dropped me back at a deserted depot still half an hour from home. No matter; I alighted and set off. It was late at night; I walked home along deserted streets, humming as I smoked a cigarette, a rare forbidden pleasure, dragging in each lungful, slowly savoring the day's events in my mind. On arriving home, I loudly announced to my mother, still awake, still waiting for me patiently and anxiously, that I had seen the greatest game of all. The next day, it was shown again on the national channel. Color television had made its debut in India the year before during the Asian Games; night cricket with colored clothes was still a rare treat. But I did not bother to see the repeat telecast. I wanted no distortion, no variation, in my memories. I did not want them made stale.

We talked about the game at school, but there was no recapturing it. You had to be physically present in that crowd, those sixes soaring, your spirit rising with them. My memories are secure; they cannot be affected by an alternative rendering of the game; they are safe from the ravages of time.

I wonder if I have told you enough to convince you I was there.*

Begging to Be Put Out of Misery

CRICKET PLAYED BY, and in, India remained dull. India's Test series against Pakistan in the mid-eighties offered ample proof for this proposition. It also showed me the Pakistani team could count on my support—even against India—when it came to Test cricket. In that domain, India's standing as world champions of one-day cricket had not intruded into my evaluative scales. My cricket fandom was sufficiently mature to realize winning the World Cup meant just that. It did not mean India was the best cricket team in the world or that it was even worth cheering for in Test cricket.

Pakistan's team—led by Zaheer Abbas—for the 1983–1984 tour was a second-rate outfit, its bowling fatally weakened by the absence of Imran Khan. We were back to playing against second elevens, condemned again to subcontinental obscurity. In the first Test, every day was affected by rain; run rates did not get to three per over. The Test appropriately ended in farce. The Indians started their second innings with no result possible; Gavaskar proceeded to bat as if playing on the first day of the Test. As time ran out, Zaheer sought to take his players off, to call a halt to the game. Gavaskar pointed out that playing conditions required Pakistan to stay on, and the net result of enforcing this regulation was that Gavaskar scored the century he so clearly desired. Gavaskar's attainment of this numerical mark seemed constitutive of Indian cricket: boring, statistics- and personal record–oriented.

The first Test had been tedious; the second Test was an utter disaster. Words do not do its boredom justice. It was a travesty, an abomination. Decades later, I shudder at describing it. It was disrupted by rain, over

---

* In September 1984, Australia played a one-day international against India at the Nehru Stadium. This time, I went alone. It could not have been anything like the Kirti Azad match, and indeed, there were no miracles as India subsided to a mundane loss. Australian power in the outfield was an awesome sight to behold. As Dilip Vengsarkar square-cut fiercely, Graham Yallop, diving to his right, plucked the ball out of the air. The sound of the ball smacking into his palm was heard around the stadium. One wag stood up and yelled out—in Punjabi—that skinny lentil-eating vegetarian Indians did not stand a chance against big beer-drinking Australians. I had not been alone in some of my privately held opinions about the Indian team.

rates were slow, and when the Indian innings began, so did the crawl. For an Indian fan in the 1980s, only two names are needed to describe this Test: Ravi Shastri and Anshuman Gaekwad, limpets at the batting crease. The latter aimlessly meandered toward the slowest double century in Test cricket; it took him 652 minutes. Had Gaekwad started batting on the first day of a Test match, he would have arrived at his mark an hour after tea on the second day.

September in Delhi is an oppressive time of year. The coolness of the autumn has not set in, the afternoons are sultry and humid, and the earth remains waterlogged after the monsoon's soakings. As I listened to the commentary, the turgid cricket in perfect consonance with the weather, a dreadful, sticky torpor settled over me. Gaekwad batted over three days because of the rain breaks and went on and on. Such was the ennui engendered by the cricket that I would nap while listening to commentary. When I awoke, Gaekwad was still batting. Mohammed Nazir, an unknown thirty-seven-year-old off-spinner playing for Pakistan, bowled fifty-two overs for seventy-six runs. Eventually, 727 runs were scored off 311 overs. I marvel at the sheer perversity of it. To think this cricket—Test match hell—could carry on, and indeed, be permitted to do so.

The third Test was another disaster, redeemed partially by a brief glimpse of Zaheer at his best. Zaheer now, in marked contrast to my first glimpse of him seven years ago, was older and heavier. He did not wear his trademark white Panama hat, and there was no kerchief tied around his neck. He wore instead the green Pakistani cap or a Panama hat with the Pakistani star. In this Test, he made eighty-five and hit three sixes while doing so. Each was effortless, and as Cardus had once written of the fin de siècle English great Archie MacLaren, the cricket ball was dismissed from his presence. Zaheer fell just short of his century to the combination I was growing to respect: "c Kirmani b Kapil Dev." As India was cruising to a draw on the fifth day, in an inspired move, Zaheer brought on Wasim Raja to bowl his leg spin. Stunningly, he induced an Indian collapse as four wickets tumbled. My heroes Zaheer and Wasim were bringing this match to a dramatic conclusion akin to the 1978 Karachi and Lahore Tests. Pakistan would chase in the last hour; those magic words—twenty mandatory overs—were going to be invoked. Wasim and Zaheer would do the chasing, and it would end in the last over. I waited with bated breath. I wanted the last two Indian wickets back in the pavilion. I wanted a run at those memories of 1978, a re-creation of that innocent mood, an evoking of a very particular time and place. But Madan Lal and Syed Kirmani, eating up vital overs and time, took India through to 262–8. This was not the series, this was not the time, and this was not the place. I was still divided when it came to Pakistan. I could still cheer for them in Test cricket. I could still cheer for them when I was watching cricket by myself.

After the game, an Indian television commentator interviewed an exhausted looking Zaheer. Captaining a weakened Pakistan team on a tour of India could enervate the most resilient of men. The commentator asked Zaheer why he had been "so negative" in the series. Zaheer's answer was testy: I have not been negative; we have not been negative. I don't know why you accuse us of being negative. I disagreed too. We had just paid witness to a series washed out by rain, played in the worst time of the year, played in dull, boring, uninspiring style by India. I had been subjected to the horror of Gaekwad's batting in the second Test. Zaheer had played the only attractive innings of the series. A few hours before, he had brought on a leg spinner, always an attacking move, and almost forced a result. And this blinkered fool was accusing him of being negative? I could have reached through the television screen and strangled the man wielding the microphone.

But the context surrounding this series was not designed to create protective feelings toward Pakistanis—even those badgered by idiotic television commentators. I was living in an India beset by the "Punjab problem," and I had, by dint of becoming aware of a Punjabi identity, started to take a keener interest in that state's affairs. That investment had started to color, perhaps irrevocably, my understanding of cricket.

As a child, I was not particularly keen to take on the mantle of being a Punjabi. My first homes were in Indian Air Force bases. There the lingua franca was English, and ethnic identities were deemphasized in favor of a more pluralistic Indian one. At home, my parents never spoke Punjabi to me, though they did so—with fluency and aplomb—with their parents whenever we visited them. I grew up listening to Punjabi but, like most urban Punjabis of my generation, without learning my supposed mother tongue.

This cultural and linguistic distancing from the Punjab had other dimensions. When an Amritsar-resident uncle invited me to spend my autumn vacation with him, I politely declined. Its historic attractions—the Golden Temple, the seat of the Sikh religion, Jallianwalah Bagh, the venue of General Dyer's notorious massacre in 1919, which told India its colonial rulers were most decidedly not benign—did not exert a strong enough hold on me. I had spent a day in Jalandhar, another modest Punjabi city, on my way to a family holiday in Kashmir and did not think much of it. Compared to New Delhi, it was impossibly small-townish. Punjab smacked of the rustic, the agricultural, and the homespun; I considered myself an urban (and urbane) Anglophone. I lived in a big city, the capital of India;

my ancestors lived in dusty villages and provincial towns. If this was my ethnic heritage, I would do better to leave it behind and take on the new one that my parents' expatriate lives—elsewhere in India, away from the Punjab—afforded me.

But migration—of whatever stripe—can change such perspectives. In my ninth and tenth grades, during two years spent in boarding school, away in India's northeast, I was not-so-gently nudged toward my Punjabi identity by my fellow students. By virtue of hailing from all over the country, they constituted a demographic similar to the one I had enjoyed on air force bases, but they were not shy about showing off their ethnic prejudices. Though the label "Punjabi" had never been applied to me, now I was one, supposedly a rustic hick, despite being from New Delhi. Confused, callow, and defiant, I sought to acquire my new identity's supposed trappings. A singular one was language. Soon I struck up a friendship with two Sikh lads and started rudimentary practice in spoken Punjabi. For the first time, I drew on a supposed ethnic solidarity with other Indians like me. My early attempts at spoken Punjabi were ludicrously bad, but a halting journey had commenced.

Taking on the language and a concomitant interest in Punjabi history and politics meant I paid more attention to the troubles in the Punjab. There, a Sikh separatist movement, initially aided and abetted by Indira Gandhi, the Indian prime minister, to undermine Sikh regional parties, grew increasingly violent and began a series of killings—first of government officials and police and later, in acts of terror, Hindu civilians. The movement thus triggered what seemed like a second refugee exodus from the Punjab—the first being in 1947 at the time of the Partition. The bitterness these killings kicked up in Punjabi Hindu circles in Delhi was contagious. The two Punjabi communities—Sikh and Hindu—came to an impasse. Sikhs wanted acknowledgment of their grievances—and no one who knew the Congress (I) and its gruesome machinations could doubt the Sikhs had real ones. Hindus wanted Sikhs to unequivocally condemn the killings in the Punjab; the Sikhs, a minority besieged, were reluctant to speak up. Meanwhile, the stories of the gruesome massacres in the Punjab became ever more lurid.

Pakistan's not-so-benign presence in my home state was no secret. The support given to Sikh militant groups—training, arms supply, and shelter—by that notorious Pakistani acronym, the ISI, was well known; this uncomfortable association had been established by dint of extensive empirical confirmation. The 1965 and 1971 wars were remote in time and space, but the Punjab problem and its Pakistani dimension were the subject of daily headlines, news bulletins, and talk in the streets. I read journalistic reports of Sikh militants trained and funded by the ISI, of the Pakistani army's Sutlej Rangers shepherding them across the border for training. While I disliked Mrs. Gandhi's "foreign hand" conspiracy theory of external interference in Indian affairs and regarded it as a sinister distraction from her complicity in the Punjab fiasco, and much to the delight of my friends, would mimic the *"videshi taakaton"* (foreign powers) line she employed at her public appearances, there was no doubt—given the investigative journalism that detailed Pakistani involvement in the Punjab problem—that Pakistan wanted the killings in the Punjab to continue, to destabilize the Indian polity.

Pakistan felt decidedly less friendly now. My father's wars with Pakistan had been abstract historical entities; the current crisis was real, here and now. I was all too susceptible to the caustic pronouncements of my mother's family and my neighbors, who bemoaned this new destruction of the Punjab by Pakistan. Once had not been enough for "them."

At one time, when Pakistan came to mind, its only accompaniment was cricket; war did not force its way into those spaces. Now I thought of a great deal else when I saw Pakistani cricketers run on to the ground, when I saw the flag on their shirts. I knew they were national representatives, and the nation they represented did not seem like a *fons et origo* of kindly sentiment toward India or Indians, a nation and a people with whom I had finally started to empathize and identify and seek solidarity with.

End of a Dream

WITH BOTH INDIAN AND PAKISTANI boards of cricket keen to flog the proverbial golden goose, India was playing cricket against Pakistan every year. Reciprocating Pakistan's tour in the previous season, India visited Pakistan in the 1984–1985 season. If the 1983–1984 series had been marked by lassitude, this was the nadir of bitterness.

For the first time, I found cause for complaint in Pakistani umpiring; now, I was predisposed to do so. In the first Test, Shastri played forward and across to a ball going down leg, attempting a flick. He missed and was struck high on the pad. The bowler appealed; up went the finger. Shastri, stunned by the decision, stood and stared at the umpire. It was a routine hit on the pad that provokes quickly stifled half-appeals from bowlers. In my years of watching cricket, I have yet to see a worse LBW decision. As Shastri walked off, I experienced a sinking feeling. It was true, then; all I had heard from those around me—Pakistani umpires were cheats. Shastri walked off the ground defiantly, holding his bat upside down, his contemptuous body language louder than overt cursing. I felt something approaching shame; I had been repaid thus for my diligent devotions to Pakistani cricket. Gaekwad's dismissal in the second innings of the second Test was worse. As Gaekwad stretched forward to defend, the ball bounced off his pad straight into the hands of Saleem Malik, who went up in appeal. A microsecond later, so did the umpire's finger. Even to the naked eye at regular speed it was a regulation bat behind the pad with no contact with the ball. My disillusionment was almost complete.

During the hellish second Test, India batted first and made 500 with Patil and Shastri—a singularly unattractive batsman in Test cricket—scoring centuries. Then Pakistan—on that featherbed pitch—went on to make 674 as the game meandered to a draw. I had now seen seven straight no-results between India and Pakistan. The pitches were dead; the crowds were thin; the cricket was uninspiring; the captains were dispirited; the umpires were under suspicion; and the commentators, both Indian and Pakistani, were busy scoring chauvinistic points. I failed to understand why these games were being played. This was not entertainment. It was a battle of attrition staged on the faulty premise that cricket would improve relations between the two countries. Cricket was bringing out the worst in both teams and their supporters (and their umpires). Some dramatic event was needed to bring India-Pakistan cricket to a close.

On 31 October 1984, the day of the second one-day international, I left Delhi University early. My U.S.-philic stance dictated that I diligently watch the weekly ABC news capsule at the American Library. I would not be denied my weekly glimpse of the most mythical land of all, albeit one denuded of cricket. My viewing the ABC news capsule was not a straightforward attempt at self-edification in world news. Rather, I was seeking the latest glimpses of a land I had already started to regard as my future home. Those news broadcasts were informational and cartographic bulletins constructing the contours of a landscape I planned soon to traverse in person.

I found my fellow students' disdainful comments about the parochialism of ABC's news capsules distasteful. I considered ABC the paragon of journalism and thought the accusations of U.S.-centric bias were off-kilter. I was particularly ignorant of, or insensitive to, the geopolitics and history that animated most radical college students' hostility toward the United States. My brother and I had frequently engaged in verbal sparring over my unabashedly pro–United States leanings. All too often he, enamored of the ruggedness of the Soviet state and its citizens, dismissed my American sympathies as the deluded fantasies of the willfully naive. And some dissonance had been stirred up within me as I had grown: I had read Dee Brown's classic, heartbreaking *Bury My Heart at Wounded Knee*; I had seen Martin Luther King Jr.'s biographical documentary; I had seen Costas Gavras's chilling indictment of U.S. interference in Chile, *Missing*; I had read Alex Haley's *Roots*; and I knew of slavery in the American South, the Civil War, the genocide of the Native Americans, the civil rights movement, and the dubious moral standing of the atomic bombs, those homicidal weapons of mass destruction that had ended that most just of wars. I had entertained much disillusionment about the political and ethical stature of the land that I dreamed would be the next station in my life. I had become aware of the nightmares that lurked at the fringes of the American Dream. But I still protected my carefully constructed vision of the United States—sometimes by inattention, sometimes by inarticulate, incoherent excuses—from these missives warning me there was trouble in paradise.

That fine morning, a couple of friends accompanied me to the American Library. We caught the 220 DTC bus from the university campus, alighted a short distance from the American Center and began walking. A man walked past us, transistor glued to his ear. We stopped and asked for the score. He irately waved us off, "Forget about the score, someone's shot Indira Gandhi!" We found his diverted attention hilarious. Our prime minister had probably been the target of some half-baked assassination attempt. Perhaps someone had pointed a gun at her and it had gone off; perhaps someone had fired a bullet in her general direction. This overwrought countryman of ours was getting his jollies listening to that trivial news rather than concentrating on the crucial business of the cricket match between India and Pakistan. I did not think my life could be exciting enough for me to live through a real political assassination. That kind of dramatic event happened in distant lands or in history books, places where history was made and written about. We were always in the wings, bearing witness to proceedings conducted far away. The events in this land did not seem to possess world-historical significance. They did not happen here, those events that got written about by those who cared and mattered.

A crowd had gathered in front of the venerable Hindustan Times Building to read the breaking news on its display board. We walked past them; it was more important to see week-old news from the United States, to pay attention to distant budgetary crises, political wrangling, international disputes, and modern versions of the Great Game than to soak up—with an Indian crowd, on an Indian street, in the Indian capital—news of the most momentous event in Indian political history in the last quarter of the twentieth century.

The news telecast ended an hour and a half later. We walked back past the breaking news board. The size of the crowd reading the headlines had grown, spilling over into the busy road that ran alongside, slowing down traffic, and bringing wheel-bound folks out to see what the matter was. I asked for details. The answer stunned me. Mrs. Gandhi's Sikh bodyguards had pumped thirty bullets into her. We fell silent. She had not been *shot at*; she had been *shot*. Thirty times. I fought off a suddenly nascent sensation, equal parts apprehension, fear, and nausea. I quickly returned home, tuned in to the BBC, and received confirmation of a fact left curiously unsaid by a timid Indian media: the Indian prime minister had been assassinated in the Indian capital. (The analysis of this event as retaliation for the Indian army's attack on the Golden Temple, de facto headquarters for the Sikh extremist leader Sant Jarnail Singh Bhindranwale, the mastermind behind the attacks in the Punjab, came later in the day.)

What happened to New Delhi and its Sikhs over the next few days is too well known—and too painful—to bear extensive repetition here. Violence revisited Indian life in independent India's modern capital: riots, retaliatory killings, beatings and burnings of innocents, pogroms that outdid their temporally and geographically distant forebears in ferocity and the eventual toll of life. There was no talk of cricket in the smoky haze that rose from the ruins of Sikh homes and families for the next few days, in the stories of families made the target of bloodthirsty mobs. Delhi became a war zone. I spent a week confined to our narrow lane in South Delhi, listening to the BBC and to the endless stream of rumors and the feverish speculation about the end of the republic that swirled about me.

Far away in Pakistan, the Indian cricket team had been given the news; the one-day international underway was canceled along with the rest of the tour. This denial of cricket did not feel like a deprivation; it felt like an appropriate sidelining of the irrelevant. I did not forget that Pakistan, the nation we were playing against, had done its share to make matters worse in the Punjab, to foster and foment the bitter divisiveness now on display. Watching its cricket team play cricket felt irredeemably tainted by that association.

Live on Channel Nine: The Indians

IN THE FIRST MATCH OF THE 1985 Benson and Hedges World Championship, which commemorated the centenary of the Victoria Cricket Association, India, chasing Pakistan's 183, collapsed, losing three wickets for very little. Imran had taken the first three wickets; for a while, we were back in the 1982–1983 series. But Mohammed Azharuddin, India's new wonder boy, and Gavaskar came together, and India strolled through to a six-wicket win on the back of Azhar's dazzling ninety-three. Besides the few members of the Indian diaspora who had come to cheer them on in Australia, the Indians could count on one more supporter far away, back in India. I had been cheering them on as I listened to Pakistan Radio's flowery Urdu commentary; it marked the first time I supported India against Pakistan in an official international game. The prodigal had returned home.

India rolled on, winning by six wickets, eighty-six runs, eight wickets, seven wickets, and then in the final, by eight wickets again. A more dominant performance in a one-day international tournament has not been seen. India pulled off this performance away from home, earning generous praise from Australian television and press—appreciation I was only too happy to echo. I did not want international television commentators talking about the Indian team the way I used to. We were the world champions, worthy of respect.

India's two stunning performances in one-day international cricket, the 1983 Prudential World Cup and the 1985 Benson and Hedges World Championship, the first achieved in England, the second in Australia, engendered an acute sporting irony: for a sworn connoisseur of Test cricket, my fandom of India began with its success in one-day internationals. It helped immeasurably that these wins occurred away from home and were telecast live back to India by overseas broadcasting services.

The first game telecast live to India from Australia was India's semifinal against Australia. I was accustomed to Doordarshan's pathetic late-on-the-ball telecasts and unprepared for Channel Nine's artfully packaged presentation of bat and ball encounters. As I watched the Indian team play on Kerry Packer's network, the one that had once stolen away the world's best cricketers and left me fuming, I felt a resurgence of the feeling awoken in 1983. Its multiple camera angles, high-resolution slow-motion replays, and stump microphones enabled an acute appreciation of the Indian team that had not been possible before, obscured by Doordarshan and my blinkered conception of myself. But now in full glory, sent to us on a telecast from afar, there they were: the arc of the Indian spinners' flighted deliveries, the wristy grace of Mohammed Azharuddin, the perfect side-on action of Kapil, Srikkanth's flashing stroke play, and Laxman Sivaramakrishnan's looping leg breaks.

On the day of the final, Pakistan, who had knocked out the West Indies in the other semi-final, won the toss and elected to bat. Pakistan's green uniforms—I had only seen them in whites or creams before—struck some deep-recessed chord. They spoke of the Pakistani flag with its white star and crescent, its green backdrop; this military-fatigued uniformed aesthetic was considerably grimmer than the blandness of the white, which had obscured national affiliations; this color conjured up uncomfortable associations political and historical. It emphasized a difference I had had made for me in writing, in images, and the spoken word. Now I could not elide the Pakistani identity of its cricketers, their entwinement in the complicated histories of our two nations.

After the openers had fallen, Kapil bowled *that ball*, a perfect yorker that castled Qasim Omar. I was on my feet, applauding and appreciating the stunning visual beauty of that feat performed on a beautiful ground far away from home and captured on an international television network. Soon after, Sivaramakrishnan came in and bowled *that leg break* to Miandad: the ball pitched on off and middle and spun to where a third off stump would have been. Miandad's first step had taken him out of the crease. He missed the line, the ball spun away, Sadanand Viswanath grabbed the ball, and the bails were off. As was I, on my feet, cheering. It was true; Pakistan was no longer my favorite in an India-Pakistan game. In India's chase of the modest Pakistani total, India's progress was slow and steady; there were no fireworks, no cascade of sixes and fours from India in the final triumphal march. Shastri kept his head down, ruthlessly eschewed all heroics, and took India through.

It had been a glorious spring day in Delhi as we watched the game. As India marched on, I sat content with my uncles and my mother, watching in rapt attention. This win was even more satisfying than the World Cup win and not just because we—there's that word again—had beaten Pakistan in the final. In the World Cup, we had been outsiders and the win was the mother of all upsets. Here, India had quickly become the favorite with a team possessing a strong bowling attack, a competent opening pair, a dazzling wicketkeeper proficient at sledging and batting, and a sharp fielding outfit, all helmed by a quiet and effective captain. This win put a little swagger in the step. Then, we had not belonged in the party we had gate-crashed. Now, the party was ours.

After the game, Shastri claimed his player of the tournament award— an Audi—the kind of award reserved for the Richardses and Lillees before him. I tensed as Shastri took the Audi for a victory lap around the MCG. He could humiliate us by confirming for Australian crowds that Indians could not drive cars like these. As the rest of the Indian team clambered onto the Audi, we watched with pride as, in the cavernous Melbourne Cricket Ground—in Australia, that glorious sunbaked lucky country with its beautiful suntanned women, its endless supply of beer and modern dazzling cricket grounds, its team of wonderfully qualified and witty commentators who had gone overboard in their praise of the Indians—an Indian team celebrated a victory over Pakistan.

The Summer of Missed Opportunity

THE 1986 BOXING DAY TEST of the 1985–1986 series in Australia was the second Test of India's three-Test tour of Australia that southern summer. By close of play on the fourth day, India had maneuvered into a winning position: Australia was 228–8, only 45 runs ahead with two wickets in hand. I wanted India to win; I was cheering for India in Test cricket. They were, after all, playing away from home. They needed my support when they traveled, away from those commentators who praised them excessively, from those fans around me whose understanding of the game I considered inferior to mine.*

I woke early to catch the radio commentary of the last day. Test wins in Australia were exceedingly rare; I wanted to be listening in when this one happened. I was visiting my cricket-crazy uncle; he joined me for my vigil in the waking hours of the day. The radio commentators mentioned impending rain in the afternoon, but I paid little heed. The post-lunch session was far away; India would have this wrapped up by then. A few minutes later, as Bruce Reid fell to Shivlal Yadav, Australia was nine down for 231. I snuggled a little tighter into my blanket on that cold Delhi morning and turned up the radio. It was still dark outside. My uncle, similarly snug in his blanket in the cold room, grinned at me. We were faithful fans; we had worked hard for this; victory would be sweet.

From there on, Alan Border and Dave Gilbert proceeded to add seventy-seven runs for the tenth wicket. Border expertly farmed the strike while letting Gilbert play himself in; he often did so by scoring three runs off the last ball. A single or a three retains strike off the last ball; the latter has the advantage of moving the scoreboard along a little quicker. These runs were gold; every one of them contributed to the steady lengthening of icicles down my spine, for the dire warnings of rain from the radio commentators had not ceased. As Australia's lead grew and as they pushed off the moment of reckoning, they crept closer to the safety of the rain, which

---

* This section borrows from my essay "Two Pusillanimous Misses," in Chopra, *Eye on Cricket*.

promised to arrive as the torrential summer downpour Melbourne is eminently capable of putting on.

Finally, Border was dismissed for 163; Gilbert remained not out on thirteen off sixty-five deliveries. India needed 126 to win. It had ample time to score these runs if it did not rain. But the rain was coming, in spades, a fact known to all; only the precise time of its arrival was unknown. Optimistically, India would get thirty overs. A sensible punter would have put good money on a successful Indian chase conducted with one eye firmly on the clock and the impending rain. A win in Australia deserved an elevation of the Indian batsmen's adrenaline levels, even if the bowlers had gone toothless in the morning.

In the most bizarre exhibition of Test match batting it has been my misfortune to witness, India dawdled. Like narcoleptics on a tight schedule, the Indian top order decided it was time for a nap. Gavaskar scored eight off fifty-four deliveries; Amarnath, three off twenty-seven; Vengsarkar, one off twelve. In comparison, Srikkanth went berserk, scoring thirty-eight off sixty-one. All the while, the commentators steadily informed us of the impending rain—presumably these missives were available in the Indian dressing room too. I stared at my radio set in disbelief, unable to fathom the tactics adopted. In disgust, my uncle stormed out to seek distraction in the form of a haircut. I slumped, panicking, wondering if there was a deeper strategy I had not divined being pursued by the Indian batsmen. None seemed apparent.

Finally, the rain came. India, chasing 126 to win, was 59–2 off 25 overs. The rest of the day was washed out. We had blown it. India could have taken a 1–0 lead and given the state of the Sydney pitch and the lack of bite in the Aussie bowling—revealed by the run fest in the next game, which again, India came close to winning—India could have had its first series win in Australia. India lacked a knockout punch—a familiar, depressing story. Nothing summed up pusillanimous cricket like India's flaccid response to the challenge of that last day.

These indications of disappointment at least revealed that I was now keen India win in Test cricket too. This conversion continued during India's series against England in the summer of 1986. India won at Lord's, the home of cricket, the temple, the sanctum sanctorum—as Vengsarkar played the kind of scrappy innings I was now happy to see an Indian play. Fittingly, Kapil Dev finished the match with a six hit off Phil Edmonds toward the Members' Section, scattering the seated and staid tie-and-blazer-clad members of the Marylebone Cricket Club (MCC), representatives of the old guard. And then, quickly enough, India romped to a win by 279 runs at Leeds. India over the old masters; victory was sweet, made more so by its venue.

India's triumph over England would remain its solitary series win outside the subcontinent for the next two decades.

The Tied Test

AUSTRALIA'S LITTLE SERIES IN INDIA that same year and, in particular, the Test at Madras, ensured—for entirely different reasons—that Dean Jones and Maninder Singh would become instantly memorable for every Indian cricket fan alive then. Jones's epic innings, played in the oppressive Madras heat while suffering from dehydration, almost killed him; Maninder's almost got him killed as well, albeit by Indian fans. On the fifth day, Border declared, setting India 348 to win. I expected a draw, because India, based on my spectatorial experiences, did not do chases. But India got off to a flyer, and the man leading the charge was Gavaskar.

The closing session, as India was well and truly on its way, was a session of personal disillusionment with the Australians. Till then, I had never taken seriously the "ugly Australian" tag—a description most often used by those who had lost to Australia. But on this last day, ugly they were, and the biggest culprit was Alan Border, the Australian captain, who was determined to waste time and lose fans as he squabbled endlessly with the Indian umpires over a series of unspecified issues. No less puerile were Tim Zoehrer and Greg Matthews, whose screaming, abusive send-offs of dismissed Indian batsmen were stomach-turning. My instincts were old ones: I did not want India to beat Australia. But this surly, unkempt bunch masquerading as cricketers was doing little to secure my loyalties. Australia seemed reluctant tourists like the English of old: irate with India, its cricketers, and all things Indian. That was damning company to keep.

As I watched the cricket and its attendant juvenile squabbling, I remembered those red-faced, irate tourists in Delhi, angrily berating shopkeepers, yelling at rickshaw wallahs, testily bargaining with village women selling handmade crafts on sidewalks in Central New Delhi, unhappy with the prices asked for, snarling at the simpering brown natives who surrounded them with their wares. They were bad travelers too. They liked yelling at brown folks who held them up, like these Indian batsmen who had so unexpectedly accepted the Australian challenge and did not play the cooperative, traditional role of supplicants who begged for favors or a little baksheesh. Those travelers, like these Australians, disliked the sand in their wheels that all things Indian sent their way. They either raised their voices and wagged their fingers, or they wrote scornful, condescending, and contemptuous memoirs when they got back home.

Underwriting the images now visible to me on a cricket field were those stories of English sahibs in distant colonial outposts, smacking their coolies and *khansaamas* who did not work hard enough for them, complaining of the dishonesty of the clerk, the babu, the shopkeeper in the bazaar, complaining of the heat. For these Australians, tourists clad as cricketers, the Indian umpires were just the cricketing versions of those brown folk, residents of the land they traveled through, who interfered with their sense of order and dominion. For the first time, while watching a game of cricket, I felt a gulf appear and grow between me and those that toured India, those whom I had previously regarded as sacrosanct ambassadors and messengers of a pristine cricketing order. It was the first Test India had played at home in which I felt an emotional solidarity with those donning whites for my nation; I felt the effect of the insults they endured.

As the last over started, all four results were possible: India or Australia could win, the game could be drawn or tied. A tie was improbable, but tied it was. As the umpire's finger went up to dismiss Maninder, I rose, switched off the television, and went running out on the streets, elated beyond belief. I had witnessed history. We had joined the select band of teams to have featured in a tied Test match: Australia and the West Indies. No such reaction was forthcoming from my university friends. They cared little for keeping such august company; they wanted to win. I dimly sensed that had India won, Australian complaints about the umpiring and playing conditions would have been as much a part of the headlines as India's spirited chase. There would have been sour grapes aplenty to have ruined the ambrosia of the win.

The Madras Tied Test is part of Australian folklore, not India's. It is Dean Jones's game. Gavaskar's flyer that got India off to its great chase finds scant mention in Australian accounts of the game; neither does Shastri's brilliant, six-laden 48 that almost took India over the finish line. I should not complain. I did not recognize these feats adequately either.

Imran's Last Frontier

IN THE WINTER OF 1986, I was still in university, disillusioned by the second teachers' strike in two years. When the university faculty returned from strike, we boycotted classes. Attending classes felt silly when the teaching faculty was absconding for most of the year. They did not do their part; we did not do ours. The mutual dislike and distrust of teachers and students was palpable. College life was wearing me out with its emptiness; not attending classes for an entire academic year will do that to you. I had lost contact with my old high school friends, most banished to universities outside Delhi—either voluntarily or by their simultaneously ambitious and desperate parents—in the hope of securing professional qualifications. At home, my brother finished college and joined the Indian Air Force to become a fighter pilot, leaving me with plenty of catching up to do in the masculinity and glamour stakes. I dreamed of leaving home like him, of striking out on my own.

The soporific home series against England and Pakistan in the eighties had ensured I regarded India as an inferior venue for cricket. That winter, as Imran brought Pakistan to India, provided confirmation of this thesis. The series was ruined by poor weather, poor pitches, and a grimness that perennially permeated subcontinental cricket. All too soon, I found I was sick of the draws, the rain interruptions, and the unenterprising cricket. I found less to admire in the Pakistani cricketer too. As I watched Miandad initiate a verbal quarrel with Indian players during a one-day international, a friend watching the game with me spoke, capturing a feeling then coursing through me, "This is ugly." In the second innings of the Bangalore Test, after Wasim Akram was out LBW to Maninder Singh, Akram walked past the umpire and screamed *"bahenchod!"* (sister-fucker) at that white-coated gentleman. There was a hint of violence in the air; I had not seen anything like it on an international cricket field. I had seen players be foul-mouthed toward umpires, but those were Delhi University goons, not international cricket players. I had entertained an excessively naive view of the gentlemanliness of cricketers. That gesture, from a young Pakistani cricketer—a rising star—expressed to an inoffensive-looking Indian umpire, was unmistakably offensive. I cursed a fair bit myself and was notorious on my college campus for my profane vocabulary. But I hardly did so in anger; my cursing was done for comic effect. To see it done—on a cricket field—with physical violence seemingly only a step away was startling. Later in the Indian second innings, the Pakistani team's ill-tempered and rude squabbling with Indian umpires grew worse—a state of affairs poorly controlled by Imran Khan who, for all his supposed iron control over his men, was reluctant to cool down his team's hotheads as they intimidated Indian umpires.

In 1978, 1980, and 1982–1983, I made few political associations with the Pakistani team; there was the cricket, and then there was the rest of Pakistan. In 1986–1987, there was a straightforward political association. Pakistan's president, Zia-ul-Haq—the martial-law administrator; the man who had put Zulfikar Ali Bhutto, the former prime minister of Pakistan, to death and had turned Pakistan into an Islamic republic; the generalissimo whose coup allowed analogies to be drawn between Pakistan and banana republics elsewhere, with his chest, like those of military strongmen the world over, bedecked with rows of ribbons and medals—came visiting to watch a game of cricket as an act of cricketing diplomacy. In keeping Indian fans, it was an association the Pakistani team could have done without. Army uniforms are green; the Pakistan team had worn green. A general was their president; their army had instigated and fought three wars with India. It was a distinctly uncomfortable set of associations and connections.

These associations allowed other perceptions of Pakistan to be constructed. At Hyderabad, as Pakistan sputtered in their chase of India's 212, Qadir and Manzoor Elahi came to the crease. Pakistan crept closer and finally needed two to win off the last ball. From it, Qadir attempted a suicidal second run and was run out. Pakistan could have tied but had lost instead. Much hilarity ensued at Qadir's expense, some of it centering on whether—as retribution for this unpardonable error against the old enemy—Zia, Pakistan's martial law administrator, would order Qadir to be publicly flogged on his return home. Joining in with my cohort's jokes—directed at Pakistan—was a first for me.

On the first day of the last Test at Bangalore, Pakistan subsided to 116 all out. I cheered on the fall of wickets. I had never, ever cheered for a Pakistani batting collapse. I liked this devastation of the Pakistani batting, and I was glad a Delhi boy, Maninder Singh, had caused it. Maninder—whose success I had long anticipated—had finally matured. A match in which India had been spun to victory by a feisty Sikh from Delhi felt like the right one with which to celebrate my continuing return to the Indian fold. By close of the day's play, India was only forty-eight runs behind with eight wickets in hand. At the crease were two solid bats: Mohinder Amarnath and Dilip Vengsarkar. India could now pile on the runs and lay the foundation for a win. The next day, with no indication of devils in the pitch, thanks to a series of poor shots, India crumpled to 145. This was the Indian team I disliked—the pathetic, weak, flaccid team I wanted to disown and had often cheered against in the past. I sensed the match was lost, that India had blown its best chance of taking a lead that would bat Pakistan out of the game. That sinking feeling coursing through me—mingled with anger and disappointment—would have been strange indeed if Pakistan was my favorite team. But it was not anymore; the pendulum had swung. I wanted the Indian team to recognize this transformation, this return to the fold. A reluctant convert had finally shown up at the temple door, and the priests had shooed him away. I slinked off, consumed by my own rage, my continued commitment to the Indian cause in considerable doubt.

India was finally set 221 to win, an awkwardly sized target on a pitch favoring turn. The Bangalore heat was intense, baking pitch and player alike and turning the sweaty conflict in the middle into a Test match classic as the Indian batsmen struggled against the Pakistani spinners, Iqbal Qasim and Tauseef Ahmed. Gavaskar though, was imperturbable, scoring almost half the Indian runs. On the fourth day of the Test, on my college campus, the roar of transistors playing the commentary was heard all over and around its open and enclosed spaces. Young men huddled beneath trees, seeking shade, sheltering from the heat, listening to the commentary and relaying scores to the numerous curious.

Later in the afternoon, I returned home to watch the game on television. Agonizingly the score inched forward. If India won, it would mark the second time I would have seen a Pakistani team lose to India in India. If Pakistan won, it would be the first time Pakistan would have won a test series in India. Gavaskar was playing the innings of his career, but in my curious blindness to his skill, his patience, his mastery of both pace and spin, I could not see it. My old dislike for him—the captain of the 1985 world champion team I so admired—still lived on. Now, at this moment, some primeval emotion corroded my desire for an Indian win. I did not want to see Gavaskar score another hundred; I did not want to see India win. I wanted to see Pakistan win, I wanted history to be made. I had forgotten this was Gavaskar's last Test. A sudden insanity came over me; I hoped the suspense created by India crawling toward victory would end with India the losers and Pakistan the winners.

And then the last wicket fell. As the umpire's finger went up, the electric tension of that moment snapped, and suddenly, there they were, the Pakistani fielders, exulting as they ran toward the pavilion. I slumped in shock, sick to my guts, haunted. I had willed this result. At that moment, I had wanted India to lose. I had betrayed India for a bunch of ill-mannered louts led by a megalomaniacal autocrat. Outside it was deathly quiet. I was by myself, well and truly alone, as an Indian fan. The volume was turned down on the television; the crowd and commentators had gone quiet. The cruelty of this blow cannot be overstated: it was the last Test of the series, there were to be no more chances for India. Imran had won. He had brought his team to India; they had squabbled their way through the land, scrapping with Indian players, umpires, and the crowds. Imran had won the series; Pakistan had made no friends; they did not want or need to. They had won the cricket; that was all that mattered to them.

The Bangalore Test would be the last I would see in India for nine years.

Part III

Crossing the Black Water

AS MY UNIVERSITY DAYS PAINFULLY dragged on to their end, I was keen to escape from home, from the drudgery and pointlessness of my university experience—three years, pardon the language, quite comprehensively pissed away—to that land of endless promise and potential: the United States. In India I was unprepared for a career, or for that matter, for any sort of "socially respectable" path forward in my life. My grades were not good enough for a desirable graduate program; I had run the Indian competitive exam gauntlet without ever holding out hope I would pass those time-bound inquisitions. I applied for jobs in hotel management and marketing, aware I was desperately unsuited by aptitude for such work. My brother was flying fighter jets for the Indian Air Force, emulating my father, setting standards of masculinity hard to match, and crucially, establishing financial independence. An aimless career, the life of a parasite—living off my mother at home where "the rent was right"—awaited me.

I took the air force's entrance exam, the written prerequisite for an interview and a flying aptitude test, but I did not wait for the results. I did not want to be a member of the same institution as my father and brother, constantly subjected to the burdens of comparison and emulation. God forbid, if I was washed out of training for actual or supposed incompetence in flying, my brother would never let me live that down. Even worse, I might become a helicopter or transport pilot instead of a fighter pilot, a diminished version of him. Instead I applied to, and was accepted into, a mediocre U.S. graduate program in computer science. I did not care; beggars could scarcely afford to be picky about the scraps thrown their way. I would be doing something considerably less exciting than flying fighter jets, but I would be traveling on a road of my choosing. Despite my avowed assurances to immigration officers at the U.S. embassy in New Delhi, I had no intention of returning; my airline ticket was one-way.

I departed on 15 August, Indian Independence Day. My mother bade me goodbye at the airport. I hugged her, grabbed my bags, and ran to the British Airways counters. My mother would be alone now, her sons living elsewhere. She would live with photographs and memories, waiting for phone calls and letters and our short trips back home. I pushed that uncomfortable thought from my mind. I was busy thinking about what lay ahead.

Flying via London, we landed at John F. Kennedy International Airport. As I waited for an old high school friend to pick me up, I—eager to show off my command of American colloquialisms—ordered a "Bud" at an airport bar. My friend soon arrived. As we pulled out of the airport parking lot, he noticed my nose wrinkle at the dance music playing on his car radio and queried, "You like rock, don't you?" He hit a button; rock filled the car. What a country. As we drove along the Long Island Expressway, I noticed—with some amazement—the size of the highway and the speed of the cars. I was suitably awestruck too, by the malls that dotted Long Island's suburban landscape—and the zombie-like humans who rang up my friend's purchases at their gleaming cash registers. The need for fifteen kinds of cereal or a dozen kinds of cheese had never occurred to me. At my friends' home in Hicksville, cold beer and microwaved pizza eased me into the evening. The bland, reheated, plain cheese, toppings-free pies were incomparably tasty; the plebian ales were nectar. I had arrived.

The next day, I took a train into Manhattan. I walked up the steps at Penn Station and found myself in front of Madison Square Garden. Large signs on its exterior said, "Tina Turner and Roger Waters tickets on sale." This was the Garden; home of the Mohammed Ali–Joe Frazier fight. I had seen photographs of it, I had read about it. Now I could enter its precincts and see those I had merely read about and imagined. The United States was not just a fantasy, it was an enabler of fantasies.

New York City was steamy, humid, and sweltering; it was home to a visible urban dysfunction. I saw the homeless, the unkempt, and the mentally deranged who occupied the dark, dirty, dingy spaces of the Port Authority bus terminal. I smelled the urine-soaked subway stations and saw the graffiti-scarred trains that rumbled into and out of them. I walked past the coke dealers, the hustlers, the pimps, and the runaway kids on the

Minnesota Strip on Eighth Avenue. As I grabbed a quick lunch at a small diner, a grimy teenaged boy—filthier than Dickensian lads—walked up to ask if I wanted to eat the rest of the food on my plate. I did not. He did; he took my plate and left. A pair of Indian students who had accompanied me on this trip into Manhattan visited electronics stores and were harassed for not making purchases. New York City—or at least the little bit of it I saw on my short walkabout that day—was hostile and unwelcoming. It cared little for my presence in its midst.

My ultimate destination was Newark, just across the Hudson River in New Jersey. The geographic distance to it was small, but the city was a world apart. I crossed the Hudson for the first time, taking a combination of the Long Island Railroad and the PATH train. I was bewildered by the dereliction and disrepair visible when I emerged—eyes blinking in the bright August sunshine—from the Newark subway station. I did not know it then, but Newark had still not recovered from the riots that had devastated its inner city in 1967. Despite hopeful talk of its renaissance, Newark remained a grim and forbidding exhibition of American inner-city decline.

Equally grim was my university, whose administration sought international students in the abstract because they paid tuition fees and made it financially solvent and then disliked them viscerally once they showed up, bringing their concrete, manifest, presences with them. Our orientation material—which had been mailed to me in India—had instructed international students to bathe and use deodorant regularly for body odor was repugnant to Americans. The campus administrative staff—including those at the international student office—was curiously indifferent to their wards' lot. So, it seemed at times, were the faculty and the local student body. Brusque, unhelpful, and rude interactions were common. An accent was a liability, an invitation to mockery and mimicry, to be disguised with a feigned one. Professors were not above the fray, and classroom jokes at the expense of Indian and Chinese students were de rigueur for some. One professor slowly repeated international students' questions in class, his giggle-ridden attempts to mimic their accents evoking perplexed silence from those in attendance. White suburban students cared little for this predominantly black and Hispanic city they commuted to; the lack of parking on campus was only the preliminary insult to encounters with minorities in the flesh. Black and Hispanic students resented the thick accents of the international students who taught many of their undergraduate classes. They had ample cause for complaint: those who shouldered these teaching burdens were frequently disinterested and unmotivated. I calculated the money my mother was spending on this experience of mine and realized it was a terrible bargain. My supposedly pristine, tree-lined intellectual haven, the American university campus, was an urban cauldron of seething resentment, prejudice, and mutually reinforced misunderstanding. There was no sign of the America I had thought I was headed to.

Once classes picked up speed, I spent increasing amounts of time in our grim library—rather inefficiently—struggling to stay awake while finishing my readings and programming assignments, parked at one of the many carrels that ran along the walls of the library. Thankfully, some of these were positioned next to windows through which one could cast despairing, if drowsy, glances at the world outside. On one of these desks I spotted a bit of illegible graffiti in Arabic. Written below it, clearly in response to its provocations, was a blunt and sharp message: "Look out of the window, camel jockey. Do you see any sand? Do you see any camels? No? Then learn how to speak English or fuck off back to where you came from."

International students were a source of considerable perplexity to the school's administration, which was flummoxed by their visible and vivid presence on campus. Administrative staff disliked the daily negotiation with unfamiliar accents and incomprehension of bureaucratic procedures; faculty were made irate by the constant, anxious requests for fellowships; and local students found the international student's impenetrable clannishness annoying and intimidating. International students found their own ways to combat this prickly response to their presence. Some retreated into cliques and others into heavy drinking, consuming cheap whisky or wine by the liter. Some began counting down the days to their graduations and future jobs or returns home. One member of my cohort had decided to lazily doodle on a desktop in the library; perhaps he was thinking about distant homes; perhaps a witticism or rude joke or dirty ditty had occurred to her, which needed immediate commitment to concreteness; perhaps, sloppily, a note was left for a fellow student.

Whatever the reason and rationale, the effort had not gone unnoticed. It had not been appreciated. It had reminded someone of the ever-present imposition of the unfamiliar; it had evoked prejudice and disdain. It provoked a sharp and pungent retort, an exhortation to the writer to remove him- or herself from the premises if he or she were unable to abide by its rules. I was not from the Middle East; I did not speak Arabic; I was not a "camel jockey." But I was unnerved anyway. I knew that for those who could and would write graffiti like that, these variations—when confronted with my accent, my brown skin, and the curious language I spoke to others who looked like me—were irrelevant.

Meanwhile the Dotbusters across the river in Jersey City suggested the campus administration was not alone in its dislike of Indians.* I now took seriously newspaper reports from my youth of skinheads beating up young Indians in England—those stories of boot stomping and shit kicking that had first served to inform me England was not the shining land I imagined it to be. Instead it was the land that called brown folks "Pakis" and black folks "nig-nogs," and my new home bore some disconcerting similarities to it. Curiously we, international students and immigrants, had been attracted to zones of rejection and disdain artfully hidden under layers of visible promise. This was a confused relationship at best. (International students were not the only "Indians" on campus. Second-generation Indian Americans might have looked like us, but they did not sound so. They disdained our accents, reminders of their parents' noninclusion in mainstream American life. We served a vital function though: we could occupy an inferior position on the totem pole and establish a marker to distance them from India.)

I had not imagined such dislike for Indians possible. But my campus and its open prejudices offered ample proof for this proposition. We were often castigated for being too insular, for banding together. To which my response—muttered under my breath—was: What the fuck do you expect? As we hunted for apartment rentals and had bids rejected by landlords, sometimes because we were students, sometimes because we were Indians, we were often told Indian food made buildings smell. Few substantive conversations about my homeland were possible; most were interrupted by questions that never rose above the level of, "You guys have highways?" "You guys have an air force?" "There are mountains in India?" This was the "abroad" I had so admired, its pretensions rapidly slipping away, crumbling under the weight of an impossible to maintain facade. For this, my mother was exhausting her life savings, paying the bills that told her I was receiving an American university education.

But I was being educated. Comprehensively and thoroughly, even if it was not about algorithms, microprocessors, and assembly language. I could feel, as a matter of everyday occurrence, a considerably less deluded self jostling for attention with the older entity that had flown across ten time zones to seek a new home here.

My new home was not a safe or reassuring place. I lived in Elizabeth, an industrial outpost just outside Newark, off exit 13 on the New Jersey

---

* Michel Marriott, "In Jersey City, Indians Protest Violence," *New York Times*, 12 October 1987, available at http://www.nytimes.com/1987/10/12/nyregion/in-jersey -city-indians-protest-violence.html, last accessed 26 January 2015.

Turnpike. On my way to campus, I drove past the grim Frelinghuysen Avenue projects, apprehensively speculating about the possibilities of my car breaking down on its poorly lit, potholed streets. HIV-positive prostitutes, crack dealers, and opportunistic muggers walked along them, past parked police cars, the armed and uniformed officers within unwilling and unable to intervene in the devastation around them. The grim Columbus Projects next to the Pavilion Apartments—where many international students lived, and where I had declined to put myself up—were unimaginably run-down and filthy, their immediate surroundings populated by threatening young men. Unbelievably, entire families lived within the graffiti-scarred, urine-soaked walls of a space used to corral human beings. Muggings in the neighborhoods surrounding my graduate school were common; students were frequently assaulted and robbed at the university's subway station just outside campus; some were relieved of their wallets on campus, in the library, and in the bathrooms of the main buildings. One Indian lad showed me a black eye acquired via an assault in broad daylight—he had not carried enough money on him. Yet another told me he had been held up at gunpoint while other students watched, too scared to intervene. "Abroad" was not just threatening to preconceived notions; it promised bodily injury and chastisement too.

In 1987, there was no coverage of cricket on radio, television, or newspapers in the United States—the final, gratuitous, heaping of insult upon ample injury. I could not hear commentary on the streets; I could not go to the university and talk about cricket. I could not switch on the radio and fill a room with cricket commentary. I could not watch cricket on television. I could not pick up a newspaper and read about cricket. The United States could never become home.

Free of India and Pakistan

THE 1987 WORLD CUP BEGAN, unnoticed, in a world I had left behind. Soon, through the international student grapevine, via the ubiquitous phone call home, I began to obtain match scores delayed by a day. Out of these tenuous connections grew a new network of relationships among exiles deprived of their central cultural passion. As the Cup went on, I continued to receive secondhand news; I was on the cricketing margins and sidelines once again. There was no radio commentary, and I was not sufficiently Internet literate to access mailing lists providing access to scores. The filtered news of the World Cup confirmed my estrangement from India. Life back there was passing me by.

But technology and graduate student enterprise came together to make possible a satellite relay of the live telecast of the World Cup final. The Graduate Student Association, which was comprised largely of Indians (this was an engineering school), booked satellite time, set up screens and viewing venues on campus, catered food and drinks, and publicized the event. Permits to show the game were organized, building forms signed, and ticket sales arranged. When it looked like Pakistan and India, having qualified for semifinals against Australia and England respectively, would set up an India-Pakistan World Cup final, the ten-dollar tickets sold out.

Pakistan lost to Australia in the first semifinal. The next day, Pakistani students lined up to claim refunds. The Indian students working the ticket stand turned them away, a touch of schadenfreude inflecting their refusals. The next day, India lost in the second semifinal. Now Indian students lined up for refunds and were refused in turn. I was not disappointed; I was relieved. India's series against Pakistan had ended a few months ago. I did not want the feelings evoked by that series intruding on my American life—one just begun a few months ago. Despite missing cricket, I did not miss some of the emotions it stirred up.

On the day of the World Cup final, from nine in the morning till noon, I endured a lecture on database management systems. I pretended to be interested in the technical details of how to make searches for a bank customer's balance more efficient, idly scribbling notes and gazing blankly at the blackboard, all the while mourning the death of my poorly defined academic dream. I then worked in the cafeteria, baking pizzas and making sandwiches till the cafeteria closed in the early evening. The student association had arranged two theaters for the telecast. One was an old lecture hall, the other an equally drab lab a few floors upstairs. Tickets were to be checked at the door, and a small snacks stall was set up. I had secured employment checking tickets and handling food stalls. I would be up all night and would continue working in the cafeteria the next day. If only I could have pulled off such all-nighters for the programming assignments I so despised and lacked the aptitude for.

Before the final began, the satellite feed treated us to highlights of the pool games. Outside the theater, a Newark police officer utterly confused by the goings-on inside, claimed that France had not qualified for this year's World Cup. As I looked at the crowd gathered in the hall, I realized some students whom I had imagined Indian were Pakistani. Their rambunctious cheering during Pakistan's matches and their pointed silence during India's gave their identity away. Thus was I exposed to the truism that "Hey, they look just like us."

Something far more discordant was taking place on the screen. In comparison with the sprawling splendor of an American football stadium, Indian cricket grounds looked ugly. The game itself looked dull, colorless, and prosaic. I wished the Cup had been broadcast live from Australia. Its slickly packaged version would have been a better advertisement for cricket. Our few American companions stared at the screen's blurred images and garbled, static-laden messages sent from another planet whose inhabitants had made it into their midst. A dirty theater—in a grimy postindustrial city across the Hudson from New York City—was showing grainy images from an obscure sporting tournament played somewhere in the Third World. It was the perfect image of the margins I imagined myself to inhabit.

Transporting cricket to newer climes was not straightforward. To relate to the game in the ways most familiar to my cricket-watching experiences, there had to be a cricketing world outside. Years later, on my journeys back to India, I made mixtapes from my newly acquired compact disc collection for my brother but realized my gifts got little play time on his stereo. But I also did not listen much to "my music" once I was back in India. The music distinctive of cultures grew out of the sounds and the aural accompaniments of the atmosphere and environment. The music my brother and I heard had to resonate, in every sense of the word, with that which surrounded us. Cricket on television needed to have cricket being played "outside"; otherwise, it was a mysterious growth, an odd imposition, a discordance.

As the night wore on, my discontent grew. I drank horrible coffee; I smoked cigarette after cigarette; I ate stale pastries that curdled my stomach. I made myself sicker as the night wore on. Graduate student life was indelibly associated with that perennial, low-grade nausea created by the relentless consumption of pungent cigarettes and bad coffee. It went perfectly with a sleep-deprived self, a harried and harassed and beleaguered state of being. That night, as I looked at the cricket playing on an old projection screen, my guts churning, I felt a curiously empty feeling. I was watching cricket, the World Cup final, but it all felt a bit flat, a bit beside the point.

More than my stomach was upset that night. I did not want England to win. England's status as a cricketing nation had fallen in my eyes shortly after I had begun to read the incessant journalistic carping about the West Indies' pace attack, the one that most recently had subjected the English to two consecutive blackwashes in 1984 and 1986. Far from being the supplier of cricketing heroes like Botham and Gower, England had come to stand for retrograde, reactionary cricket, holding on to colonial fantasies, being dragged kicking and screaming into the bright new world of non-Anglo-Australian-dominated cricket. Sometimes the English journalist and commentator, or retired player, which sometimes came to the same thing, complained about declining over rates, sometimes about ascending bouncer rates, sometimes about excessive subcontinental appealing, and sometimes about a less than sanguine response to umpiring misfortune. The very suggestion that English umpires—those professional arbiters of cricketing fortune—could ever make a mistake or ever be any less than impeccably impartial and evenhanded in their dealings or that they might ever be tainted with the dominant stereotypes or prejudices of their culture seemed to have been taken particularly poorly by the English writer. County cricket, that land and season and clime of cricketing excellence, which I had once admired from afar, seemed to have its virtues overemphasized. The relentless invocation of its essential place in the education of any successful cricketer anywhere had become tedious. English cricket continued to be the supposed fount of cricketing rectitude from which all manner of sporting and moral goods flowed outward to the rest of the world, which seemed less than appropriately grateful for the many bounties sent its way.

There were no two ways about it: an English win in the World Cup would be intolerable. I had realized my relationship with English cricket had changed much in the way my relationship with another area of human endeavor and lore changed—the story of mountaineering, and especially Everest expeditions. In the beginning, it was all English glory, involving endlessly repeated stories of George Mallory and Andrew Irvine, the relentless flogging of that legend of admittedly admirable men, the story of the 1953 Coronation Year Expedition, so ably led by an upstanding veteran of the British army, John Hunt, that put a Commonwealth climber, Edmund Hillary, and his loyal Sherpa, Tenzing Norgay, on the top of the world. But I no longer wanted those Everest stories. I wanted the stage, the summit, to be populated by someone else. And the stories surrounding Everest changed. The Everest narratives became free of English influence and free of English understandings of what was good and great in mountaineering. Everest was populated by great climbers from elsewhere. There were Poles and Finns and Ecuadorans and Basque and Korean and Japanese climbers. The stories of Everest acknowledged that climbing talent could be found elsewhere. Mountaineering was not endlessly oppressed by older histories and standards. It was generous in its acknowledgments of climbers and styles of climbing that were not English. The English had supplied their precious oxygen to the Sherpas who took them to the top; I did not want to breathe it anymore.

Close Encounters of the Cross-Border Kind

DURING MY FIRST INTERNATIONAL STUDENT orientation at graduate school, as some Indian students and I mingled with a motley crew of Taiwanese, Lebanese, Israeli, and Chinese students, a young man walked up to us and asked us if we were Indian. We assured him we were. A nervous-looking older man stood behind him. The young man introduced himself and his friend; they were Pakistanis. The older man was like us, a new student, and he was worried about being in Newark by himself. The young man had to drive back to Long Island and had a request: Could we look after his friend? We agreed. Our interaction was polite; we made small talk. From now on, encounters with the rest of the world would not be mediated by geographical distance but by a mutual willingness to participate. They would be dependent on the negotiated parameters of our conversations and interactions.

Pakistani students offered me my first extended contact with Pakistanis in the flesh, the first chance to observe them and to interact in social and academic settings. That anthropological description smacks of exoticizing, but it does justice to the differences I perceived and encountered. Pakistani students worried about halal meat and dietary restrictions and disdained alcohol, while the Indian students I knew were scarfing down beef burgers and chasing them with cheap beer. Even after accounting for the legendary vegetarianism of Indians, it was easier to find a beef-eating Indian than that mythical creature, a pork-eating Pakistani. (Cigarettes were a vice that bridged the gustatory gap here.) Pakistani students spoke approvingly of the Ayatollah Khomeini's fatwa on Salman Rushdie, that reckless blasphemer, the figurative defiler of the Koran. My roommates and I often sang dirty songs based on the Hindu epic *Ramayana* in which Ram and Laxman cursed like Delhi University students and spoke of threesomes with Sita, Ram's consort. Pakistani students offered little critical commentary on Pakistani politics—but that might have just been sensitivity in the company of Indians. Indians were happy to critique the Indian government, especially the Congress (I)—even on Kashmir—with little regard for the audience.

Much history was skirted in these conversations. Pakistanis did not regard an Indian audience a safe context in which to think aloud, critically, about the land they had left behind. Indians, for their part, often regarded Pakistanis as wayward brothers to be persuaded back into the fold. Unlike other Indians who wished the countries would be reunited as a measure of their affection for Pakistan, I felt no such desire. I knew Pakistan had its own identity—no matter how tenuous—and I knew enough of the history of the two countries to know a polar vortex would descend into hell before the two would reunite.

I was acquiring too, defensiveness about a nation I had never cared to defend before in any forum: I did not like hearing Pakistani critiques of India. I bit back the retorts that came to mind when Pakistani students critiqued Indian teaching assistants—How many graduate students does your country supply?—or Indian politics—Why don't you get a democracy first? A young woman from Karachi complained there were too many Indians on campus—and too many blacks and Hispanics in the city around us. She had imagined her American experience would be more densely populated by those of a whiter persuasion. I suggested to her that to our sullen college administration, she looked just like the Indians she disliked. Between my defensiveness and the differences between us, companionship was not easy.

But I made a Pakistani friend, another graduate student. I played the Punjabi card—it seemed like a more probable point of contact than any other. I told him I was Punjabi, that my grandfather had attended Government College in Lahore, and that our old ancestral village was now in Pakistan. We traded jokes and tales of our hometowns in Punjabi; but we too, skated around each other. We occasionally spoke—in platitudes—of the political distrust between India and Pakistan. He spoke of the "lunatics" on the Pakistani side of the border. I dutifully did the same for the Indian side. We offered bromides and clichés about the terrors of the Partition, about how Indians and Pakistanis needed to disdain blind prejudice. We resolutely skirted the awkward business of those who were not "lunatics" but still contributed to the contentious, edgy relationship between the two countries. The substantive issues at the heart of the India-Pakistan divide lay untouched, a live wire too threatening to approach.

Cricket on the Internet

I DID NOT LIKE to be reminded I was a foreigner in the United States. I was embarrassed when I was reminded that I mixed up my *Ws* and *Vs*— wax instead of vax, wallyball instead of volleyball, wodka instead of vodka—that my vowels were not as short and clipped as American ones. I was mortified when my accent's distinctive intonations and my idiosyncratic emphases of syllables bemused my audiences, sometimes, humiliatingly and embarrassingly, forcing me to repeat myself. I was awkwardly self-conscious in groups of Indians in public settings. Clusters of brown men, long before 12 September 2001, were problematic in American spaces. My supposed Western education, acculturation, and Anglophone background had only equipped me with a veneer of Westernization; my physical appearance was enough to mark me as a foreigner. My audiences could not hear me talk because they were too busy processing my difference from them. A year after I arrived in the United States, I had shaved off my mustache and bought new clothes, a makeover to hopefully make me look "more American." If only I could have lost my accent and my brown skin as easily. Even harder to lose would have been the twenty years I had lived in India before I came to the United States—a span of time that ensured a distinct and locally unfamiliar source of material for self-conception.

But I was also Americanized. A Cuban American friend informed me he would, if he could, grant me U.S. citizenship, so Americanized did I seem to him. I spoke formal and colloquial English fluently; I was comfortable with American pop culture; I followed American sports and immediately cottoned on to its great rivalries, adopting the New York Giants and New York Mets as my favorites. (I was nothing if not a bandwagon jumper; these teams had won the Super Bowl and the World Series respectively the previous year.*) I had read a great deal of U.S. history: the Revolutionary Wars, Wounded Knee, the Alamo, Pearl Harbor, Dr. King, and other prescribed landmarks were familiar navigational aids for it. I listened to jazz and blues and rock and roll; I understood and used pop cultural references; I had grown up on Hollywood; and I had spent years haunting the American Library, enculturating and indoctrinating myself. Still, no one here cared very much. And there was a huge, aching gap in the center of my American life. There was no cricket. There was, especially, no cricket played by the Indian cricket team.

Since I had left India, every Indian cricketing achievement had become larger than life. They now became objects of pleasure, to be gloried in and used as fodder to build a new self. My retrospective glances at the Indian feats I had once disdained were now inflected with longing and admiration. Don't know what you got till it's gone, indeed. What grim irony then, that the one game India was any good at—or could be good at—was a game the United States ignored and despised. I wanted reflected glory from those who knew of cricket—other fans from other countries. My community lay there, not in Newark. If someone would acknowledge my

---

* Samir Chopra, "Confessions of a Mets and Yankees Fan," The AllRounder, available at http://theallrounder.co/2014/10/08/confessions-of-a-mets-and-yankees-fan/, last accessed 14 April 2015.

distinctiveness, see through my outer brown accented shell, it would be cricket fans. Not Americans.

I found cricket on the Internet. I had discovered Usenet newsgroups in 1988, shortly after I began work as a research assistant at a campus lab. I "worked" long hours in the laboratory; e-mail and newsgroups occupied much of that time (in between writing and debugging code and stepping out for coffee and cigarette breaks). I considered myself well-read, but this inflated estimation of my edification was soon revised.

In the late eighties and the early nineties, Usenet newsgroups were largely populated by those with university affiliations: faculty, students, staff, and postdoctoral fellows. Commercial affiliations were not unknown, but these were outnumbered by academic ones; the .edu address was most commonly visible. That demographic, unsurprisingly, was voluble and prolific in its writing. (To the eternal credit of the hacker community, many of its members wrote often and well on newsgroups.) I read newsgroups daily; these were the time sucks of their day. You could spend hours and hours reading, responding, and engaging in flame wars. They were how you filled lunch and coffee breaks, making you stay up late at night and logging in frequently to see whether new articles had shown up, to see if anyone had responded to your post, and to engage in (often seemingly endless) refutation and disputation.

It was here, in Usenet newsgroups, that I read many, many well-written, articulate, and clearly argued and defended points of view on topics I had never read, or never had the opportunity to read, before: free speech absolutism, the legalization of recreational drugs, Palestinian self-determination, women's reproductive rights, privacy rights, gay and lesbian rights, free software versus proprietary software, flag burning, feminism, interpretations of the U.S. Constitution, and First, Fourth, Second, and Fifth Amendments debates. (I also spent a great deal of time discussing the Grateful Dead in rec.music.gdead, obsessing about tour dates, tape trades, and set lists.) When world-shaking events like the fall of the Berlin Wall or Tiananmen Square occurred on the world stage, they provoked almost immediately, corresponding discussions in the relevant groups. I read furious debates; refutations and counterrefutations; angry tirades; racist and xenophobic rants; calm, reasoned, erudite quasi-dissertations; deflation of pretension and artifice; and satirical humor.

I had often entertained conventional views on these topics before I encountered newsgroups; very few of them survived their encounter with newsgroup discussions. I read a great deal of revisionist history, which offered me alternative perspectives on world historical events I had glibly thought I understood well. I had been complacent; I was no longer so. The sense of instability in my beliefs was alarming but exhilarating. I learned that seemingly air-tight arguments and refutations often contained fatal fallacies and weaknesses that could be exposed by close reading and careful attention to their logical and rhetorical form. I never forgot those early readings that produced in me a distinctive shock of the new. Many, many thanks are due to unnamed teachers of mine.

But in those early days, in the newsgroups, a new personality of mine found expression: a defender of India. I ranted about how Indians did not stand up for themselves; I disliked "destructive criticism" of India made by 'outsiders'; if I could say anything about India in contradistinction to its culturally dominant image as an obscure, forgotten, poverty-stricken land, I would. Now, the lens through which I viewed India was considerably more tinted than the one I had used when I had lived there. It was easier to defend an abstract notion from a distance, easy to forget my own discomfort in my skin when I had lived in the concrete reality of the abstract nation and its ideals. I was easily provoked and intemperate, a new emotional core uncovered, one whose rage and resentment and sense of grievance was primed by my weekday life. Those intemperate pronouncements of mine still survive in the Internet; they have not lost their capacity to embarrass and make me wince.

In 1990, the cricket newsgroup rec.sport.cricket was born. That summer, on India's depressing tour of England, as India went down to defeat in time-honored fashion—its weak bowling attack allowing huge English totals to be racked up and placing unbearable pressure on its batting lineup—I learned of Sachin Tendulkar and grew excited at the thought of a new Indian superstar. I thrilled to read of Kapil Dev's hitting Eddie Hemmings for four straight sixes at Lord's and saving the follow-on, though not eventual defeat. It spoke of defiance; we could act boldly. Away in New Jersey, I gloried in that minor act of resistance, that getting in line, that refusal to step back and away.

Sometime in 1989, cricket scores had begun to be posted on the rec.sport.misc, soc.culture.indian, and soc.culture.british newsgroups.* The cross-posting of the scores of games not involving England to the third group was made under the innocent but mistaken assumption that members of the Commonwealth possessed a neutral interest in cricket. For this "invasion" of British cyberspace almost immediately led to an epic flame war between the two online communities. The English suggested Indians deserved to be recolonized, to be taught appropriate manners and deco-

---

* This section borrows from, and draws upon, the chapter "Cricket and Media," in Chopra, *Brave New Pitch*.

rum all over again. Indians suggested the English needed to recover from their colonial hangovers. I jumped in and fired off a flame or two. I found myself possessed by a rage I had not known lurked within me; I was arguing with online representatives of a culture I had once uncritically idolized in dimensions other than the cricketing. My reactions—born of my life in Newark, my displacement from India, my post-1983 World Cup self, my new understanding of cricket rhetoric and history—were unsurprising. I was a jilted, disillusioned lover, possessed by an unhinged fury. My carefully constructed fantasies had crumbled around me: "All too often, when we love somebody, we don't accept him or her as what the person effectively is. We accept him or her insofar as this person fits the co-ordinates of our fantasy. We misidentify, wrongly identify him or her, which is why, when we discover that we were wrong, love can quickly turn into violence. There is nothing more dangerous, more lethal for the loved person than to be loved, as it were, for not what he or she is, but for fitting the ideal."*

Nothing quite demonstrated this failure to match up to excessively romanticized ideals like my relationship with Pakistani fans on the cricket newsgroup. Where I hoped to build a community, mostly by informing Pakistanis how much I admired their cricketers and how they had affected my cricketing sensibilities so deeply, I found no reciprocity, no outstretched hand that would accept my proffered handshake. Where I hoped to talk about what my being a fan of Pakistani cricketers had meant to me, I found my pronouncements blocked by an unrelenting hostility toward Indian cricket—as part of a larger hostility toward most things Indian. I had experienced difference with Pakistanis in person and in the political relationships between India and Pakistan; the interactions in these virtual spaces offered adequate confirmation of the problematic nature of this relationship. There was no mistaking the hostility that suffused online interactions, unaided by visible body language or expression, no mistaking the curiously diminished and impoverished vision Pakistanis had of India.

The difficulty of this relationship was exacerbated by the nature of the Internet—its anonymity and asynchronicity offered an easy, cost-free medium to express hostility and rancor. Unsurprisingly, newsgroups were prime forums for demonstrations of nationalist aggression, often populated by those like me, clinging to imagined conceptions of unrealized ideals, fiercely rejecting all that could disturb those complacent, safe assessments. The cricket newsgroup was no exception. Flame wars were

---

* Slavoj Zizek, *The Pervert's Guide to Cinema*, available at http://www.imdb.com /title/tt0828154/quotes?item=qt0524189, last accessed 14 April 2015.

common, there was little mediation, and no one wanted moderation. I read a great deal of quality cricket writing on rec.sport.cricket; it is a tribute to the quality and range of this corpus that the writing of professional journalists often paled by comparison. But it suffered from those things many newsgroups suffered from. There was a cyclical nature to most discussions; and members would troll—make outrageously provocative remarks—all too often.

On the Internet, you can write anything, you can read everything. I grew tired of the endless Pakistani descriptions of the physical and mental weakness of the Indian, of the silliness of the explanations of why Pakistani produced pace bowlers and why India produced spin bowlers. In its barest form, this argument presented the meat-eating, tall, virile, fair-skinned Pakistani as the pace bowler and the rice-and-lentil-eating, cunning, wily, dark Indian as the spinner. Indians were weak and devious, preferring the backdoor entry of the spinner to the break-down-the-front-door spirit of the pace bowler. Fitting these bizarrely essentialist views into Pakistan's troubled history with ethnicity and nation—especially as manifest in the creation of Bangladesh in 1971, when a racially inflected genocide had been carried out on Bengali Pakistanis, then described as "small and dark" in distinction to the "tall, fair" Punjabis and other West Pakistanis*—was especially galling.

There were tit-for-tat wars aplenty. Pakistani fans trudged through mounds of statistics to devalue Indian cricketing achievements; Indians did the same, suggesting all Pakistani cricket performances at home be discounted. The Pakistanis on the Net who attacked Gavaskar's statistics were doing what I had once done, mounting objections—runs made at home, against weak bowling attacks—that could have been made to anyone's statistics, for all Test batsmen have fattened their averages so. But Pakistani forensic analyses seemed infected by a virulent, directed spitefulness. To make this objection against Gavaskar and not against Gary Sobers or Don Bradman was silly. Few Pakistanis devoted as much energy to attacking the statistics of other countries' players. Many Indians, of course, took the time to painstakingly document the glaring difference between the number of times Javed Miandad was given out LBW in Pakistan by Pakistani umpires, and the number of times he was so out playing away.

---

* Pervez Hoodbhoy, "Shahbag Square—Why We Pakistanis Don't Know and Don't Care," *Express Tribune*, 15 February 2013, available at http://tribune.com.pk/story/507834/shahbag-square-why-we-pakistanis-dont-know-and-dont-care/, last accessed 26 January 2015.

There was no denying Pakistan had a more distinguished cricketing record than India's, that from the eighties onward Pakistan fielded a more talented side than India, that the gap grew with the arrival of Waqar Younis and Wasim Akram, two of the greatest pace bowlers of the modern era. None of this meant Indian cricketing history was worthy of denigration—the kind I had indulged in once. None of it meant no Indian player had done enough to ensure a place in cricket's pantheon—an older assessment of mine. The most historically ignorant fans on rec.sport.cricket were Pakistanis; they too, had their reasons for ignoring and abnegating the history of Indian cricket. It interfered with their conceptions of themselves—like it had with mine once.

My praise of the Pakistani team meant little to the Pakistanis. They did not care I had Pakistani cricketing heroes. They enjoyed my appreciation of their cricketers but did little to earn my friendship or solidarity by sending praise for Indian cricketers my way. This was analogous to a larger problem with my life in the United States. There was little point in telling Americans I admired the U.S. marines; that I had studied the U.S. Navy's Pacific campaign in the Second World War, the history of the Revolutionary War, and the civil rights movement; and that I understood how the American budgetary process worked. Americans expected and demanded such homage and fealty. I spoke their language. I learned their history. I knew their jokes. I had left my country for theirs. They did not need to understand me. I was another brown man laying flowers at the altar of American homage. I was used to making unilateral concessions in the United States; I wanted this parade of subjugation to stop somewhere. It stopped at the door of the Pakistani cricketing fan.

So I neatly reversed roles. I defended Gavaskar against the charge of being boring and a home-track bully and went from being the one carrying out the vilification to being his defender. I was now able to appreciate what Kapil Dev had done in those years when he bowled innumerable overs on dead pitches to take hundreds of wickets even as he conceded a mountain of runs. I now spoke of the virtues of Indian cricket and the Indian team, and found dimensions to their performances I had never explored. I found talents and skills previously left unpraised.

Because I regarded Pakistanis as a bloc on rec.sport.cricket, I regarded their most disturbing aspect as being the visible lack of community restraint. When Indians transgressed in making bigoted remarks, in making comments designed to provoke and irritate rather than contribute to meaningful discourse, they were often subjected to sustained critique from other Indians. No such restraint was exercised by Pakistanis on the Net. While you could write anything on India if you were Pakistani, the one thing you could not do was criticize another Pakistani. Ramblings that spoke of ignorance were not embarrassing; criticisms of your countrymen were. They were a minority here; they were besieged. I was a minority elsewhere. We closed ranks and drew back into zones of comfort and safety and imagined solidarity.

That I would ever meet a Pakistani cricket fan capable of admitting defeat fair and square to India, that India had played better in the 1979–1980 series, that Indian players had made a mark in cricket, or that India had cricketing achievements to be proud of struck me as an absurd fiction. I wondered whether a Pakistani youngster had any Indian cricketing idols; I could not imagine one. I searched in vain for some measure of acknowledgment, some recognition of Indian talents. There was a fundamental asymmetry to the relationship, a lack of reciprocity. Pakistani fans owed me no favors; they were entitled to their opinions. I went on hoping they would acknowledge the figurative hand I held out, but they did not see it. They could not; their sheer bloody-mindedness about the Indian team had me all too quickly decide not to praise anyone from the Pakistani team, to not wax nostalgic about the Pakistani cricketers I had so loved and admired.

I sometimes engaged in mild banter with Pakistani members of rec. sport.cricket, sometimes by e-mail, sometimes on the group itself. These encounters were the virtual equivalent of my interactions in physical space with my graduate school Pakistani friend. A Pakistani student at Cal State Chico whose writings I considered an exception to the usual puerile ramblings of his countrymen did not fail to disappoint when he wrote, "When Pakistan toured India in 1986–87, they did not just sleep with Indian women; they also won the test series." I thought of my fandom of Pakistan in years past: all that emotional investment in a team whose supporters despised us and gloated over their wins.

Pakistanis viewed gestures of friendship from Indians that ignored the border as moves to erase Pakistan's identity. Their studious distancing from such advances enabled their construction of a Pakistani identity free of Indian interference. Such Pakistani insecurities quickly became tiresome for they were understandable only at an intellectual level, not at a visceral, emotional one. Their insecurities were unattractive; as lovers find out, few relationships survive in which one partner is constantly, narcissistically, insecure. When this applies to both partners, the mutual reinforcement of insecurities and paranoia makes for a truly ghastly relationship.

I once suggested to my Pakistani friend something I heard many Indians say: "If the two countries put together a combined team, we could be world champions." I wanted to talk about the cricketing possibilities involved. Sachin Tendulkar could open with Saeed Anwar; Pakistan would supply the pace attack; and Anil Kumble could form a deadly spinning combination with Mushtaq Ahmed on the right kind of wickets. My friend's reply was that Pakistan was world champion on its own and did not need India. An admirably spirited reply—and a rebuff. I could have pointed out that India beat the West Indies in the West Indies before Pakistan did, that India beat England in England before Pakistan did, that India won the World Cup nine years before Pakistan did. None of this came to mind as I thought, "God, you're a prick. Could we just talk cricket for a bit?" But he was right. Why did I, an Indian, want to talk about the possibilities of a combined India-Pakistan team? Why not a combined India-England team? An Indian friend once remarked to this same Pakistani friend that (a) there was "no difference" between India and Pakistan, and (b) she hoped the two countries could be one again. I restrained a giggle. The irony of saying this to a Pakistani who did not think those were remotely friendly comments was not lost on me.

Meanwhile the news from India informed me of the Kashmir problem growing and festering. India and Pakistan had drawn close to war in 1989 and were perennially on the edge of another armed conflict over that disputed land. The Pakistani posters squabbling with Indians on rec.sport. cricket were appropriately representative of their meddlesome country. The hostility I read about in Pakistani headlines and in their governmental pronouncements was mirrored in the hostility their countrymen expressed on this cricketing forum. When I had lived in India, the Kashmir problem had not had the same violent dimensions it acquired in the 1990s, the decade in which I encountered Pakistanis on the Net. The Pakistani involvement in its strife, like its entanglement in Punjab in the 1980s, did not feel benign. Despite my liberal inclinations in U.S. politics, I was susceptible to Indian nationalist commentary on the Kashmir problem. The fuse of anti-Pakistani sentiment was lit in me all too quickly because, trivially enough, I felt rejected by Pakistanis in the United States and on the Internet. But the personal was supposed to be political, wasn't it?

When Pakistan toured England in 1992, I found the cheating allegations—leveled by the English press against Pakistani fast bowlers—easy to believe. I had disdained Fleet Street's commentary on the West Indies' overuse of pace and intimidation, but I found it remarkably on target when it came to Pakistani perfidy. Later, when I read Mike Marqusee's *Anyone but England,** I found his neo-Marxist analysis of English class and political prejudice, of cricket's irredeemable grounding in commercial

---

* Mike Marqusee, *Anyone but England: An Outsider Looks at English Cricket* (London: Aurum, 2005).

interests and its creation myths of a pristine, unspoiled, wholly amateur past grounded in the village game congenial and perspicuous. And I agreed an insurrection was underway in the world of cricket, one stoutly resisted by its former masters. But I did not feel the sympathy Marqusee clearly expressed for the Pakistani team of 1992. It had taken ten years, but the defender of Imran's 1982 team was the accuser of the Pakistani team in 1992. Subcontinental solidarity was found wanting here. Amid an ostensible growing political sophistication, I was still infected by a personal animosity that could easily tilt my political scales.

An Awakening

BY 1992, at the age of twenty-five, I had spent five years in the United States, three weeks of those five years in India—the spatiotemporal distance between home and me had grown. I had finished graduate school and turned in a singularly uninspired performance. I had been unmotivated and keen to move on from my depressing campus, my poorly structured and taught graduate program. I had taken the easiest classes I could to finish my degree for I suspected I had little aptitude for computer science. I was now well and truly adrift, unsure of what career to pursue, mystified by where my inclinations lay.

I found a job I was overqualified for: system testing of voice and data systems at Bell Laboratories. I took the job, because it seemed like the only one I could get. I could not have made a worse decision. A suitably trained chimpanzee could have performed the work assigned me: blindly following testing plans, pressing one key sequence after another. It was mind-numbingly boring, and I immediately began scheming for a transfer to another department where I would be more intellectually challenged. Still, Bell Labs often provided a salubrious, laid-back environment with regard to its dress code and working hours and thus offered many options for playing hooky. I went running or played long basketball games at lunch. I spent much time reading the Grateful Dead newsgroup. I often left work early to smoke pot at home (and sometimes, on the way back, lighting up in my car as I drove along the Garden State Parkway). I spent hours reading rec.sport.cricket, checking again and again to see if new articles had been posted. Reading and arguing about cricket provided solace during those long, dreary afternoons stuck in the labs. Little had changed: once I used to be bored and lonely in graduate school labs, now I was bored and lonely in corporate labs.

I had found love though, striking up a relationship with a fiery Irish American radical feminist, a technical writer preparing for a long leave of absence to study literary theory at New York University. As we dated, I struggled to explain the significance of cricket to her. K eschewed the usual American cracks about cricket that so alienated me and tried to accommodate my passion for it—she could sense it was more than a game. Best of all, she joined me in some gentle ribbing of her English brother-in-law on matters cricketing. True gestures of an enduring love, I thought.

Our relationship was bookish; we bought each other books as gifts. On the four-year anniversary of my arrival in the United States, K bought me Toni Morrison's *Sula* and Richard Wright's *Native Son*. The first one changed my understanding of sexual politics forever; the second, my understanding of my place in this world, the external construction of my internal self. I had not heard of Wright; I had not read *Native Son*. A few days after receiving this generous gift, I began reading it. I will long remember the day I did. It was summertime in New Jersey, the nights came late, providing relief from the muggy heat of the day. I had driven back from work, eaten an early dinner, and then retired to my tiny bedroom. I had solitude and time, near perfect conditions for reading. I propped my pillow up against the wall, rested my head against it, stretched out on the modest futon mattress that served as bed, and read *Native Son*.

I read *Book One: Fear* and *Book Two: Flight*. As I read *Book Three: Fate*, and as Bigger Thomas approached his final, irresistible fate, I felt as if the world, and the place I had previously inhabited in it, was fast becoming unrecognizable. And yet, simultaneously, I was becoming more comprehensible to myself; suddenly I understood. As I lay there, slumped, stunned, struggling to take in the dramatically new portrait that Wright was painting for me of race, class, subjugation, and resistance, I felt as if the walls of the room I was in were moving back, somehow expanding to accommodate a growth I felt within me of something I had never experienced before. I could not stop; I continued to read, sickened and fascinated in equal measure by the tragedy whose contours were traced out so eloquently by Wright. I knew I would never see my past life in the same way again; I did not think I would ever feel as I had before I read *Native Son*.

Now, whenever I think of *Native Son*, I think of that evening, that room and its walls, seemingly being pushed back by the expanding consciousness they enclosed. I understood myself a little better. I understood—just a little better—why I had felt the way I had growing up in India. I was not a black American, and I had not grown up in the United States, but *Native Son* still spoke to me. It did not induce solidarity with my subcontinental "brothers"—that part of the analysis did not work on me. In that domain, a corrosive anger born of rejection, a jilted lover's disappointment, still infected me. But other parts did resonate: the sense of being diminished by a system that had denied a fuller appreciation of my past, my culture; a system that had prevented me from forming a fuller sense of myself. I felt I understood how I had co-constructed those ideological lenses through which I had viewed the world and understood my place in it. I understood cricket a little better; I viewed its history differently. I knew why my watching and following of it was no innocent, apolitical act. Then, I had still not read C.L.R. James's *Beyond a Boundary*, a curious lacuna in my cricketing education. When I finally did, I realized with a start that part of the journey I would have undertaken with James had been accomplished by reading Wright.

Pakistan Triumphant

BY THE TIME OF THE 1992 WORLD CUP, I had made my first serious stab at integration into American life—via a romantic relationship. And I had become disillusioned with Pakistan.

As the World Cup wore on, I was averse to cheering for Pakistan, resistant to join the company of those who sparred with me in online flame wars. I was not crestfallen by Pakistan's losses in the preliminary round games or by the personal failures of those I had once admired—like Miandad and Imran. The thought that these setbacks would shut up those louts on the Net was deeply satisfying. As Pakistan stuttered in its opening matches, I remained indifferent to the possibility they would be knocked out of the World Cup. Meanwhile India blundered on, their campaign quickly running aground. Their galling failure in the Australian summer of 1991–1992 had lowered my expectations that their World Cup magic would be repeated at the site of their triumph in that magical Benson and Hedges World Championship seven years ago.

India was derailed after a series of mediocre performances. Pakistan steamed on, to the semifinal and beyond, to a Cup final encounter with England. I could have watched the final at Indian and Pakistani restaurants in New Jersey and New York, but I was not going to watch it in the wrong—that is, Pakistani—company. I could not cheer for England either; I did not want to put up with English journalists and fans—always convinced of their country's eternal high ground in cricketing history—persuading all and sundry this win spoke of inevitable English mastery of a format invented by them. Increasingly, my responses to cricketing events were being driven by my acute anticipation of the responses they would evoke in the online forums I participated in.

Finding the final utterly noncompelling, I settled for checking the scores at work—well after the game had ended. My lack of interest was complete. I was no longer a neutral fan of the game; I could be disinclined to support anyone out of sheer bloody-mindedness. At work, I read the transcript of the commentary that described England's fall in its chase to reach the Pakistani total. My mood changed to relief; I would not have to listen to triumphalist descriptions of a resurgent England. An English lecture was less tolerable than Pakistani gloating. There was a distinctive hierarchy visible in my prejudices and disinclinations.

The next day Pakistani students raised the Pakistani flag at my old university, only to have it torn down the next day by unknown miscreants. While it would have been tempting for Pakistanis to have thought this was the handiwork of disgruntled Indian fans—a charge immediately leveled—they might have been flattering themselves. Bigotry at my alma mater was blunt and inchoate, directed at anything not white and not American. It did not matter whose flag it was; an Indian flag would have received the same treatment.

At work, a Pakistani colleague brought a video of highlights of the Cup final to one of those ubiquitous celebrate-world-culture-for-the-sake-of-diversity-in-the-workplace parties that had sprung up over the American corporate landscape. These accompanied sensitivity training seminars and affirmative action training sessions, all in the name of multiculturalism and a kinder, gentler, United States. At the party, the video played in the corner, as discordant a presence in that scene as the assorted food items and music. I brought in Ugandan pop music; it narrowly edged out my original choice, the Clash. I could no longer abide those polite, superficially curious conversations about all matters Indian conducted over a plate of samosas—and they would certainly be prompted if I brought in a sarod recital by Ali Akbar Khan. As I stood there watching the cricket, I realized I would be asked about the game; those men on the screen looked like me. The inevitable query about this baffling game soon came. So, I explained how cricket was played and who was playing it. As I did so, I admired those beautiful deliveries by Wasim Akram that destroyed the English batting. I still enjoyed watching the Pakistani team. Now, of course, there were other images to link with the Pakistani team: they reminded me of their fans on the Internet.

It was supposed to be the other way around. I was supposed to leave India with my sensibilities corroded by tribal passions and be reformed by the West and its liberal melting pot societies, which would show me that ancient hatreds had no place in modern life and society. The stellar examples of Indians and Pakistanis living and working together would show me that friendship was possible between these supposedly estranged communities. The Pakistanis would realize we meant them no harm. How could we when we admired their cricket team so much, when our women swooned over their cricketers, and when, as a child, I had not fallen for the jingoistic nonsense sent my way? But the most modern tools of electronic communication had served to drive us asunder, creating spaces for displays of facile patriotism and carefully constructing virtual arenas used for flexing nationalist muscles.

Channel Wars: The Internet Relay Channel

IN 1993, I discovered the new dimension that the Internet Relay Channel's real-time conversations afforded to cricket coverage on the Internet. The format of IRC commentary was simple: one person with access to radio or television typed in a line-by-line report on the match. The channel members read the commentary and chatted on another channel. (IRC commentary was a live version of Robert Elz's line-by-line, ball-by-ball descriptions of Tests during the 1991 Indian tour to Australia. You opened a text file, started reading, and made your way through the match. When a wicket fell—in the line-by-line descriptions—the shock felt was close to that experienced as you watched on live television.) Sometimes cricketers gave interviews on IRC; an IRC member sat them down at a terminal, solicited questions from channel members, and typed in their answers. (In 1997, I moderated an interview with Aamir Sohail, the Pakistani opening batsman. Sohail sat in Lahore with another IRC regular as I was sent questions by private messages. I typed in the questions; Sohail's answers were typed in by his companion.)

I followed cricket on IRC intermittently: leaving in 1997, returning in 1998, and then sporadically checking in before I finally signed off in 2000. I discovered community on IRC. I met cricket fans from all over the world. I would log on to chat, to assuage loneliness; nothing was quite as melancholic as logging on and finding only strangers online. There were many long rambling conversations on IRC; small splinter groups of like-minded friends evolved. The need to put faces to names grew strong; websites with photographs of IRC contributors were put up.

The highest quality interactions I had on IRC were with a small band of Indian fans who had set up a private channel to chat during India's games. Much of our chatter was nostalgia-mongering: talk about the Indian resurgence in the 1980s, about "that ball" as Greenidge shouldered arms to Sandhu in the World Cup final or Kapil bowled Qasim Omar or "that shot" as Patil crashed a screaming straight drive past Mudassar, who nimbly skipped out of harm's way. Those memories were rapidly acquiring a golden hue, becoming immortalized and sacrosanct. We all peddled nostalgia; it was all we had to offer.

The need for that private channel hints at what was problematic about IRC; it was never more than a lightly organized anarchy. While IRC was a great medium for tracking live scores and good for simple one-liners as comments on a match, it was a horrendously bad medium for reasoned discussion or argument. Inevitably, on the cricket channel, the same patterns of behavior observed on Usenet newsgroups emerged. And again, the worst culprits were Pakistanis and Indians, with the former again, lacking in self-policing and community-enforced restraint. There was little South Asian or color solidarity between Indian and Pakistani fans. Pakistani views of India often resembled those of ignorant, Orientalist, racist whites—jokes about Indian poverty and dark, vegetarian Indians, for instance. ("If Venkatapathy Raju went to night school, the teacher would mark him absent.") I did not like North Indians or Punjabis who made those kinds of jokes about South Indians; I did not like these Pakistanis either.

The flame wars between Indians and Pakistanis grew tiresome and quickly clogged the channel. There was no way of stopping them other than via the operators, those privileged human users of the IRC channel who assumed their positions through a rough, loosely organized system. But human operators have nationalities, and very soon, battle lines were drawn. English and Australian operators were of a simple opinion: Pakistani and Indian fans were rabid fools; to allow them self-expression was to open the gates to the barbarians. The bickering between IRC residents and the heavy-handed, inconsistent application of rules by channel operators became increasingly problematic. Too soon, any edgy conversation between an Indian and a Pakistani—or worse, between any subcontinental fan and operators who were English, Australian, New Zealander, or South African—ended with the operator exercising her or his authority and banishing the user from the channel.

Even more than the intra–South Asian flame wars, I despised the patronizing attitude of the operators, the regarding of all South Asian cricketing opinion as fundamentally unhinged and irrational. Too often, operators on IRC were concrete instantiations of the paternalistic, colonial attitudes their countries had embodied. If I ever came close to experiencing solidarity with Pakistanis on the Internet, it was when I would see a sanctimonious operator urge *us*—a rarely used word by me—to learn some manners before we got back on IRC. The cricket channel suffered from the "*The New York Times* Kashmir reporting syndrome": subcontinentals were locked in a cycle of incomprehensible tribal conflict.

But what finally turned me off cricket on IRC for a long time were the pronouncements of Pakistani fans during the third game of a one-day international series between India and Pakistan in 1997. I woke early at a godforsaken time, logged in, and "watched" as India made a mediocre score that was easily chased down thanks to a pair of thunderous innings from Ijaz Ahmed and Shahid Afridi. As Pakistan's six-laden chase began, so did the comments from Pakistani fans: talk of thrashings, humiliations, beatings, and wars won on figurative battlefields. There was little moderation; there were no operators present, and no Pakistani called for restraint among fellow fans. I retreated from the channel and took to watching the scores flash by and chatting with another Indian fan, one with Pakistani friends at his university with whom he often played cricket. Finally, appalled at the language visible on the channel, he said, "Only net Pakistanis are like this." I did not reply in the affirmative; I had become convinced it was not "only net Pakistanis" that were "like this."

In those years of online cricket fandom—starting from the first posted scores on rec.sport.misc in 1988–1989, continuing on to rec.sport.cricket till 1994–1995, and to IRC starting in 1993 and my sporadic presence there till 1998—I made a few friends and learned a bit about cricketing cultures worldwide. Pakistan's fans did a bad job representing theirs. But all subcontinental fans came across badly on rec.sport.cricket. Australian fans said they found Sri Lankan fans intolerable with their endless complaints about racist Australian umpires and their defenses of Muttiah Muralitharan's bowling action. English fans complained often, and profusely, of the postcolonial fan's excessive sensitivity to perceived insult and constant prickliness about suspected condescension. I suspect I did not contribute much to rec.sport.cricket either, that I often got caught up in flame wars by falling for transparent flame bait.

For Pakistani fans, IRC was the forum for an aggressive expression of their nationalism, a virtual battleground far away from physical home. Much of it was directed at a team and a country I had only recently started to consider mine—ironically, after I had left it. I had acquired an indulgence in romanticization, even as I grew more distant from India in time and space and in my growth in my personal life. (My relationship with K, a divorced Catholic woman eight years older than me, had provided the first inkling that a personal relationship could drive a wedge between my family and me; marrying her might have engendered a profound crisis.)

These encounters on IRC drove me further from any imagined place of safety with Pakistan and its people. The spaces on the Internet played host to a proxy war. Battlegrounds are no places to make friends, so I left. Battlegrounds leave scars; I took mine with me.

Hudson Crossings

IN THE SPRING OF 1993, I traveled to India to attend to my mother, who was now terminally ill with metastasized breast cancer—an unwelcome reincarnation of an earlier occurrence in 1988. She was painfully weak and could do little except rest all day. Her chemotherapy and radiation treatments were soon brought to a halt; they were pointless in the face of the advancing death within her. Among the few pleasant memories of her last days—otherwise marked by hospital visits and her agonizing pain and discomfort—were those of watching Pakistan play the West Indies. Amazingly enough, satellite television had brought home international cricket. It was now possible to watch live cricket of matches that did not involve India—the distance between India and the rest of the world had shrunk. Just my bloody luck, I thought, all this happened after I left India. My mother told me I could and should watch all the cricket I wanted while I stayed at home with her. I often did, lying next to her on her bed where she rested, our heads propped up on pillows, watching Akram and Younis bowling to Desmond Haynes and Richie Richardson.

On 25 April 1993, after a five-year struggle with her illness, my mother passed away at the Pune Military Hospital. With her passing, I was cut loose from home, family, and country; I could find no anchors with which to tether myself. I had left home physically six years ago; my mother's death cut me frighteningly loose in an even more fundamental sense. A link with my past, with its most visible and powerful symbol, was gone. I spent two more months in India, moping and mourning, watching two-hour highlights of Alan Border's Australians thrashing England in the Ashes, playing with my year-old nephew, drinking whisky with my brother, eating my sister-in-law's home-cooked food, and watching MiG-29 and Jaguar fighter jets take off from the nearby air force base. I was delaying my return to life in the United States; I knew a deeper and more acute loneliness and despondence awaited.

I returned to the United States and moved to New York City—swapping a New Jersey address for a New York City one felt as big a change as moving to the United States from India—and began graduate school in philosophy at the City University Graduate Center. I had often crossed the

Hudson from New Jersey to New York, seeking samplers of New York City's many offerings: food of all stripes, art house movies, live music, raucous bars, bustling street scenes, and crowded sidewalks at two in the morning. Sometimes I took New Jersey Transit trains to the stuffy, ugly Penn Station and then headed for the subways; sometimes, I took PATH trains to their steaming, malodorous Manhattan stations. In the early 1990s, the subways still featured ample displays of graffiti; these served as a garish welcome to the new urban landscape I entered after my subterranean travels. These were journeys that never quite lost their mysterious magic: a displacement from my weekday trials to endless diversion. My returns to New Jersey—after the night's engagements were done—required expert knowledge of the times of the last train. A delay entailed a sleepless, weary return at dawn. New York remained the destination of choice after I began work at Bell Labs. I had begun my graduate student career there while commuting for night classes as a nonmatriculate student at the Forty-Second Street site of the old CUNY Graduate Center. I continued to dream about life in the city—that looming, towering, cosmopolitan haven that beckoned me, away from the gray, postindustrial towns on the New Jersey side of the Hudson. Finally I moved across the Hudson, up the West Side to Ninety-Fifth Street and West End Avenue. I sold my pickup truck, shook myself free of my ridiculously overpriced auto insurance policy, and began buying subway tokens. I was now a New Yorker.

The nine-to-five life was not for me. I had returned to the academic fold, deciding to leave my computer science education behind and strike out anew in philosophy. K's example—of studying literary theory on her long leave from work—had inspired me sufficiently to have taken two philosophy classes as a sampler. (I wrote amateurish but adequate papers for my classes, writing them well enough to secure a recommendation for admission.) Our relationship though, had ended the day Bill Clinton was elected president; a twenty-five-year-old romantically immature man was a poor fit for a thirty-three-year-old vastly more experienced woman. K, much to my eternal gratitude, had brought me to a distinctive station in my emotional and intellectual travels; from here, I moved on without her.

I found a room for rent on the Upper West Side with a gay Italian Egyptian American studying algebraic group theory, a diligent, sober-minded Indian Muslim studying chemical engineering, and a Jewish American woman studying Adorno. We formed an odd quartet, eccentric at the margins, each dealing with a distinctive angst about graduate school and our self-worth. I attended philosophy lectures and wrote papers on epistemology, philosophy of language, and logic. But graduate student life was disappointing. I felt bitterly alienated in my aggressively male, Anglo-Americananalytical-philosophy-oriented department. I had expected bohemia, imagining graduate school to consist of endless opportunities for intellectual dilettantism and café conversations. None were to be found. Most graduate students were rushing from teaching jobs to class, to back home; there was a great deal of tedious making ends meet. My roommates were busy with their academic work, their running from laboratory to library to part-time job. Few graduate students had the luxury of that most prized of possessions, a fellowship. Graduate school in New York City was marked by a lack of intellectual and personal community. Yet again, with unerring perversity, I had found an uncaring space in America.

My apartment, my ostensible home, was often deserted. I found little to hold me there, and I consciously resisted going home to work, sometimes looking for drinking dates, for alcohol guzzling sessions that could last till dawn, sometimes dawdling on the streets. I found my reading assignments—often of unfamiliar, turgid writing—impenetrable; I found concentration on philosophical theory and argumentation elusive. I had not adequately mourned for my mother and caught up with those emotions as the months went on. The city felt lonely and cold, sometimes literally so as I walked along its windswept canyons. I was plunged into deep melancholy at the realization that several years of this life lay ahead of me.

Two of my classes that first semester were attended by a student whose accent reminded me of the voices I had heard on Channel Nine telecasts. It was distinctive and singular; it was not American. One day after class, I asked him for a light for my cigarette. As we puffed away, I asked if he was Australian. Silly question; with an accent like that, there was only one country he could be from. On being confirmed in my conjecture, I persisted in my curiosity. What part? This brought forth a puzzled look. Are you familiar with Australia? Yes; I know where all the cricket grounds are. On hearing my companion was from Melbourne, the conversation rapidly turned to the MCG, venue for India's famous triumphs in both Test and one-day cricket. D had been present at the "underarm game," when Trevor Chappell, under the captaincy of his brother Greg, had bowled a pitch-hugging delivery to deny New Zealand six runs off the last ball in a one-day international. D had been working in Bay 13, serving food and drink; there, from the stands, he had sledged Greg Chappell after he had been spectacularly caught by Martin Snedden but was bizarrely not given out: "Walk, ya cunt, walk!" This felt like a brush with fame, with someone—refreshingly enough—unafraid to call an Australian spade one. We were off to a rollicking start. A few days later, we had our first beers together and talked more about the movies and cricket, two common passions. I showed D how to buy pot on Thirty-Ninth Street; he was impressed by my swagger as I conducted street deals with

Rastafarian dealers, as I hid my fear of arrest with loud bluster about how I deserved more contraband for my twenty-five dollars.

More importantly, D was impressed by my knowledge of cricket history, statistics, and technique and by my acknowledgement of Shane Warne—a Victorian no less—as a big turner of the ball. Apparently, Indians cared little for spinners from elsewhere. But I had seen Warne bowl in 1993 in England, and I had seen those big ripping leg breaks that spun many feet from leg to off. I told D we had a star on our hands. He told me he had enjoyed watching Indian cricketers play in Australia; he had watched Srikkanth lash a ton at the Sydney Cricket Ground during the 1985–1986 tour. This was the kind of cricketing friendship I desired, one imbued with reciprocity. I should have been the ideal friend for any cricketing opponent; I always remembered their best and brightest feats against the Indians. In D, here in America, I had found my first true-blue cricketing companion and friend away from home.

D was lonely; his lovely girlfriend was back in Melbourne. My home and my family were nowhere close. We both loved cricket. We were destined to be friends. D made my fantasies of a bohemian life in graduate school come true; we would stay up all night smoking pot, talking about cricket, movies, politics, and philosophy. Besides the Indian cricket team, D was curious about Indian philosophy. I claimed ignorance—being Indian had not made me an expert in Indian philosophy, Western philosophy was my first and only language for philosophical expression—but tried my best to explain the little I knew. Far more important for me was the friendly interest evinced in a matter Indian.

With D, I would talk about every Test involving Australia I had paid attention to; I gave full expression to my admiration for every Australian Test cricketer I had read about. That I knew something about Ian Redpath—a Victorian with a short Test career—was the clincher for D, the final confirmation I was a genuine cricket fan. Of the cricket fans I had met, whether online or off-, Australian fans were the most knowledgeable of cricket history, and D was a distinguished member of their cohort. I introduced D to cricket on the Internet, to the commentaries on the IRC, to the live score relays and to Cricinfo when it made its debut. When Mark Taylor's Australians toured the West Indies in 1995, I found radio commentary on WBAI in New York and sent its details on to D. I had done my duty; finding commentary for a fellow cricket fan felt like a noble deed. When I finally wrote the acknowledgments to my doctoral dissertation, I thanked D for talking to me about cricket over the years we were graduate students together. Our "mateship" was, quite simply, the most important personal relationship of mine through those years, and our love for cricket underwrote it at every step.

My friendship with D was crucial, for in cricketing terms, New York City like the rest of the United States, displayed the same sheer, benighted ignorance and aversion to the game; deliberate hostility was indistinguishable from indifference. The American understanding of cricket had not changed in the time I had lived in the United States: a quaint, slow, boring, incomprehensible game, five days long, played by posh Englishmen and slavish colonials. It made my past life a mystery to me, my interest in cricket a freak show exhibit. Despite the size of immigrant communities in New York City, there were no cricket magazines at newsstands, even at newsstands that carried hundreds of publications from around the world on topics most Americans found just as obscure. The magazine store at the corner of Sixth Avenue and Eleventh Street in Manhattan that carried journals so esoteric that their total readership in New York would not exceed a dozen diligent readers did not carry cricket magazines whose potential readership in New York City could run into the thousands. To buy a cricket magazine, you had to go to an Indian or Pakistani store. You had to go to the ghetto to get that fix.

When I talked about cricket in the United States, a cricketing version of Groucho's immortal line was sometimes visible in American responses: How good *could* this game be if India played it and even won its world championship? I was grateful again, that England and Australia—two "white" nations with respectable standing in the United States—played the game. I cringed when I thought of the American reaction to my imaginary announcement that I was a fan of a game played only by India, Pakistan, Bangladesh, and Sri Lanka. My assignment to the utterly insignificant would have been quick. But then, I would not have been a fan of the game if those countries had been the only ones playing it. The validation of cricket by England, Australia, and the West Indies had been just as essential for me.

Talking about cricket inevitably induced eye-rolling in Americans, a steadfastly alienating experience. It did not matter whether my audience was liberal, conservative, white, black, or Hispanic. Sometimes the ones rolling their eyes were second-generation Indians. Cricket was a reminder of their parents and their accents and of all they had tried to leave behind as they attempted to assimilate. Dissing cricket was a good way to remind your American friends you were not as Indian as they might think; their disdain of cricket could serve as a good indicator of how acculturated they were to the United States.

Thanks to D's presence, I was able to create a new conversational space. Now in company, I could bring conversation around to cricket. Cricket was easily dismissed when invoked by a mere brown man, but not so easily when done by a white one.

The Sublime and the Sordid

IN THE SPRING OF 1996, I was living on Manhattan's Upper East Side in Turtle Bay, safely ensconced on the thirtieth floor of an apartment building catering to corporate tenants. I had not acquired sudden riches. My Indian American girlfriend worked for NBC; we shared her paid-for corporate studio, luxurious digs for a grubby graduate student like me. Another experiment in relationships had begun. Perhaps I could overcome my prickliness about this distinctive breed of Indian, one whose relationship with our supposed homeland was as complicated as mine.

The 1996 World Cup featured the sublime and the sordid—in India's quarterfinal and semifinal. I paid little attention to the political and financial subtext of the Cup's staging in the subcontinent, to the solidarity shown by India and Pakistan in playing a friendly game in a Sri Lanka racked by political violence—in response to the fears of inadequate security expressed by non–South Asian teams, apparently stark evidence of a "color line" in cricket.* My following of cricket still concentrated exclusively on the action visible on the pitch, on bat and ball; I was sensitive to cricket's older colonial contexts but failed to see them manifest in these newer administrative developments and their surrounding discourse. Most crucially, I made little of the fact that the World Cup's return to Asia had required financial backing by a board of control—the Indian one, the Board of Cricket Control in India—that was rapidly becoming cricket's most powerful entity.

I watched a telecast of India playing Sri Lanka in the preliminary rounds at an Indian movie house on Lexington Avenue. I paid my ten dollars and, walking through the theater's doors, found a zone beloved of immigrants: the re-creation of familiar spaces left behind and only imperfectly remembered. Masala chai and samosas were sold in a lobby festooned with Bollywood posters while *paan*-chewing Indian fans smoked cigarettes and walked around chatting loudly with friends in a potpourri of Indian languages. On the screen inside the theater, Indian commentators described a game being played in New Delhi even as the panning cameras showed the ramshackle arrangements at Ferozeshah Kotla, the

---

* Mike Marqusee, *War Minus the Shooting: Journey through South Asia during Cricket's World Cup* (London: William Heinemann, 1996).

Delhi skyline—lit up by the hazy winter sunshine—serving as backdrop to the sweater and scarf– and shawl-clad crowds. I watched the Indian innings and then, made somnolent by the overwarmed theater interior and a belly full of alcohol and food, I gathered up my sleeping girlfriend— she who had so patiently accompanied me—and went home. I awoke the next day to find India had lost to a furious assault by the Sri Lankan openers, Sanath Jayasuriya and Romesh Kaluwitharna. It was the last time I underestimated Sri Lankan abilities. Seventeen years after the 1979 Cup, Sri Lankans were still performing their David and Goliath routine.

Through pay-per-view deals on cable, the 1996 World Cup was available on television. Cricket had finally come to the United States. I desperately hoped I could introduce American friends to cricket, perhaps via Indian glory and my basking in it. But India's semifinal placing was flattery—and my friends stayed steadfast in their neglect. Cup games began in the morning and ended in the evening: precisely the time I was at work up in the Bronx at a job that would pay graduate school's bills. I could tape the games and watch them on my return but matters were not so straightforward. The matches ran a little over seven hours with a lunch break. Even an extended-play tape would not do. I needed two tapes. At lunch, about four hours into the game, on extended mode, the first half of the match—and some of the second—would have been captured on the first tape. If the tape was changed, I could record the entire match.

My girlfriend worked at Rockefeller Center on Fiftieth Street and Sixth Avenue; our apartment was on Fifty-Second Street and First Avenue. Miraculously she, utterly uninterested in and ignorant of cricket, became my tape-changing angel. She would return to our apartment at lunch, change the tape, and then walk back to work. I would return home at six, pop the first tape in, and commence watching. Because I had no Internet access at work, and because I was in the United States, there was little danger of my learning scores during the day.

After my working day ended in the Bronx, beside myself with impatience, I would run to the Fordham Road station, catch the D train, and ride down to Rockefeller Center before briskly walking back home along Fiftieth Street. R would return late at night; her corporate work hours were brutal. Normally I resented their intrusion on our domestic life, but now they let me watch cricket in pleasant solitude. After eating, she slept; I continued to watch with the volume turned down, resigning myself to a late night and an under-slept state the next morning.

India met Pakistan in the quarterfinal, the de facto final for Indian and Pakistani fans. The game was to begin at four in the morning. I would meet some graduate school friends for drinks at a Hell's Kitchen dive before being picked up by an Indian friend to be driven across the Hudson to his apartment to watch the game. Back in our apartment, a cordial evening had degenerated into arguments and recrimination. I sought relief in glass after glass of wine. As the evening and my holding pattern wore on, I drank more. Finally I decided it was time, said goodbye to R, and stepped out into the cool spring night. Earlier, as I planned my trip to New Jersey, I had asked R to accompany me to watch the game. I had thought of our watching the match together as an opportunity for her to experience an essential historical component of myself, a participation in an old cultural ritual of great personal significance, one that might conceivably strengthen our relationship. (In my view, the need for understanding ran only one way; she was the one in need of cultural and historical edification, not me.) But now, with our verbal brawl sitting squarely between us, it was not to be. I was disappointed, but also relieved. I could focus on the cricket without catering to the persistent inquiries of a neophyte. And perhaps an old jealousy would have flared up as she paid attention to the Pakistani players; she had had a Pakistani boyfriend once.

I was worn down, tired by the wine and our squabbling. I walked to the curb, hailed a cab, and as one pulled up, opened its door and sank into the back seat. The cabdriver's name tag displayed a Muslim name that sounded Punjabi—it ended in Chaudhary. I leaned over and inquired in Punjabi, "So, are you looking forward to tonight's match?" My alcohol-infused tone was jovial; I was curious; I wanted to know what he thought of Pakistan's chances. Yes, he had heard about the match, but he was not going out of his way to follow it. Many Pakistani youngsters he knew were. He thought they carried on unnecessarily and made too big a deal out of it. I listened with interest and prodded him to say more. They act like it's a war, like they're going off to fight a battle. I pressed on; this man had given me the opening I wanted. Why did he think the youngsters talked like that? He had no answers.

I responded with a story of my own. Once at my old university, while I had been talking to my Pakistani friend, he had introduced me to a pair of young Pakistani undergraduates named Javed and Asif, a pair of monikers that had their own, private, cricketing significance for me. I had made perfunctory noises as our conversation meandered to a finish; I had only come out for a smoke. Soon, a Sikh friend strode over to join us. The young Pakistanis politely said hello, and the conversation resumed. I greeted my Sikh friend in Punjabi, a tad self-consciously. I was aware the Pakistani youngsters were Punjabis. I wanted them to realize they were talking to Indian Punjabis, a Hindu and a Sikh—folks with whom they shared a language and other cultural components, even if not a political sensibility.

Then, rather plaintively, I asked my cabdriver, "We're all Punjabis, aren't we? Punjab has Hindus, Muslims, and Sikhs. Why can't we respect this *Punjabiyat*?" I had tried to forge relationships with Pakistanis by disowning my national identity—holding on to it had not helped online—and by emphasizing ethnic identity in my personal interactions with them. I was trying to move past and over the India-Pakistan border, using the Punjabi route. Speaking in Punjabi with my Sikh friend was my invitation to those young Pakistanis to come join me on it. We could be fellow travelers there, even if not elsewhere. But perhaps for those racked by insecurity about their national identity, such a move was not possible. My invitation to be Punjabi with me was just another variant of the "if only we could put together a joint team" fantasy.

When my stop came, I jumped out and reached for my wallet. The cabbie shook his head; I could keep my money. He would tell his friends about me, about how he had met someone he liked, who made sense, who spoke to his sensibilities. Had I not blundered on in that drunken haze, I would not have spoken so volubly. I was the classic self-pitying drunk; I only sought reassurance for myself. But he had been sober, and he had spoken his mind to an Indian on the night of the 1996 India-Pakistan World Cup quarterfinal.

I walked into my Hell's Kitchen destination and met my Australian and American friends. Over drinks, I told them I was on my way to watch the World Cup quarterfinal. Much hooting ensued: "Go India!" My friends certainly knew what to say to me when they knew India was playing Pakistan in a cricket game. Then I told them a Pakistani had driven me to the bar. One of them turned to me and said, "Did you let him know who's boss?" Yeah, I said. I had let him know. My conversation with my newly acquired cabdriver friend would have sounded sappy to this crew, ignorant of the Punjabi context and eager to hear evidence of edgy trash talk between folks ostensibly at each other's throats—all for the sake of a game. It was easy to regress, easy to remember that till that point in time, few Pakistanis had volunteered friendliness to me.

In New York, I was often offered free rides from Punjabi cabdrivers from India, both Sikh and Hindu. That ethnic connection had not always worked with Pakistanis. My rambling conversations with Pakistani cabbies followed a pattern. I would speak in Punjabi and ask them where they were from. After they responded, I would tell them my father's village was Dilawar Cheema in the former West Punjab, now Pakistan, that I was from Delhi, that my mother was born in Batala, Gurdaspur District, and that my grandfather had moved from Dilawar Cheema to Maihar. The Pakistani responses to these confessions, these opening moves in a putative conversation, these icebreakers, were mixed. One Pakistani cabbie told me he had an Indian girlfriend in Queens; she was stupid and complained too much; his Pakistani girlfriends would not have behaved thus. Some Pakistani cabbies offered expressions of envy and regret; India was becoming rich and more technologically advanced, its computer industry was taking off and leaving Pakistan behind. One Pakistani cabbie told me he did not care for a religion that worshipped cows. Then too, I was drunk and woolly-headed, but his comment cut through the haze. I handed over the fare, mumbling inanities as I left.

So I chimed in with the crowd, with my American and Australian friends. They wanted me to play the part of the edgy, tribal subcontinental, giving vent to festering, irrational, exotic frustrations and hatreds. They would have done the same with Croatians and Serbians, or Celtics and Rangers fans, or any of those other tribal divisions, so distant in space and time and sensibility. Americans found these sporting tribal conflicts fascinating; the Yankees and Red Sox rivalries were not bloody enough. They wanted to watch the car wreck of this conflict, and I provided it. A little something for the boys, I thought. They'll go home, they'll go to work the next day, they'll tell their friends, girlfriends, and wives that they had met their X'ian friend, rushing off to see his X'ian team play in the blah-blah competition against the Y-ian team. And don't you know it, X and Y have fought these wars and they hate each other's guts, so just imagine what these games must be like. And this guy, check it out, he was going to stay up all night to watch the game, and is that crazy or what? This must have been exciting and thrilling in some exotic way, like watching stories of distant conflict on the nightly news, in which one tribesman slaughters another in the name of undying, unresolvable hatreds. I gave it to them. It was harmless—a little provision of entertainment from an expected source—wasn't it?

The quarterfinal's atmosphere was charged, its fuse waiting to be lit by a cricketing spark. On television the Pakistani captain Aamir Sohail said the Indian crowd's partisan cheering would egg the Pakistanis on instead. Imran Khan, clad in flowing *salwar kameez*, reminded television viewers Pakistan had won here in 1986. The years had rolled by. Instead of pace bowling and captaincy, I saw the Koran-quoting politician, pontificating on international affairs and on many other matters well above his pay grade. Now more than ever, the dark Pakistani green looked sullen and grim; the Pakistani team colors evocative of fatigues, military grounds, uniforms, and regiments. They remained, somehow, representatives of a military regime.

Although Tendulkar did not make a big score, the rest of the Indian batting lineup made amends. India, long unable to fight off Pakistan's dominance in the one-day format, finally asserted itself at the right time, in the right place. Ajay Jadeja's pyrotechnic display at the end was the most astonishing assault I had seen on a Pakistani fast bowler by an Indian batsman. It took a Delhi boy to do it. The bowler who bore the brunt of Jadeja's attack was Waqar Younis, the whirlwind head of the Pakistani pace attack. Through the late nineties, no other fast bowler gave me as much pleasure. No other bowler captured quite as well the power, aggression, and strength of fast bowling. His bowling run-up—a near sprint—and action displayed an acute marshaling of the pace bowler's physical resources in a manner unmatched by his contemporaries.

Ironically then, this match, in which Waqar received his worst hammering ever—at the hands of Ajay Jadeja—is still one of my favorite matches to watch him in action. In that hothouse, cracklingly electric atmosphere, Waqar hurtled in at full speed, giving no quarter, holding nothing back. It was thrilling to watch; I was in awe at this display of the most elemental of cricketing powers. I feared he would break through the Indian batting lineup, that India's World Cup dreams would come to an end at the hands of a Pakistani in front of an Indian crowd.

In Pakistan's reply, Sohail and Saeed Anwar got off to a rollicking start that sent Indians panicking. Even after Anwar was dismissed, Pakistan was clipping along, well on their way to the Indian target. Soon, Sohail came down the wicket to smash Venkatesh Prasad over cover and then cockily pointed his bat at the bowler, telling him where the ball had gone and how he should go fetch it. Away in the commentary box, Imran Khan could barely contain his glee; Sohail the Pakistani street fighter could do nothing wrong. On the next ball, as Sohail went for another swing, the ball crashed into the stumps. Prasad came charging down the wicket, dispensing a vigorous send-off with a hand wave and an easily lip-read "Fuck off" instruction. Sohail complied. Sohail's hubris had bit back hard. Pakistan had it all; they were heading for a win; Sohail had had other thoughts. On air, Imran was on the back foot; the speed at which he ate his words could barely have been matched by his quickest deliveries. I sensed India would win. Nothing could stop them now.

There was more to it than that. Jadeja—the Delhi boy—had smashed Younis out of the ground; that had been sweet. This was sweeter. Sohail—the tough Punjabi from Lahore—had charged down the wicket to show the dark, skinny, rice-eating South Indian, Prasad, who was boss and had received a rather efficient comeuppance. I was worn down by all I had heard about meat-eating fast bowlers, how tall Pakistanis would always trump dark Indians and vegetarian *baniyas*. And now, here in a World Cup quarterfinal, a skinny South Indian was running down the pitch, telling Sohail, the Punjabi Lahori kebob-eating street fighter, to measure with all due precision, the number of steps back to the pavilion. The Pakistani dressing room knew their captain had thrown his wicket away in front of an Indian crowd and handed the initiative back to the Indian team. The Indians in the field—and those in the stands—knew Pakistani swagger was hollow, worn out from within. The wind had to go out of the Pakistani sails. It did; India slowly choked Pakistan off. I cheered as Javed Miandad was run out in his last international innings. Seventeen years ago, Asif Iqbal's run-out at Calcutta in the last Test of the 1979–1980 series had reduced me to tears. Now, I shed none as another childhood hero faded.

Grief awaited elsewhere, in the India-Sri Lanka semifinal. It began in stunning fashion: both Jayasuriya and Kaluwitharna were gone in the first over. But Aravinda de Silva's brilliance—and the rest of the Sri Lankan lineup—left India needing five runs per over. India began in uninspired fashion, and it never got better. As the game drew to its disastrous close after Tendulkar's stumping and Mohammed Azharuddin's duck, as Calcutta fans rioted at India's lame collapse, I sat in my Upper East Side home, angry and humiliated, close to tears. I was angered at the way the game had ended; I was angered the Indian team had collapsed so totally and utterly; angered by the failure of Tendulkar to make that crucial match-winning innings, the one Indian fans would urge him to make throughout his entire career. A second World Cup final, staged in Lahore, had awaited; now that chance was gone.

I knew that under my veneer of cricketing loss there lurked an emotion that recurs all too often in a diasporic Indian worried about what home looks like from a distance. Unruly hooligans rioting does not look good on live television. That excitable response was more ammunition for the sub-continental-crowds-are-one-step-away-from-a-riot understanding of Indian cricket. Expatriate Englishmen worried similarly when soccer hooligans ran amuck in Europe, but the anxiety is worse when the predominant preconception about a broader culture is precisely the one reinforced. English hooligans were a counterpoint to tales of English reserve and gentility, an aberration of sorts; Indian riots were merely confirmation of the natives' mental and emotional instability. One step forward with the new financial power of Indian cricket, the hosting of the World Cup in the Indian subcontinent for the second time, with the advance to the semifinal. Several steps backward with the collapse and this sore losers' riot.

The Desi Watercoolers

Manhattan's Little India and Pakistan, a few blocks on and around Lexington Avenue, between Twenty-Fifth and Thirtieth Streets, features a by-now-familiar-to-Americans mix of Bangladeshi, Indian, and Pakistani restaurants and stores selling assorted foodstuffs, spices, and gifts. On my visits there, mostly as an intrepid guide for others' dining adventures, I was often obliged to decode the semiotic indicators of the nationality of the restaurant owners. The Bangladeshis sold "Indian-Pakistani-Bangladeshi food" and spelled *saag paneer* as *shaag ponir*. Pakistanis utilized green decorative motifs in their awnings, and "Pakistani-Indian food" was the order of the hard sell. The South Indian restaurants were vegetarian and kosher, certified as such by rabbis with impressive titles and affiliations.

Like any good desi neighborhood, this one had *paan* shops, selling betel leaves stuffed with those mysterious ingredients that seem to lack counterparts outside India. These establishments assuaged a privation unique to the Indian and Pakistani exile: the lack of the after-dinner walk to the *paan* shop to purchase and chew this unique supposed digestive. After trying out several *paan* shops, I settled on a Pakistani one for my indulgences. (To most middle-class Indians, this taste betrayed me as a hopeless hick beneath my urban veneer. *Paan* chewing was an activity best left to villagers and crude small-towners, quasi-bovine ruminators who spat betel juice over their immediate surroundings and turned them a ghastly orange-red.) Pictures of mosques were prominently displayed on the shop's walls, and prayer calls often played on the store's battered cassette player. In a nod to New York's melting pot, the space was shared with an Orthodox Jewish locksmith. I conversed with the *paanwallah* in a mixture of Urdu and Punjabi; he replied in Urdu and the occasional Punjabi sentence. He was unfailingly courteous and assumed I was Pakistani. I did nothing to dispel this impression. We would sometimes talk about cricket; nothing I said gave away my Indian allegiance. I resolutely stayed in this closet, fearing the characteristics of my online interactions would follow me into physical space.

I also found a Pakistani store renting cricket videos. These were mostly of one-day internationals with a few dedicated to Test cricket. The store's owner soon began curating a wider selection dedicated to World Cup and Test series highlights. I forked over $100 for my unlimited rentals membership and began dipping into this hoard, steadfastly ignoring the owner's frequent suggestions I rent the Sharjah game in which Javed Miandad had hit a six off the last ball, Pakistan's most famous one-day victory over India, supposedly the harbinger of an endless funk in both the Indian cricket team and its fans.

D and I were companions in enjoying these bulletins from a world apart. We watched England's fall for 46 at Port of Spain in 1994 and Brian

Lara's magnificent, star-heralding 277 against Australia at Sydney in 1997. Most enjoyably, I rented videos of Pakistan's tour of England in 1996. I enjoyed watching England get beaten; I enjoyed watching Waqar and Wasim bowl. These two inclinations were satisfied by that series. I watched Younis dismiss Graeme Hick twice, and both times my enjoyment at seeing Hicks's stumps rattled was a pure unilateral expression of pleasure. Besides these inevitable depictions of Pakistani fast bowling excellence, two sequences of batting action in the Lord's Test stood out. In one, Saeed Anwar leaned forward and wristily square-drove—pure genius. In the other, Inzimam sat on his haunches and drove through cover; the lazy power, the casual assertion of authority, was incredible. I still enjoyed watching Pakistan play cricket, and in my cricketing hierarchies of preference, I still cheered for Pakistan against England. Postcolonial resentment trumped personal and political slights.

Another viewing experience showed the extent of my rift with Pakistan and the internalization of what can only, charitably, be termed paranoia. I rented a video of India versus Pakistan in the 1992 World Cup and noticed that large portions of the tape—including the section with Tendulkar's batting—were missing. I immediately suspected deliberate butchery. It did not strike me as coincidence that a video rented from Pakistani store, whose only possible customers would be Indians—no Pakistani would be interested in seeing *on tape* a game Pakistan had *lost* to India—would include all Indian wickets to fall, very little Indian batting, and only a few Pakistani wickets.

Little of the game itself was notable. That great pair of all-rounders, Imran and Kapil, looked faded and spent. But the cricketing conflict was palpable and thrilling, best captured in Manoj Prabhakar, India's aggressive allrounder from Delhi, dismissing Saleem Malik. As Kiran More took the catch, a charged-up Prabhakar ran down the pitch straight at More, past Malik. Prabhakar could be seen vigorously mouthing that most common of North Indian expletives, *bahenchod*. I loved it now. I loved Prabhakar's pumped-up excitement. Finally, someone who could mouth off the Pakistanis, someone not afraid of a rumble.

Surrogate warriors indeed. We waged battle on their behalf on the Net; they on ours on the field.

Back and Forth to India

IN 1996, en route to India for a trip on which, besides meeting family, I hoped to watch India play Test cricket live on television for the first time in nine years, I stopped over in London and visited Lord's. A pilgrimage to that historic venue seemed an obligatory rite of passage for an ostensible cricket tragic. A gaggle of young Australian tourists accompanied R and me on our paid tour. We took the usual photographs on the players' balcony, in the stands, on the pitch, struck poses with cricket bats in the adjoining gift shop, and gingerly stood on the hallowed turf. I struggled to explain to R why we were enacting these secular rituals in this supposed temple of cricket. I wondered what this Indian American woman—who knew little about cricket and had never seen it played in a ground—made of my interest in an empty, bitterly cold, windswept, not-particularly-remarkable sports stadium.

With the Australian lads clustered behind us, we perused the honor board of centurions at Lord's. As they stepped closer to photograph the entries that showed three Australian centuries in the same innings of the 1993 Ashes, I remarked loudly, ostensibly for R's benefit, "See Dilip Vengsarkar up there? He's the only batsman to have scored three hundreds at Lord's." Gratifyingly, a couple of the Australian youngsters followed my pointing finger. There it was: Vengsarkar in 1979, 1982, and 1986. The last one, part of my conversion to the Indian team, had won India the Test. I had learned cricket history from Australians all my life; perhaps I could send a few lessons their way too.

Lord's was just another cricket ground. English magic did not work on me anymore. I sensed an archaic monument to an old ordering of cricketing goods, one used to maintain old hierarchies of appreciation and to sustain a particular reading of cricketing history. It was no longer a temple, and I was only going through the motions of paying homage; an old inner impulse had turned my steps toward St. John's Wood, much like a lapsed Catholic could still cross himself at a reluctantly attended mass. But to R, I spoke instead of Lord's place in cricketing history, its status as the home of cricket, and its place in an older imagination of mine. I could not bear to tell her I had come here too late, long after my illusions were dispelled, long after carefully constructed fantasies had crumbled. I could not bear to acknowledge that my past, which I had often sought to familiarize her with, was rapidly fading and becoming ever more irrelevant. I could not admit I could not go home again.

I flew on back to India. There, I soon immersed myself in the daily rhythms of life in an Indian household during cricket season: the waking up in the mornings for live telecasts; the breaks for lunch, which allowed errands to be run; and tea, which provided enough time for a quick walk to the corner shop for a cigarette. The buzz on the streets from radio commentary was markedly quieter; television and its endless commercials now ruled the roost. During the first Test at Ahmedabad, I noted the birth of a new star: V.V.S. Laxman who, on his Test debut, scored a gallant fifty on a bad pitch against a good bowling attack and ensured India would have enough runs on the board to defend in the fourth innings. I reexperienced the pleasure of keenly fought Test cricket as it was that day when India strove desperately to put some runs on the board.

South Africa ran out easy winners in the second Test. In the second innings, as South Africa piled on the runs, I was appalled to see Anil Kumble persistently bowl down the leg side, a reminder of the times when India could only contain and never attack. Things got worse when India batted. Rahul Dravid pushed and prodded, making no attempt to get the South African bowling on the back foot; Tendulkar scratched around endlessly before pushing an innocuous off-break from Pat Symcox straight to forward short leg. By close of play on the fourth day, India was shattered.

The Indian team had not lost its ability to provoke, to push buttons I did not know existed in my apparatus of sporting appreciation. Once, they were worthy of defeat; now, I desired their victory and found their defeats mortifying. In their confrontations with adversity, I craved a form of visible resistance that would, on my behalf, an impulse—part historical grievance, part redressal of personal insult and injury—that ran through me. Their failure to instantiate on a sporting field a resistance that I now felt was my current and favored mode of interaction with the culture that underwrote the historical cricketing world, was especially galling. The South Africans did not have a long-standing rivalry with the Indians; I bore them no animosity. But they were still India's opponents, ones who could, when they and I wanted, be instantiations of an older established order I wanted displaced.

I taped video highlights of India's series-clinching triumph in the third Test—and went through the expensive process of converting them into the appropriate format for viewing in the United States. Not only could I watch the games back in New York but just as importantly, share them with D. They would be the perfect accompaniments for a quiet smoke and a beer and a mope, feeling homesick in New York City, dreaming of grounds far away. I brought back the sights and sounds of India in the winters, the movie advertisements, the opening music of the highlights show, and the bouncy, irrepressible commercials between game segments. The cricket was center stage, but I peeked around the edges, seeing in the sidelines those sights denied me in the United States. I was guilty of not wanting India enough to want to live there but still needing it to make me whole, to secure me in ways not available in my chosen home.

Ironically, technology, precisely by bringing me into closer contact with loved ones and old haunts, by ostensibly assuaging loneliness and longing, had made things worse. It reminded me ever more acutely of what I was missing. That deprivation seemed at odds with the footloose sensibility supposed to be the hallmark of the connected, wired, constantly traveling world. But the homesickness that afflicted the immigrant never went away; it had become more persistent. Technology—whether through the call back home or the ethnic cable television channel—did not cure this homesickness. It only served to remind me that nothing could replace the felt sensation of place, the encounter with sounds, light, and smells bearing the imprint of childhood experiences long ago internalized, that are a feature of physical contacts with home, that tap into sensations long ago integrated into mind and body. The phone call and the web camera will not assuage these longings. Nothing will replace the walk out of the customs hall, past the immigration desk, out into the arrival hall, and the drive back home.

The year 1996 was when the "Toronto scene" began; it would remind me of another offshore battle.

Offshore Proxy Wars:
Toronto and Sharjah

I FIRST SAW CRICKET IN SHARJAH shortly after the 1985 Benson and Hedges World Championship. The contrast between the two venues, Melbourne and Sharjah, was great and unpleasant. The physical environment was discordant: the harsh glare of the desert sun beat down on a slow, low pitch that perennially wore a glassy sheen. The cricket was an indulgent *tamasha*, a public theatrical performance, staged by a rich sheikh to satisfy not only his own cravings for the game but more importantly, those of South Asian expatriates in the Gulf. Indian and Pakistani cricketers played for their pleasure, supplying the missing ingredient in this otherwise blessed life away from my birthplace. Sharjah was about the local landed hobnobbing with cricket board officials, Bollywood stars and starlets, underworld match-fixers, and even the occasional gangster. It was about rich and fatuous impeccably coiffured Bollywooders coming to be seen, watching cricket through oversize, expensive sunglasses; it was about the Azharuddin–Sangeeta Bijlani marriage, the quintessential Sharjah rendezvous between Indian cricketer and Bollywood starlet. Match-fixing, rumors of which often swirled around the cricket in Sharjah, was an entirely unsurprising and appropriate accompaniment to these liaisons.

At Sharjah, India and Pakistan waged proxy wars offshore for immigrant communities. The entertainment their nations' leaders were unwilling and unable to provide by crying havoc and letting slip the dogs of war could be found here. The pitch could become the battlefield; there were medals to be won, calls to combat, rousing slogans to be raised, and battle honors and standards to be proudly flown over the vanquished. Pakistan fans cheered their team as they beat India so that they could mock their Indian neighbors; they offered sweets to their Indian "friends" after their team—a visible symbol of Pakistani sporting superiority and thus, presumably, of the validity of the two-nation theory—spoke up for them. After the Indian team was jeered mercilessly by an Indian crowd angered by the loss of diasporic bragging rights—after they had lost yet another game in Sharjah to Pakistan—Tendulkar said he never wanted to play in Sharjah again. When the BCCI eventually declined participation at Sharjah following yet another match-fixing scandal, I felt no regret. The farce was coming to an end. Cricket had felt cheapened at Sharjah, too easily taken over by the sense of a mercenary engagement.

In 1996, India and Pakistan began playing one-day internationals in Toronto. Supposedly, playing cricket in Toronto would popularize the game, bringing cricket to North America and bringing the Indian and Pakistani communities together. But Pakistani and Indian fans went to see the other team beaten; they were not interested in building bridges. Instead, the scores on the field would contribute to tallies off it. Cricket in Toronto provided an opportunity for the Indian diaspora to hope to see India's pride vindicated abroad, to see the hopelessly underperforming Indian stars stand up against the Pakistanis, and to provide them enough gunpowder for a rhetorical salvo or two in their off-the-pitch rumbles. The atmosphere in the Toronto stands confirmed bridge building was the furthest thought on anyone's mind: Pakistanis taunted Indians, hoisting giant Pakistani flags, raising martial slogans, and gloating over Pakistani success. When India beat Pakistan 4–1 in the Toronto series in 1997, groups of fans appeared holding Indian and Pakistani flags, proclaiming Indo-Pakistan friendship. Such flags were not quite as visible when Pakistan won 3–2 in 1996 and 4–1 in 1998. Pakistani fans were pleasantly accommodating when on the losing side but hardly so when they were winning.

In 1996, for the fifth and deciding match of the Sahara series, I traveled to Jackson Heights, Queens, to watch its telecast at the Eagle Cinema, then becoming known for—in addition to its regularly scheduled Bollywood programming—live telecasts of cricket. Besides the cricket, there was pleasure to be found in other things in this little South Asian enclave: *pakoras* with chai, reminiscent of tea breaks at Delhi University; a cigarette while chewing *paan*, the now fragrant and flavored smoke effortlessly evoking memories of breaks with college mates while watching university cricket; a spicy eye- and mouthwatering chicken biryani at a Pakistani restaurant which also made the best *ras malaai* in New York City. As I ate, I eavesdropped on an animated discussion between two Pakistanis seated at an adjoining table. One of them, a newsstand owner, informed the other that newspapers being distributed by him would no longer be displayed in his store because their headlines—pertaining to internecine Sunni-Shia violence in Pakistan—would incite trouble in the local neighborhood. My curiosity provoked, I sought to join the conversation but was curtly told—after finding out I was Indian—the matter was for Pakistanis only. I wondered whether Mohammed Azharuddin, the Muslim Indian captain, realized he would not be made privy to this sectarian debate either.

Back in the theater, as the match drew to a close, and as a Pakistani win approached, the chants from the Pakistanis in the theater started, their call and response building and holding, growing louder and louder. "Pakistan *Paindabad*" and "*Naara-e-Takbeer*" rang out again and again. The former was similar enough to "India *Zindabad*" to not mystify me, but "*Naara-e-Takbeer*," which I was hearing for the first time, most certainly did. It sounded like a call to the faithful or a war cry, not an exclusively sporting chant. (I learned later it meant "Shout out Allah-O-Akbar; shout out God is great.") A young Pakistani man ran down and danced in front of the screen, now a figurative Indian grave. I wished someone would bell the cat and tell him to cease and desist, but that would have been asking for too much. Self-policing had never been a strong point in the Pakistani communities I had had contact with—whether online or off. I did not have the guts to tell the young man to get off the stage either; I feared I would provoke an international incident—right after I got lynched. An Indian fan sitting next to me, a resident of the local neighborhood, shook his head and said India's loss meant *beizzati* (dishonor) would follow. The Pakistanis loudly celebrating in the stands and in front of the screen were relieved of such worries. They did not fear *beizzati*; they had escaped the gallows of sporting defeat to India.

As the postgame ceremony was telecast and an Indian woman from the Sahara group handed out prize money checks, lewd hooting and catcalls from the rafters began. Losing to Pakistan in the deciding game of a five-game series was bad enough; losing to them in that company, while being subjected to that cheering, was worse. Cricket in the diaspora was a sordid and miserable affair; all of us, far from home, were fighting these ludicrous replacements for the real thing. This was a far cry from the days when I had cheered for Pakistan, for Zaheer, Majid, and Asif. I had not realized then I was cheering for a team supported by Pakistani fans in all their complicated glory.

Toronto's crowning moment came in the 1997 Sahara series.* On 14 September 1997, I was following the second one-day international of the five-match series on IRC, safely ensconced at the CUNY Graduate Center's dungeon-like library—a venue invariably starved for books and pleasant reading space. Guaranteed to induce sleep with its endorphin-expelling powers, the library was not a venue for scholarship. It was a forum to sink deeper into melancholia, to stare at its dank walls and idly note the absence of the books you needed. It was easier, far easier and far more pleasurable, to log in to one of the conveniently provided computers and follow cricket instead. As the match dawdled along, commentators noted a disturbance in the crowd. A Pakistani cricketer had attacked a spectator. Someone had been persistently heckling Syed Inzamam-ul-Haq, calling him an *aloo* (potato), mocking his rotundity and his glacial presence in the outfield. Finally, the normally placid Inzamam had lost his patience and run into the crowd, determined to teach the offender a lesson.

But Inzamam had not run into the crowd unarmed. He had entered the fray with a bat brought out by the twelfth man. Inzamam had not had a spur-of-the-moment reaction to abuse, a hotheaded and impulsive moment in which he had seen red. Rather, he had initiated a premeditated assault on the fan. The heckler had jeered Inzamam mercilessly, he had been an irritation, an infuriatingly loud annoyance armed with a megaphone (which should have been confiscated by ground staff). But other than his amplified volume and persistence, he was like spectators all over the world who heckle and cheer without being assaulted. Inzamam had thought it acceptable to call for a bat, have it placed on the boundary line, and then use it as a weapon to assault the fan.

In modern professional sports, when players assault fans, severe penalties—the lightest of which are long bans—are imposed. Conversely, when fans physically assault players, they are usually arrested and charged with criminal offenses. When Manchester United's Eric Cantona assaulted a fan in 1995, he was given a two-week prison sentence, which was subsequently overturned, and he was banned from play for nine months.†

---

* Martin Williamson, "Inzimam and the Canadian Aloo," ESPNcricinfo, 22 April 2006, available at http://www.espncricinfo.com/magazine/content/story/245024 .html, last accessed 26 January 2015.

† "Eric Cantona," Wikipedia, available at http://en.wikipedia.org/wiki/Eric_Can tona#1994.E2.80.9395_season_.E2.80.93_Ban_from_football, last accessed 26 January 2015.

In instructive and appalling contrast, Inzamam was suspended for two games and was playing again by the end of the series. The Pakistan Cricket Board made the mildest of castigatory comments, content to dish out token punishment so the clamoring for discipline would stop and business could go on as usual. He had only assaulted an Indian.

In the commentary box, Wasim Akram piously proclaimed that because Inzamam was such a nice guy, his actions could only have been brought on by severe provocation and needed to be viewed in a more empathetic light. My immediate reaction to this kid-gloves rhetorical treatment was impatience. Little had changed; Pakistanis would never find a Pakistani's actions indefensible, especially if its subjects were Indians. Pakistani fans online defended Inzamam as a matter of course. These defenses were inexplicable, a bizarre symptom of groupthink. I imagined that some of the boundary-line heckling in Australia that Inzamam would have experienced in his career would have been just as tuneless and castigatory. But an Indian fan's heckling—expressed in Hindustani—was especially intolerable. One Pakistani fan provided Inzamam's cricketing statistics and listed as one of his "miscellaneous" achievements: "Slapped an Indian."

I did not miss Pakistani fans online; I could not cheer for the team they cheered for.

The Traveling Patriot

IN 1997, it was time for me to perform another cricketing pilgrimage. India was touring the West Indies. Kingston, Jamaica, was my destination. Of all Caribbean cricketing venues, this one, even more than Port of Spain, was mythical. It was a venue shrouded by history and incident and drama of cricketing and noncricketing kinds; it was wrapped up in cricket and politics and race, the most interesting and potent mix of all. (Besides, in a more frivolous dimension, I could "go Rasta" and indulge in a bit of the fine herb.) In preparation, I purchased tickets over the phone from the West Indies Cricket Board (WCIB) office in Kingston. The casualness of the procurement process was disarming; I was told to pick up my tickets from the board office on arrival. I had heard Caribbean accents many times in New York City; hearing one speaking from the West Indies was especially evocative, instantly transporting me to a long-imagined land whose giants had regularly slain the mere mortals who had dared step on its shores.

As R and I flew to Kingston over the azure waters of the Caribbean, its island tops boldly poking out, their foundations visible clearly below the limpid waters that surrounded them, memories and visions jostled for attention: Ian Fleming novels, Kingston 1976, memories of tuning into Sabina Park at night, and the Caribbean cricketers who had so inflamed my cricketing dreams as a teenager. I was reminded again that the life I was living away from an older home had started to make manifest dreams from a childhood lived in it. I was being brought into contact with the hard edges of wispy fantasies. Finally, we landed at Kingston. I walked off the plane, stared at the towering, aptly named Blue Mountains looming from behind a misty backdrop, lit up a cigarette, and puffed away on the tarmac, doing my best impression of an MI5 operative arriving on a clandestine mission. That suave touch came to an end as I was asked to stub out my cigarette by a gruff airport security guard. Bet that never happened to James Bond; it was not all "No problem, maan" here. As I rode into town, I looked around eagerly. There were no sunny, white-sand, clear-water beaches to be seen; no Caribbean tourist haven, a refuge from bedlam, was visible. Instead, the approach to Kingston reminded me of Indian small towns: decrepit buildings; open-air refuse stands; roadside stalls selling cigarettes, soft drinks, and assorted knickknacks; dusty side streets; and urchins running dangerously close to our rental car.

Suddenly, we were at Sabina Park. I gazed at the lettering that read "Sabina Park" on the back of the stands that faced the street, looking for evidence of world-historical significance. The faded sign peered back. This was where the action had taken place as I had tuned in to the commentary during the first Test in 1983, where India had been bounced and battered into submission in 1976, the home of the legendary playing surface that struck terror into the hearts of those who took guard and faced a West Indies quick marking out his run. We parked our car on a road that ran alongside one edge of Sabina Park. I entered the ground and walked out over on the grass; security here was considerably laxer than it had been at Lord's. Sabina Park was less pompous, less suffused with a sense of its self-importance than Lord's had been. The stands, the walkways, and the interior spoke of a ramshackle fading glory. Australia had beaten the West Indies here two years ago, bringing the West Indies' reign as the world champions of Test cricket to an end. Sabina Park seemed resigned to the lowered status that came with that demotion in cricket's pecking order. I quickly picked up our excellent tickets: on each of the second, third, fourth, and fifth day's play, we would be behind the bowler's arm in the George Headley Stand.

As I strolled out from the WICB office onto an adjoining street, I noticed on a nearby corner, a dreadlocked old man wearing the distinctive Rastafarian hat smoking a giant joint. Overcome by sudden boldness, I walked over and asked him for a puff. A little surprised, he passed over his spliff. As I inhaled and exhaled, my Caribbean dream taking on an ever so slightly psychotropic hue, a security guard came running out. The young woman who had sold the tickets had realized I might not have had enough sense to leave Sabina Park's precincts and had sent the guard out to make sure I left. Daylight was fading, and the formerly bustling parking lot was now deserted. I took his advice and left. As we walked to our car, parked on a side street outside Sabina Park, a car pulled up alongside. In it were four young men, boisterous and loud. Their catcalling, directed at R, felt hostile and threatening. Shaken, we walked on to our car, clambered in quickly, and drove to our hotel. But not before suffering another scare, as we proceeded to get lost in Kingston's unfamiliar streets. In my jittery state, I did dare not ask for directions. Finally, with darkness settling in around us, we arrived at our hotel and checked in, tired and relieved.

Cricket at Sabina Park was a supremely self-indulgent experience. You could buy food and drink—Red Stripes, Heinekens, Guinness, goat and chicken curries with rice—at your seat, from peripatetic vendors. If you asked around, you could buy very good marijuana—huge amounts for very little in U.S. dollars—and then walk up the George Headley Stand to smoke. Which I did frequently, puffing on a large joint—rolled for me by one of my friendly neighbors—and sipping on a Red Stripe while I watched the game. Putting a damper on the euphoria generated by this lethal daytime combination of curry, beer, ganja, and cricket was the crime-ridden city around me. The unease created by that first day was not shaken off easily. I was restricted in my movements once I left Sabina Park, able to travel only to those places for which I had clear and unambiguous directions. Once I left the ground, my mood quickly took on a darker, more anxious tone. I might have been brown, but I looked like an American tourist. My claims to being a cricket fan—"Don't mug me; I'm only here for the cricket; I admire your team, always have"—would not help me. Cricket was not that important; there was much more on folks' minds here. Newark, Sharjah, and Kingston were united in one aspect at least. There was cricket, and then there was the illusion-dispelling reality outside.

Besides Jamaicans, there were fans from other Caribbean nations in the stands. The most memorable members of this traveling cricketing circus were folks from Trinidad: Ramsammy, Zafar—who had dyed his hair with henna marking his trip to Mecca—and Rajan. Ramsammy and Rajan drank lustily, passing around a steel tumbler filled with ice and Trinidadian rum, all the better to fuel their boisterous cheering. (Zafar was content to teetotal, to watch his friends' excesses with amusement and then drive them back to the hotel at the end of the day.) My Trini friends were forthcoming and friendly. They had welcomed me as a brother of two stripes—as a cricket fan and as representative of a homeland long lost to them. They assured me they would always cheer for the Indian cricket team. Except when they played the West Indies, of course. They would have passed the Caribbean version of the Tebbit test; they had made a new nationality for themselves and kept a long-departed homeland in their sights. In my permanently inebriated state, I enjoyed my repartee with them and imagined myself to have connected with Caribbean Indians, away from the despotic ignorance of cricket in the United States, from the feigned hostility to cricket of the Indian American community. I learned Trini slang, and my use of it with gusto was greeted with rambunctious cheers. I was at home, talking about cricket, showing off the statistics I knew, and dishing out one accurate prediction after another. I was at ease. I was among friends now.

The days in Kingston—few as they were—passed quickly. I awoke early, drove to the ground in time to watch pregame practice, and stayed till the last ball of the day was bowled. The day's excesses—the Red Stripes, the rum, the ganja—took their toll. I was a "burned-out case" by day's end. My Trini friends remarked on my capacity for inebriation, but I had to show them that an Indian could party as hard as they could. It was a familiar feeling. In the United States, I had often drunk male friends under the table, drinking the strongest bourbon on offer; downing Jack Daniels, Maker's Mark, Wild Turkey, and Jim Beam; chasing my glasses of whisky with bottles of beer; swigging forty-ounce bottles of malt liquor— trying to fit in, fighting hard to dismiss the emasculation of being Indian. No one else had had to perform the same contortions. I was the one on the outside looking in, not they. So it was in Jamaica. I was still on the outside, still looking in, still knocking on the glass pane.

There were discordant notes in this otherwise pleasing chorus of cricket fandom. I heard an older Jamaican man refer to the Indian players as "coolies"—evidence of older prejudices that still stalked this land. Other cranky old-timers did not take kindly to having a "youngster" in their midst, especially one escorting a young woman who looked Indian and sounded American. She *was* American; I had not lived in India for ten years. But we were stuck with ambassadorial responsibilities, with copping the hostility occasionally sent our way for being representatives of cultures only incompletely accepted here.

I spent the washed-out last day dodging the rain, hoping my stay in the West Indies would not end with a damp whimper. But it did. The Blue Mountains remained hidden all day, as did the sight of men in white playing on the Sabina Park pitch, now placid and serene in sharp contrast to the bumpy terror of the 1970s. While loitering by the boundary line, I managed to say hello to Saba Karim, an ex–Hindu College wicketkeeper, doing reserve duties for India. I was invited back to the hotel to meet the rest of the Indian team, but sadly, I had to decline. My flight left the same evening. Thus did travel logistics interfere with a brush with glory, for a chance to meet those who bore the responsibility of assuaging my doubts and insecurities, of addressing my many grievances against foes both real and imagined.

R and I broke up later that summer and I became a nomad, moving to temporary digs in Harlem, not-yet-gentrified Brooklyn, and then back to the Lower East Side in Manhattan. My departure from cricket on IRC—after that tirade by Pakistani fans—happened at the same time. But my ongoing relationship with Pakistan was not terminated so easily.

Rewriting Lives: The Military History Connection

At year's end in 1997, I took a temporary hiatus from academics. I had passed my oral examinations—with distinction—after swearing off the twin distractions afforded by alcohol and pot. But I was broke, and I had run up debts. I needed to pay graduate school tuition bills and rent. My landlord was indulgent, making polite inquiries about my delayed payments. But he was persistent too, and his knocking on the door of my rented room in his young son's apartment reminded me of my delinquency a little too frequently. I took up UNIX system administrator duties at an online brokerage and joined the Internet gold rush. I would save money till I could return to writing my dissertation. My place of employment was populated by hypermasculine, aggressive young men, racist and sexist, committed to a workplace atmosphere profoundly hostile to women and minorities. I engaged in some verbal jousting but soon retreated into indifference; I was casting pearls before swine. My commitment to the job was minimal; I was only too happy to let my companion system administrator take on all duties. I would get coffee; I would get lunch; I would take a coffee break; I would browse the web; I would dream of returning to my Ph.D.

Early in 1998, I began investigating on the Internet, Indian and Pakistani military history. Finally, eleven years after I had left India, I had begun personal archaeology, a not so thinly disguised attempt to find my missing father. One morning at work, as I browsed and searched and otherwise occupied my time, I found a website on the Indian Air Force—and, indeed, one dedicated to a war my father had fought in: the 1965 war for

Kashmir. I looked for mention of my father. I found indirect references—here, there was a note about his squadron; here, the mention of a battle I knew he had fought in. Now suddenly fascinated, intrigued by the prospect of solving a mystery that had long perplexed me, my forensic sensibilities suddenly aquiver, I entered a short note in the guest book about my father's medal in the 1965 war, promised the webmaster I would aid his historical research by procuring more details about my father from his friends still serving in the air force, and carried on. (Three years later, we would begin a collaboration on writing histories of India-Pakistan aerial conflicts that has to date produced two volumes on the 1965 and 1971 wars.)

I found too, sites dedicated to Pakistani military history. My father's life had been intertwined with Pakistan, and I could not avoid these virtual reminders of that entanglement in its history. I expected the Pakistani narrative to be different from the Indian one, to be replete with disagreeable material, with stories never told or accepted as true by Indians. I found tall tales of Pakistani glory. Apparently, Pakistan had won the 1965 war, humbling the Indian "aggressor," and lost the other—the 1971 Liberation War for Bangladesh—only because of its perfidious countrymen. Page after page was filled with stories of airborne supermen who shot down incompetent, cowardly Indians by the score. It was the military history version of those Pakistani tales in which the world's best cricket team—powered by virile pace bowlers—destroyed the puny, timid Indians. Pakistani military historians sounded like Pakistani cricket fans on the Internet, the ones who ignored statistics that did not confirm their hypotheses about Indian weaknesses.

I had grown up on sanitized and romanticized histories of the First and Second World Wars. In those chronicles, pilots were possessed of a chivalry and respect for their aerial opponents. The battles that took place in the air seemingly soared high above national differences, untainted by the grubbiness of the bloodshed below. In the histories I was now reading, I found chivalry aplenty on the Indian side—in the admiring assessments by Indian Air Force pilots of their Pakistani counterparts, as in their praise of a Pakistani bomber pilot who carried out multiple bombing runs on Indian air bases, all the while in grave danger from antiaircraft fire. They even gave him an admiring nickname: "Eight-Pass Charlie."* I found no such testimonials from Pakistanis. Praise for Indian pilots was not forthcoming in any shape or form from Pakistanis. The furious assaults by on-line noncombatant enthusiasts were unsurprising, but the real blow was

---

* P. V. S. Jagan Mohan and Samir Chopra, *The India-Pakistan Air War of 1965* (New Delhi: Manohar, 2005), 241–43.

struck by Pakistan Air Force pilots, who were equally ungenerous, oblivious to the wisdom of Nietzsche's dictum that the glory of our enemies is ours too, for in doing battle with them we are made stronger. The closest Pakistanis came to acknowledge the presence—and thus the human skills and virtues—of Indian pilots was when a retired Pakistani pilot offered some grudging compliments to an Indian pilot he had shot down. But I did not need the praise associated with being a brave loser anymore.

"South Asian" in the Time of Indo-Chic

As India celebrated fifty years of independence in 1997, the United States kicked off a great love affair with India. Indo-chic was the rage. Bhangra parties were chockablock full, their dance floors filled with Indians and Pakistanis and Bangladeshis—and their American friends, come to ogle those dusky beauties who were suddenly visible on New York City's streets. The *New Yorker* published a special issue on Indian writing; to be South Asian was hip, a culture now deemed rich, made ripe for marketing and appropriation. Exoticization—the henna parties, the Ganesh tattoos, the Indian motifs on backpacks—was cool again. That summer, shortly after breaking up with R, I began a friendship with another Indian American woman. She too, like R, identified as 'South Asian.' As we first met and flirted, she told me of her handsome Pakistani boyfriend and his dance moves on bhangra floors. I retaliated with stories of India's wins in Toronto as Saurav Ganguly won match after match for India. I suggested she would do better to find a consort from the winning side.

A couple of months later, the charade came to an end: she broke up with her Pakistani beau, and we began dating. A's identification as South Asian—some notable manifestations of which included her frequenting South Asian party scenes, dating Pakistani men, and participation in South Asian activism—made me think anew about my South Asianness. I had never called myself South Asian, never joined a South Asian organization, never felt the need for such alliances. I thought South Asian diaspora literature was boring and reductive, its narratives invariably centered on sexist, racist, patriarchal, and terribly dressed Indian men, speaking with comical accents and being rejected by Indian women who sought the company instead of white men who did not quite "get" them. Their titles spoke of mangoes and monsoons and arranged marriages and chutney. I do not know if there is a diaspora novel that meets this template, but I was convinced it was the dominating cliché.

The most common understanding of South Asian was simply "Indian and Pakistani." I rejected such an association for I did not comprehend the logic of diluting my identity. I was struggling to establish its outlines, to make it sharper. I saw little point in diffusion, in merger into a conglomerate. I was not Turkish, trying to become European. But there was more at the heart of my rejection: a deep defensiveness. The South Asian groups A was a member of were radically critical of India in numerous dimensions, many of which I agreed with. But in the United States, I could not bring myself to join them. Here, I was beleaguered. By association, my home country seemed to need all the help it could get.

In the United States, I felt, deeply and persistently, a toxic, corrosive shame at India's many ills, viewed from afar: the abiding sexist and violent abuse of women; the persistent caste- and religion-based violence; the deep tribalism; the filthy cities, dominated by a sheltered, indulgent, self-centered middle-class; the irredeemably corrupt and venal political sphere; the shameful poverty; and the terrible human development indexes. India's food was varied and delicious; its clothes, festivals, and weddings were colorful; its women were beautiful; its landscapes were wondrous; yoga could make you supple and limber; some of its writers wrote well in English; and many other Indians wrote a lot of computer code. But that, it seemed, was that. At least as far as the image of India in the United States went.

It was easy to jump on the critical bandwagon, and South Asian groups were adept at doing so. I soon found myself mouthing that most inane of responses to such critical engagement with India: Why not stay in India and improve it rather than offer critiques from afar? I took myself to have indulged in a virtuous turning away from home. I had been angered and infuriated by an opaque and cruel Indian bureaucracy, by my catastrophic university experience, by the mistreatment of my father by the Indian Air Force, by the distinctively Indian chauvinism and sexism my mother had faced in the world of business after his death. I had been angry enough to want to immigrate. I had chosen to not serve the nation. I had declined service in its armed forces. I was supposedly honest enough to acknowledge I had left India behind. South Asians should have done the same.

I had come to regard South Asians as self-hating Indians, faithfully parroting critiques of India that would echo the preconceptions of, and find them favor with, the white folks they dragged along to their soirees and whose approval they craved. They could get themselves reckoned rebels and radicals and brave warriors by the simple dint of speaking up against India. The irony. Surely, I had once been one of 'them' when I lived in India—in dimensions beyond the sporting. I found this mixture, this straightforward contradiction, this unresolved tension in myself, dizzying. There had been a time, had there not, when I had channeled my dislike of my Indianness into delight in Indian humiliation on sporting fields? But then, I told myself, I was surrounded by Indian critique of our social ills, our political pathology, our disgraceful colonization. Joining in that critique—even if only in my perverse way—felt like the right thing to do. I was at home safe and secure. Once I moved to the United States, those same critiques came to be directed, by others of considerably less benign disposition, at matters far more personal: my past, my childhood, my family. In resisting critiques of India's militarism, for instance, I sought refuge in defensiveness because my father and my brother had been members of its armed forces. A criticism of those entities was a criticism of their lives and their choices.

But I was made uncomfortable by those who agreed with me. I realized with some alarm that I often spoke and wrote like those whom I despised in other forums—the angry, unhinged Indians who called insufficiently nationalist Indians "sepoys." Mostly they were unrepentant ideologues, sanctimoniously religious, pompous defenders of the Hindu faith, speaking up on behalf of Hindus—apparently only Hindus could be Indians—everywhere. They spoke, yet again, of temporally distant glories, lost to traitors and invaders, of a rejuvenated, more muscular Indian nationalism, resisting modern insults and injuries unknown to our ancestors. I did not want membership in that group either. Indian assertion on a cricketing field would do me just fine. My nationalism or patriotism, such as it was, was carefully circumscribed, kept within the boundaries of cricketing arenas.

Going to a South Asian event was alienating, not because I was among white folk, but precisely because I was among brown folk, trying to re-create a land and time and clime that could not be. I did not feel like celebrating Indian festivals in the United States. I did not want to splash colors on myself for Holi or light candles for Diwali. Those celebrations felt inorganic and out of context in the United States. I wanted invitations to Thanksgiving dinners; I wanted to watch the NFL on Sundays; I wanted to attend Independence and Memorial Day barbecues. Celebrating Indianness in America was a reminder you did not belong, that you had left behind that which was once yours and could never be regained. I did not attend South Asian functions, and neither did I march in the India Day parade or go to the celebrations of Indian festivals or other paeans to Indian culture. Art house movies, the occasional classical music recital, Indian food, Indian American girlfriends. That was about it. And yes, cricket—the one zone in which I let myself be unambiguously Indian.

These unvarnished resentments are not sophisticated. They implicated me in a glaring inconsistency. When it came to U.S. politics, I was a liberal and a progressive; in the Indian context, I had bristling apologetic and protective inclinations. I was dimly aware I was conforming to a ghastly stereotype: the overseas resident patriot.

Return of the Prodigals

BY 1999, A and I were living together in a tiny studio on the Lower East Side. Our lives were frugal. We rarely ate out; we snuck into movie double features; we worked through graduate reading lists in philosophy and sociology. I had sworn off alcohol and pot to finish my doctorate, and though I did not sense a new work ethic or diligence or academic acumen magically spring to life, I was sober and more likely to be found using a word processor than sitting at a bar or racking up a game in a pool hall.

That year, accompanied by the expected hype associated with the resumption of cricketing ties, Pakistan was to tour India. Indian and Pakistani papers were agog with talk of the security risk to the Pakistani players from Hindu extremists, who warned that if Pakistan "meddled" in Indian affairs and aided and abetted terrorist violence in Kashmir and elsewhere, its players were not welcome in India. I cursed that neofascist Bal Thackeray and his merry band of chauvinist thugs, the Shiv Sena, for making it transparent there were idiots on the Indian side of the border as well. In response to the Sena's provocations, there was ample commentary on how the "common fan" wanted to see Indian and Pakistani cricketers play each other. Pakistani and Indian players chimed in by issuing pious statements on the desirability of restoring cricketing ties.

There was little mention of the surrogate conflict that India-Pakistan cricket represented, and none of the crowing, the preening, the strutting, and the taunting that would follow if either of the teams would win. The folks claiming cricket would produce increased friendship between Indians and Pakistanis had spent little time online and never participated in its brutal flame wars. They had never been to the Eagle Theater in Queens to watch an India-Pakistan one-day international. If they had, they would not have thought India-Pakistan cricket was a bridge builder. They would have known cricket could spark illiberal, chauvinist tendencies even in those who considered themselves American progressives and could construct and deconstruct intricate philosophical arguments.

India and Pakistan resumed cricketing ties in 1978 and continued playing test cricket regularly—even ad nauseam—till 1990, at which point ties were broken off. Relationships between the two nations did not improve in the slightest by playing cricket. Instead, thanks to Pakistan's nonbenign involvement in the troubles in Punjab and Kashmir, matters grew considerably worse. Amazingly, India and Pakistan were able to play a Test series seven years after the Bangladesh war but were unable to do so in the nineties. Improved bilateral relationships brought about more cricket; more cricket did not improve bilateral relationships. The proponents of cricketing ties between India and Pakistan had the direction of causality precisely reversed.

But the cricket went on. The first Test convinced me anew of that old Pakistani ability to seize the crucial match-winning moments. As India was set 271 for victory, it responded with excessive caution, an attitude bound to trip it up in a quest that depended on runs being scored, and not just wickets defended. It did. India was soon reeling: 82/5 in 41 overs. Tendulkar and Nayan Mongia, the Indian wicketkeeper, dug in and defended grimly. I stayed awake, late into the night, and into the early morning, following IRC commentary, brewing one cup of tea after another as tension grew in both Chennai and the Lower East Side. Finally, as Tendulkar began to complain of a sore back, Mongia, after a few loose swishes, lost his wicket. Sunil Joshi then walked in and hit a six. These strokes seemed indications of desperation; India was self-destructing. But the cauldron of an Indian crowd had started to influence the Pakistanis. Soon enough, Moin Khan the Pakistani wicketkeeper, missed a stumping and induced panic in the Pakistani ranks. Tendulkar's back injury, which was hampering his movements, could have been an asset had he called for a runner and worked runs in singles. Pressure would have been on the Pakistani fielders, surrounded by a cheering Indian crowd, on the verge of going down 0–1 in an away series.

But it was not to be. Predictably for the skeptical, Tendulkar, his mobility restricted, was out lofting a ball in the air. An aggressive forcing stroke had been too difficult to pull off. Seventeen runs were still required. Four runs later, three more wickets had fallen, and India had lost by twelve runs. India had fought back from an almost impossible position but tossed it away at the end.

It was a shattering denouement. Bitterness rose quickly within me. Tendulkar could not finish off games; the Indian lower order was spineless. The next morning found me still stunned and disbelieving. I felt an old, scalding anger at the Indian team return. I saw too, in the failures of the Indian team my own failures. I was an underachiever, an underperformer, mired in mediocrity; I had attended mediocre universities and secured mediocre grades; I had never found a way to become excellent; it was only natural I would be stuck with an underachieving team. Their failure made me want desperately to transcend what seemed to be an innate Indian and personal penchant for falling at the last hurdle, a perennial also-ran status. I conflated the Indian team and myself; their failures were mine, mine theirs. I shrank from this identification. As the years would go by, as I accumulated mediocre displays of academic competence, I thought of my criticism of the Indian team. How could I criticize that lot—for underachieving, for not excelling—when I was guilty of the same crimes? That's what being Indian meant: lacking the instinct, the drive, the ambition, and the hustle for true excellence. At those unguarded moments, I was ready to believe the facile psychologizing and amateur social science I disdained in my more measured moments. Cricket could easily disrupt my sophisticated exterior, stirring up the considerably less measured interior.

I discussed the Chennai Test with my "friend," the Pakistani *paanwaallah* on Lexington Avenue. I did so briefly, for the Test still rankled. His comment that Tendulkar never made any runs against Pakistan irritated me. What did he think that 136 was? I heard no praise of Tendulkar's batting, his fightback from the edge to near victory. I was talking to the cricketing version of Pakistani military histories; appreciation of cricketing prowess did not extend to their foes. The Pakistani shopkeeper was only leveling the same accusation against Tendulkar I had—that he did not play match-winning innings—but I was not interested in joining Pakistanis in their critiques of Indian cricket. Adopting that critical deflationary perspective was my prerogative.

In the second Test, India won as Kumble took all ten wickets in the second innings. But I felt curiously empty. The Ferozeshah Kotla pitch in Delhi was one of those spinning, bumpy, scarred tracks India always did well on. The Pakistani collapse was a little too obliging; the Indian win a little too facile. I wanted India to win on all kinds of pitches; I wanted them to win the hard way—as they could have in Chennai. Here, the Indian team had given Pakistan a thumping and still failed to please me. Beating Pakistan was not enough. India had to do it the right way—the right kind of qualities had to be instantiated in its wins, ones that would assuage my felt needs.

I would watch most of the third Test in Little India, at a Bangladeshi restaurant. The telecast timings were, to put it mildly, inconvenient. New York was in the grip of a typically freezing winter, and my venue of choice was a half-hour walk from home. Company would be nice in my cricket-watching endeavors. I asked D if he would join me for the first session of play on the second day. He was unenthusiastic. He did not have a dog in this race; why would he want to go out on a cold winter's night? Sensing his hesitation, I played my trump card: "There's a new Pakistani quick playing. I've heard he's bloody fast." At this, D's ears perked up, and a few minutes later, bundled in heavy jackets, scarves, and gloves, we stepped out to make that long walk. A new Pakistani quick—in this case, Shoaib Akhtar—was still occasion for excitement.

At our viewing venue, the food was tolerable, the television screen large, and the volume turned up. There were many Bangladeshis in attendance. I wondered who they were cheering for. Were they appropriately grateful for the deliverance of 1971? Did they find solidarity with Indian Bengalis easier than with Pakistani Muslims? Who were their cricketing heroes? I was imposing my own version of the Tebbit Test on Bangladeshis. Watching Test cricket through the night was made harder by the lunch break; with the television then devoted to showing Bollywood songs, there was little I could do to entertain myself. It was close to three in the morning. I was cold and sleepy. The draft of the January night from the constant closing and opening of the restaurant's door had chilled my bones. A young Pakistani sat next to me—with his Bangladeshi friend—carrying on loudly about dishonest Indian umpires. The cold and my companions got to me. I left for home. It was a narrow escape; I still shudder to think of the roars when a few minutes later, Dravid and Tendulkar were dismissed off consecutive deliveries from Shoaib Akhtar, the new Pakistani pace find. Pakistan was still capable of the stunning and dramatic, the heartbreaking.

I was a sucker for punishment. I returned on the day of India's run chase. India did not lose wickets in the first session. I felt hope, confidence, and nervousness stir within me, though memories of the catastrophe at Chennai still lingered. Laxman looked good; India would go through with him in command. But disaster waited.

As the first wicket fell, a group of Pakistani men walked in. They spoke loudly in Punjabi and crowded around the table where I sat, even as I squirmed at the thought of Indian wickets falling with them present. My companions made no attempt to strike up conversation. I continued to watch Laxman and Dravid take India onward. I rather pointedly applauded the pair's stylish strokes, hoping not to be mistaken for a Pakistani, hoping not to be drawn into a confrontation. I did not want to hear taunts; perhaps the knowledge I was Indian would act as a damper on my companions' responses. What if I let go unchallenged some jibe at India, failed to defend India adequately against some offensive barb sent its way? I imagined telling the story to my Indian and American friends and cringed at the thought of their reactions. "What did you say then?" "You didn't call them out?" Better to let these Pakistani fans know I was Indian so they could exercise any restraint they possessed.

Then Laxman fell, his dismissal greeted by cheers from my table companions. Tendulkar walked in, and soon *that run-out* happened. Tendulkar drove to long on, took off for two runs, came back for the third, and collided with Shoaib Akhtar as the throw from the boundary landed on the stumps. Much as I would like to blame Pakistani obstruction for Tendulkar's dismissal, I could not. Akhtar was doing what any bowler would have done: backing up behind the stumps, waiting for the throw. As the stumps went down, a roar broke out at my table. Tendulkar was in trouble; replays showed his bat was not grounded. Rather than sprinting with his head down, Tendulkar had been ball-watching as he ran into Akhtar. When he did so, rather than barging on or pushing Akhtar aside, he had reached with his bat between Akhtar's legs, a bizarrely diffident act. Now infuriated by finding further confirmation of my gloomy thesis of Indian incompetence in pursuing victory, I burst out, "It's Tendulkar's fault." Several pairs of curious eyes turned to me. I continued in Punjabi, "I don't know what he was doing, looking at the fielder as he ran." My speaking in Punjabi, my criticizing an Indian, and a demigod at that, might have ensured the tolerance of my presence among my companions.

As I spoke, bottles came raining down on the ground. I stared at the television in dismay, feeling a warm crimson flush grow and spread as I realized that additional heaping servings of humiliation were on the menu. The Calcutta crowd had provided grist for the tale that we were so desperate not to lose to the Pakistanis that we would riot. Pakistanis were supposed to be the sore losers, not us. When riots had occurred during the 1996 World Cup semi-final against Sri Lanka, it had been excruciatingly cringe inducing. Now that they had been instigated in a Test match in India against Pakistan, it was worse—much worse. And I was stuck in New York City watching this mortifying spectacle with a group of Pakistani men. Thanks, countrymen.

One of my newfound "friends" finally spoke, "This did not happen in Madras when India was losing." Yet another replied with much conviction, "In Madras they are Christians; the Bengalis are Hindus." Christians were civilized; they gave the Pakistanis a standing ovation. Hindus were not; they rioted. It was a masterful piece of sociocultural analysis, albeit possibly confusing to the orthodox Brahmins in the Chennai crowd. I was nauseated yet again by India-Pakistan cricket; it was the most sordid business of all. I left soon after, trudging back through the wintry New York night back to the relative safety of my apartment.

The next day I left for Brown University for a graduate student conference. I spent the following night in conversation with other graduate students. We talked about mental causation, epistemology, belief revision, and the philosophical foundations of quantum mechanics. But my mind was on the cricket. The next morning, armed with a coffee and doughnut, I went looking for an Internet terminal. I found one and, sitting on the third floor of the beautiful dark-wood-paneled student center, learned India had quickly collapsed to defeat after the resumption of play. Their failure was seen by few. The stands were empty, because the Calcutta police had escorted everyone out after rioting had begun again on the final day. When Tendulkar went on to score a century in the drawn Test against Sri Lanka in the Asian Test Championship, my disdain grew. A century scored on the last day of a dying match when the crucial innings should have been played earlier was a true continuation of the Gavaskar tradition. But Tendulkar could not be blamed for the collapses the Indian line-up produced against Pakistan in that series.

Conversation with my Pakistani *paanwallah* had remained polite during the Test series. The *paan* shop had become a venue for me to show off my Punjabi and to attempt to establish, yet again, an ethnic alliance. One night my national and religious identity finally became an issue. The night started well. In the midst of a group of customers clustered around the shop counter, I jocularly suggested to a Pakistani youngster ordering a sweet *paan* he would be better off eating *aam ka murabba* (sweet and savory mango chutney), a quip received with hilarity by the other Pakistanis present. Just then, an older *maulvi* (priest) walked in and offered a *Salaam Aleikum*—the traditional Islamic greeting—to everyone. He leaned forward and offered me his hand. Suddenly confused, not sure whether there was a religious gesture involved that I might perform incorrectly and cause offence, I folded my hands in the Indian *Namaste*, a traditional Hindu greeting. I was stupidly naive. The *maulvi* glared at me, took a step backward and spoke, his voice dripping with suspicion and anger, "Are you Sikh?" I truthfully replied no. He persisted: "But you're not a Muslim." "No," I said again. The possibilities were being rapidly eliminated. One of the Pakistani men, not quite following the conversation, asked the priest, "What made you think he was Sikh?" The atmosphere was still lighthearted. The *maulvi* continued, "I came in and said *Salaam Aleikum* and shook everyone's hand. He was the only one who refused to shake my hand. Right away, I knew he was not a Muslim." Another man laughingly said, "*Maulvi saab ne te fatwa nikal dita!*" (The priest has issued a fatwa!). He had not seen my folded hands; he still thought I was Pakistani. A young man who had thus far been speaking to me in Punjabi now addressed me in heavily Punjabi-accented English: "Where you from?" "Delhi," I replied. (I suppose I could have said the Lower East Side, but I suspect he was not looking for that answer.) He turned away as he heard my reply. I turned to look at the man who had made the fatwa crack. He looked away. There was silence in the shop. I turned to the shop owner, now studiously gazing at the *paans*. He indicated they were ready. I paid, picked them up, and walked out. Far friendlier spaces for social interaction beckoned.

A few months after the Pakistan tour, as peace talks went on between Indian and Pakistani political leaders, the Pakistan Northern Light Infantry occupied the Kargil Heights in Kashmir.

Cricket and Kargil

AS THE 1999 WORLD CUP BEGAN, I was slowly making progress on my Ph.D. A publication or two had added lines to my CV, emboldening me to press on with my dissertation. I was not so optimistic about India in the World Cup. On the day it started, I was at MIT attending a logic conference. As speaker after speaker droned away on model and set theory, I sneaked into a nearby lab to check the scores. India had begun its campaign badly with a defeat in its opening game. Indian fans would soon consume trillions of CPU cycles calculating what India needed to do in later rounds to qualify for the semifinals.

A few days later, the Kargil war started. I mark its commencement with a call I received late one night from my sister-in-law in India. She spoke calmly, but I could hear the fear in her voice. My brother had been deployed to a forward base with his squadron; she did not know when he would return. I could call him but could not ask questions—on an open phone line—that could be deemed "sensitive." I called my brother. In the background, I could hear the hustle and bustle of a pilot's crew room. We spoke quickly; he had no more information to offer. I put the phone down and slumped, sick with apprehension and disappointment. I had booked tickets for India that summer; my plans included hiking in the Garhwal Himalayas with my brother. Now I might have to cancel or postpone my trip. Our grand vacation, planned and paid for, taking A to meet my family, to introduce her to the land and times and peoples I had grown up in and with, was now in jeopardy. I wanted A to meet my brother, my sister-in-law, my adorable nephew. She would see a real air force base, with its *dhabas* and leafy cantonment roads, a venue of childhood legend and imaginings. She could experience, even if only in mediated fashion, places and times formative for me. Those plans were to be held in abeyance; my personal relationships were to be impoverished. And a Pakistani military misadventure would be to blame. I cared little for Kashmir and its geopolitical significance at that point. My mind was focused almost exclusively on the danger to my brother, the stress on my sister-in-law, and my foiled pathetic attempts to forge a deeper relationship with my romantic partner.

Meanwhile the World Cup was on. On the day of my nighttime flight to India, I planned to watch the India-Australia match in Little India. Rising early, I walked uptown to an Indian tea shop known for a large-screen television that showed the usual Bollywood fare. Perhaps they would show the cricket. I was right. This venue was then known among young, tragically hip South Asians as the place to go after nightlong dance parties to recover—to sit back and snicker at the other customers, the plebian types who spoke in comical Indian accents and consumed its exclusively vegetarian offerings. Even the afterglow of party drugs could not make you feel better about being Indian.

By the time I arrived, India's middle order was back in the pavilion. As Ajay Jadeja and Robin Singh fought back with a few sixes, I jumped up to cheer. To my amazement, the proprietor walked over and asked me to keep it down; I was disturbing the peace. Showing the cricket World Cup was a business proposition, not an invitation to participate in a sporting and cultural ritual. Showing cricket would bring in the customers; they would drink chai, order a samosa or two; maybe they would bring their friends in with them and stay for lunch. The Indian owner's relationship with his Indian customers ended with their wallets; he cared little for their involvement with cricket beyond their merely passive, wallet-opening consumption of it. I doubted a Brazilian restaurant would stop its patrons from cheering loudly during a Brazilian free kick during the World Cup. The Pakistani description of India as a land of bean-counting shopkeepers ill-suited for actual sporting pursuit seemed apt.

I was leaving for India that day. War raged far away as the Pakistani army's Northern Light Infantry—described by the Pakistani government as "Kashmiri freedom fighters"—having occupied the strategic Kargil Heights and its passes, was now locked in a fierce battle with the Indian army, which had launched a series of courageous, but expensive in men and material, raids to regain them. I arrived in Delhi, and as we drove back from the airport, my cousin, come to pick me up in lieu of my brother, filled me in on the details of the day's games. War news was scant, cricket scores were not. On the day of the India-Pakistan match, I woke early and caught the Shatabdi Express from New Delhi to Ambala to meet my brother's family. As I read newspapers and looked out on the countryside rolling by, my mind was on the cricket. The train took us quickly to Ambala, even as I fretted it would be delayed, leaving me high and dry, missing the must-see game of the World Cup. The train was obligingly punctual; we pulled in well ahead of the game's starting time. A smart uniformed serviceman stood by with a car to take us home. As we drove through the broad tree-lined avenues of the Ambala cantonment, the unmistakable thunderous sound of a fighter jet's engines at full throttle reminded me I was back on an air base. I looked up as a Mirage 2000 flew overhead, taking off for missions in Kargil, its delta-winged flight an awe-inspiring and somber sight. Besides the hype of the World Cup—the "epic contest," the "marquee game," the crowds in England, the diasporic fans in the United States—there was this relationship between the countries, one that the faux bravado of online patriots and warriors invoked and squabbled over.

My disquiet grew after we arrived at my brother's home. I sank into a couch and watched my sister-in-law bustle about. There was plenty on her mind; her husband was four hours away, preparing for war. She prepared lunch, fighting to stay calm. After lunch, we sat sipping tea, making small talk. There was a knock on the door. My brother's colleague—a pilot from his squadron—stood on the porch. He had come to convey greetings and news during a short furlough from his forward base deployment. We sat him down and plied him with questions. He could only offer noncommittal replies; military caginess prevailed—"loose lips sink ships." I gave up. The India-Pakistan encounter—thankfully a day game—was to start later that afternoon. I was hit by attacks of drowsiness and struggled to keep awake with cups of tea and games of Scrabble with my nephew.

Finally, the match began. Just as it looked like Tendulkar and Dravid were taking Pakistan apart, Tendulkar charged Azhar Mahmood and drove straight into Saqlain Mushtaq's safe hands. I swore bitterly; once again, Tendulkar had failed to dominate a marquee match. I had struggled to stay awake during the Indian batting, nodding off to sleep, waking up when a boundary was hit. I was exhausted and jet-lagged. I had spent two days in the Delhi heat tramping about, stuffing myself with junk food and staying out in the sun. Now it was all catching up with me; my body's systems shut down. I sat a few feet from the television as the greatest event of the cricketing season went on while I fell in and out of sleep. Jets roared overhead, headed to and from Kargil.

Equally loud roars from the television screen informed me things were better for India than I imagined. Three Pakistani wickets were down; the Indian quicks were on top. Saeed Anwar was batting fluently, raising danger signals. But India continued to take wickets, making this my favorite kind of one-day match, one in which a middling target was defended. The real danger came with Moin Khan, who had patented lower-order blitzes. I watched nervously as he compiled a quick 34 off 37 balls. But this was

India's day. Prasad dropped short, Moin pulled, but only straight into a gleeful Tendulkar's safe hands. The last three wickets, all sweet ones, Inzimam, Saqlain, and Akram, went down in consecutive overs. As Akram swung and was held by Kumble on the boundary, the game, the hype, was over. India had cantered to an easy victory.

Sea green and light powder blue swarmed across the ground. The crowd surge came to a halt in front of the pavilion; a few firecrackers were set off. The taunting that had gone on in the stands did not degenerate into violence even as some Pakistani fans burned and stomped an Indian flag. When I saw a photo of the incident, I considered sending it to A and her friends in New York with the caption, "There's South Asian unity for you." Those Pakistanis reminded me of the Hilfiger-wearing lads from Queens who hung out at bhangra parties in New York, the Medina Boys gang members who attacked Indian DJs and harassed Indians at parties. I did not consider the Indian flag defiled at Old Trafford. I did not ascribe religious status to the Indian flag. I cared little for national icons; but I still experienced the gesture as an unnervingly hostile figurative act. I knew those doing it intended to unsettle me, and they succeeded. In 2001, as riots broke out in Bradford, North England, I felt little Asian solidarity with the rioters. I saw them as Pakistanis with English accents, like those who had burned the Indian flag. That Bradford racists would call them "Paki" and would call me one as well meant little. I did not think having a "common enemy" meant a shared friendship.

The Kargil conflict was not an abstraction to be discussed over morning cups of tea. I had a personal stake in it, more important than any national one: my brother was possibly to be pressed into service. At times, absurdly, I wished for war so my brother could be baptized by fire. I wondered whether he resented my father, that ever-present absent figure who had shown off his training in war. My brother had earned more peacetime laurels as a pilot than my father, but he had not flown in war. I wondered whether he even sought such an examination himself; he did have a family waiting for him to return safely. The queasiness I felt at the thought of my brother coming to harm—and at Pakistani hands—was debilitating. I had good cause for such fears: an Indian pilot taking part in the air operations who had worked with my brother as a flight instructor at the air force academy had been shot down. After bailing out behind Pakistani lines, he had been captured, tortured, and killed.* A day or so later, the bodies of the six Indian soldiers captured and tortured to death by the

---

* Wikipedia, "Ajay Ahuja," available at http://en.wikipedia.org/wiki/Ajay_Ahuja, last accessed 26 January 2015.

Pakistani army were brought home. Their injuries indicated extensive and prolonged antemortem torture and mutilation.* This was all too close to home; I was receiving this news in the company of those whose attitudes were hardened by years of proximity to tales of Pakistani perfidy. It was, just like those days in the eighties when I had heard stories of the killings in the Punjab, a time to be vulnerable and susceptible to the knee-jerk reaction, the unthinking response, the pushed button.

I did not remain unaffected. I was susceptible and vulnerable, and I spent much of my time in India nauseated with anger as I read reports in the U.S. press that were inadequately critical of Pakistan, or that gave Pakistani spokespeople column inches. I was an easy target for wartime rhetoric, highly susceptible to its provocations. I found few internal resources with which to combat it. In the rawest of moments, I would look resentfully at A and wonder how she could ever have slept with the enemy.

I spent the long, hot days after the India-Pakistan match with my brother as his squadron deployed for possible operations. His commanding officer had generously allowed me to stay on base; I slept in the small officers' billets. My brother left at six in the morning; we ate lunch together and went for long walks in the evening. I watched news and updates on Kargil; I watched highlights and live telecasts of cup games. It was wall-to-wall cricket and war. At night, pilots spoke of homesickness, India's chances in the World Cup, and the heat. They were curious about my life in the United States and persistent in their questioning. I answered as well as I could and drank on with them. Thanks to his indulgent commanding officer, my brother secured two days leave to accompany me back to Ambala. We would watch the World Cup final together.

India did not make it to the final, Pakistan did. Two World Cup finals involving Pakistan; I had been unable to cheer for them in either game. I had no Pakistani friends to commandeer my support for their team. My best friend, curious and inquisitive about India, was Australian, someone who spoke of the Indian team with respect. Cheering for the Australian team was a foregone conclusion. I still looked forward to watching Pakistan in the field, to seeing its fast bowlers operate. But I most wanted to see the Pakistani crowd shut up. As I watched the game, I thought about the Pakistani fans on IRC and on rec.sport.cricket and dreamed about their comeuppance.

Pakistan started slowly and then collapsed. In 1979, I had stayed awake to listen to Majid and Zaheer take on the West Indies, hoping they

---

* Arifa Akbar, "Pakistan 'Tortured Indians to Death,'" 12 June 1999, *The Independent*, available at http://www.independent.co.uk/news/world/pakistan-tortured-indians -to-death-1099605.html, last accessed 26 January 2015.

would triumph. I had mourned when Pakistan had collapsed against the West Indies—a team that, under normal circumstances, Indians cheered for. During the 1983 World Cup, I had switched off the commentary during Pakistan's last pool match against New Zealand because the possibility Pakistan would not make it to the semis was too upsetting. Now I cheered as Pakistan collapsed in the World Cup final, as Pakistani wickets fell, yelling at the TV screen, "Off with you!" As the Australians romped to an easy nine-wicket win, the most crushing ever in a World Cup final, my seven-year old nephew and I chanted, "Aussie, Aussie, Aussie, oi, oi, oi." As Darren Lehmann hit the winning runs, and as my nephew posed next to the television screen for a photograph I would take back for D in New York City, my sister-in-law turned down the television so I could hear firecrackers going off outside. I was not the only one celebrating a Pakistani loss. I knew when I got back to New York, I would recount the day's happenings with much gusto to D. And that's exactly what I did.

Part IV

All Shook Up
Down Under

IN 2000, ensuring further psychic disorientation, I moved to a new home. I finished my doctoral studies in philosophy and scouting for a postdoctoral fellowship, found one in Sydney at the University of New South Wales. I received strange looks from other academics—who considered Australia an academic backwater—when I told them of my intended move. But it was no accident I had sought out Australia. Sydney was beautiful; it was the city that—Gore Vidal had once said—is the one San Francisco imagines it is. D's friends in Melbourne, many of whom I had met on their trips to New York, awaited my arrival, for their chance to show me the pleasures of a new city. I dreamed about road trips to the outback. And there was a cricket season to be experienced during the summer—the same glorious summer I had caught glimpses of on television as a child. I could, and would, make cricket a part of my daily rhythms. I could return home from work, switch on the television, and watch the cricket as the summer went on its merry way outside. I could and would play cricket. I would be surrounded by a cricketing culture, an immersion deeply pleasurable and whole-making.

I would be living in a country though, where the Indian cricket team had done its best to sully the waters for me—by going down with nary a fight in the Test series in the Australian summer of 1999–2000. Indian complaints about the umpiring conspiracy against Tendulkar left me unmoved. India could have done better with more spunk and with a little less of its asinine reliance on the Little Master. We had been out-aggroed, out-batted, out-bowled, out-caught, and out-fought. We had deserved to lose 0–3. I would have to dispel some long-standing and recently reinforced cricketing impressions once I got to Australia. Thanks, boys.

A Sikh cabdriver drove me from Sydney's Kingsford Airport to the university; we chatted in Punjabi on the way. He spoke with some feeling of how it felt to be a *pagbandha* (turban wearer) in "this racist country." I pushed away my unease at hearing this; it was too soon for such sullying of the limpid waters here. On arrival at campus, like many Punjabi cabbies in New York City, he refused my fare.

With a little thrill, I realized that my university was in the Randwick of the Sydney Cricket Ground's Randwick End and that one of my colleagues lived in the Paddington of the ground's Paddington End. Other signs of cricket surrounded me: a cricket calendar on a student's desk and conversations with postdoctoral fellows about attending the Sydney Test in the New Year against what promised to be a weak West Indies touring party. One day, as I took a bus back from Sydney's city center, I saw the Sydney Cricket Ground itself, its distinctive green stands and beautiful light towers rising out of an imposing sports complex. I was in yet another place I had thought I would visit only in my dreams.

Soon, the Olympics came to town, bringing with them the Indian hockey team. I could have bought tickets for two games featuring India, but I stayed away from the match that featured India and Pakistan playing on the same day and settled for one. I did not want to be in the stadium when Pakistani fans would cheer for India's opponents. After years of cheering for Pakistan no matter who they played, to be in a stadium with Pakistanis sure to be possessed by the anyone-but-India sentiment was not how I wanted to spend a beautiful Sydney afternoon. This was pristine, unspoiled. I did not want to infect Sydney with an old, corrosive emotion. The off-line representatives of online louts would not spoil Sydney for me.

During the India-Poland game, I struck up conversation with a neighboring Canadian couple, bragged about Indian ball-control skills, and gloried in being from the same state—the Punjab—as not just the Indian hockey team's best players but also the drummers in the stands who had set up a stirring, syncopated *dholak* beat around the ground. During the second half, I shouted loud encouragement in Punjabi as India mounted an inspired counterattack. As I did so, a young Indian turned around and made a wincing gesture, covering his ears; I had been cheering too loudly. He told me I should make my noise elsewhere. I told him—in the vernacular—to get fucked. He reminded me of the New York restaurant owner during the 1999 World Cup who had told me to keep it down. My Canadian friends were shocked by my outburst. They clammed up and made no more conversation. My anger at the lack of solidarity shown by an Indian, at his attempt to police me, was enough to swamp worries about a poor showing in front of my newfound friends. I had sanitized myself too often to gain entrée; the time for that was over.

Around me, there was little solidarity with the Indians as a crackdown on the Indian drumming began. Sydney police moved in on the young lads pounding away in the stands and told them to put the drums away; their protests were unavailing. I associated this behavior—a dull, ignorant stupidity backed up with crude force—with New York City club bouncers or the New York Police Department. Not the police of this beautiful, friendly, lovely city. It did not matter; brown folks were brown folks, loud and undisciplined, and they needed policing. I yelled out bitterly, "Hey copper, what have they done?" No one, neither Indians nor the other spectators present, supported me in my protests. A few minutes later, Poland equalized with a late goal and knocked India out of the tournament. I left disgruntled, wet and freezing, as the rain came pouring down. Twenty-four years after I had first paid attention to the Olympics, nothing had changed; we were still hopeless in world sport.

Two months later I took up U.S. citizenship, losing my Indian one. Ironically, my decision was prompted by my leaving the United States. I was a permanent resident, equipped with the famed green card. But not wanting to deal with the immigration authorities looking askance at my prolonged absences during my extended stay in Australia, I applied for naturalization. My desire to not be hassled by immigration officials at ports of entry had overridden my desire to remain an Indian citizen.

On a bitterly cold December morning, I lined up at the Federal Building in New York City, submitted my papers, and took my place in the cheerless waiting room along with dozens of other applicants. The room was a veritable United Nations. The expressions of the citizens-to-be reflected a similar diversity of emotions, ranging from boredom to hope to eager anticipation. Finally, my turn for my interview came. The immigration officer, a young man in his thirties, sat me down, turned to a brisk inspection of my passport, quickly—at times brusquely—querying me on the contents of my passport: what was this trip for, when, for how long, and so on.

Then, pointing to a visa stamp made by the Jamaican border authorities, he asked, "Were you visiting Kingston for a holiday?" I replied that I had traveled to Kingston to watch a Test match between India and the West Indies; I had spent five days in Jamaica, all of them at Sabina Park. I expected my reply to be met with incomprehension. Instead, my interviewer put down my passport and began a conversation about cricket. He had studied the work of a certain Neville Cardus in a class on creative writing in his university days. To describe my reaction as flabbergasted would be to severely understate matters.

My interview was comprehensively sidetracked. Bureaucrat and supplicant chatted about cricketing rivalries, the game's modern innovations, my favorite players, and so on. Eventually, with some regret, the immigration officer looked at his watch and suggested we wrap things up. There was one last step left. I had to write a sentence in English that would attest to my mastery of the language. The topic of the sentence—cricket—was immediately suggested, based on our conversation, by my new friend. "I prefer Test cricket to the shorter version of the game." I duly complied and finished the remaining formalities. A handshake later I was done. When I stepped out into the windswept, icy corridors of downtown Manhattan that afternoon, my naturalization papers in my backpack, I was disbelieving. Unimaginably, I had had a conversation about cricket in my U.S. citizenship interview; I had sealed my American deal with an expression of my preference for Test cricket.

In taking on U.S. citizenship, I lost my Indian one. Now I would need a visa to travel to India. I had been thirteen years gone from India; notions of home had grown ever more confused. Because I was a voluntary exile and my identity was now a contested notion, questions of citizenship did not feel as infected with nationalist or nativist urgency as they might have. In choosing U.S. naturalization, I did not find myself in the grip of an existential question; rather, I was dealing with a more mundane concern: Which travel document would work best for my career? My academic work required me to travel—for conferences, for instance—and a passport that meant fewer trips to consular offices was a blessing. The Indian passport had been an invitation for suspicious scrutiny by consular and immigration officers the world over. I felt no desire to continue suffering in solidarity in that dimension with other Indians. I knew I could not, would not, go home again. My visits to my brother, now living his own life, with his family, the two of us now parentless, had convinced me India was not where I would find home; my older one was irrevocably gone. Relinquishing my Indian citizenship was an act of distancing from a shared past and culture and history, from family and home. I did not think of it as a betrayal, though some unkind friends did urge this interpretation on me. I had turned my back on an older me.

My swearing in that cold December morning marked the first time I had deliberately chosen the citizenship of a nation. My Indian one had come to me by birth. My first passport had been mine to ask for; a set of allegiances lay waiting for me to take on. Here, I had inserted myself into the process of gaining a nationality; previously, I had been born into one.

My older passport had been the culmination of a long series of experiences that had reinforced my nationality; my newer one was the first contributor to the building of a new edifice of identity, a hyphenated or qualified one. From now on, I would be an American of Indian origin, an Indian American, or an Indian-born American. One that cheered for India in cricket.

Cricket in Oz

THAT SOUTHERN SPRING IN SYDNEY, a university friend asked if I was interested in "having a net." I was. We met at the beautiful Waverley Oval on Bondi Road for our session of preseason exertions. While the nets were unremarkable, putting on pads and gloves and picking up a bat was not. I was playing cricket in Australia, landscape of my cricketing dreams as a child. I was facing a true-blue Australian fast bowler. When J asked whether I would be interested in playing cricket with his team, I was simultaneously eager and nervous. I would not just be playing cricket on the weekends. The game in the middle would not be a simple bat-and-ball business; I would be waging my own personal battles every time I went out to bat or bowl or field. I could be a bad ambassador for Indian cricket, a batting incompetent, scared of fast bowling, backing away to square leg, a timid, easily subjugated subject of sledging. My teammates might think I could only bowl spin. Perhaps I would be a poor fielder, unable to match the catching and throwing athleticism of my Australian counterparts. Recreational weekend cricket on Sydney's beautiful grounds would be integrated into the larger symbolic order of international clashes. It would be another domain for the channeling of Indian aspirations, for the contestation of stereotypes established elsewhere.

My friend wrote to his captain recommending me for their team. He was nice enough to compliment me on my cricketing knowledge—reading all those *Wisdens* had to pay off someday—and my unflinching acceptance of a hard knock on my knuckles by a full toss. As he described it, I had been "Akhtared on the hand." I was especially grateful for the nod to my supposed cricketing courage against a quick. I was damned if Australians were going to see an Indian cower in the face of fast bowling.

My first net practice was in Mosman, close to Sydney's azure waters. We drove down in the heat and humidity; summer had arrived early. To my relief there was a healthy mix of body types on my team: skinny, plump, tall, and short. Not everyone in Australia was a blond, tanned surfing god. My team was curious about my background; my Indian origin and my American residence had given me a split identity. I had thought I would be seen as Indian, but my teammates saw me as American, as well. I hailed from New York City; my accent was muddled. This gave my teammates ammunition for two kinds of jokes: the ones about Americans who called football soccer, ate too much, and called the baseball championship the World Series, and those about incompetent Indian cricketers on the last tour. This banter, and my willingness to give as good as I got, ensured I was on everyone's radar. I had not felt this comfortable in the years I had played softball in the United States. Then, my teammates had been excessively polite; their wariness had made it clear I belonged outside, not in.

My first big day that season—and my first runs—came after I returned from New York City as a spanking new U.S. citizen. After dealing with the cracks about a cricket-playing American on the team, I went out to bat. (As an Indian, I had made zero runs for my team.) What followed moved me to write the following e-mail to friends in New York and elsewhere:

So, now, I can die a happy man. Pardon the breathless tone of what follows, but this was about the most fun that I could imagine having. This past Saturday, I turned out for my first cricket game since coming back Down Under. Our team, the Centrals, was playing a 2-day game (spread out over two weekends). Our opponents: the Kirribilli cricket club. We were batting first, lost a couple of early wickets, got a small partnership going, and then the third and fourth wickets fell quickly. In I went at #6. Embarrassingly enough, I had not scored a single run in the season so far and was desperate to get off the mark. I told my batting partner, Teddy, that I was keen to get off the mark, and would be looking for a quick single. He agreed to cooperate in the hunt for that magic first run. It came soon enough with a firm push past mid-on for a couple off the leggie.

The real fun came a few overs later. As Teddy and I hung in there getting singles and twos, the opposition captain decided to bring back the main fast bowler, a demon who in his opening spell had the stunning figures of 6 overs, 5 runs, 1 wicket. He was quick, the wicket was bouncy (grade C plays on hard Astroturf pitches with a fair amount of bounce) so I was not really looking forward to facing him. Teddy got a single off the first ball, and I went on strike. I was in a bit of a mood by this point. Some of the close in fielders had been chatting it up a bit in the middle when the spinners were bowling, and I had been keen to start dishing it out to them as well. The first ball I faced went quickly past off-stump. The second was a bouncer, coming in at me. I fended, missed, and the ball thudded into my chest. Much cheering from the fielders and a grin and a wave from the bowler. Teddy asked me if I was OK, and I waved back. All right, I said, muttering a few choice Punjabi expletives under my breath, No More Mr. Nice Guy. The next ball, I gritted my teeth and drove through mid-on. A sweet sight, as it raced to the boundary. Cheers from the pavilion. The next ball, quick and on offstump. I slashed; the ball went flying over slips, 4 again! The quick was pissed off now, but then, so was I. The next ball was a bouncer. I had already made up my mind to go for it. I pulled off the eyebrows, the ball screamed away behind square leg, thudding into the metal fence with a loud bang. Loud cheers from the pavilion, as I turned and stared hard at the bowler. He stared back, knew he was done in, dropped his eyes and walked off. The fielders went quiet, the pavilion did not! He did not bowl any bouncers after that. I reckon it's every kid's fantasy, to take the quick on, after copping a bouncer, and it was great fun making it happen. Even now, thinking about it, I get a big goofy grin all over my mug. I got run out stupidly after the break, but what the heck, it did not matter.

PS: Apologies for the overwrought prose above :)

I feared fast bowling, but I was in the middle with my Australian teammates watching me. I was an Indian facing a fast bowler. I was acutely conscious I had found the bounce on Sydney's pitches disconcerting. That's what Indians supposedly did not like about playing cricket in Australia: its playing conditions, its fast bowlers. I had a chance to prove them wrong. This was a Test match and World Cup final rolled into one. For months afterward—and till I left Sydney—the memories of that innings sustained me. A little detail I had left out of my e-mail was the nationalities of the players. The fast bowler was Australian; the fielder at short leg whose sledging irritated me was Sikh. Nothing got me more fired up than an Indian initiating the sledging; nothing got me more fired up than being able to curse in Punjabi under my breath. An Australian friend described me as a "pugnacious Punjabi." I liked the sound of that.

In another game, an opposing batsman looked "subcontinental." As I bowled, I found myself hoping he was not Pakistani. If he smacked me for a couple of fours, my mates would not let me live it down. He was caught behind, refused to walk, and was declared not out. I was furious and became more so when he hit me for four on the next ball. I called him a cunt—not loudly, for the C Division had a strict disciplinary code—and then at the drinks break, walked over to the scorebook to check his name.

Much to my relief, he was Indian. Further encounters with him later in the season, while edgy, were considerably less demanding. An Indian-versus-Indian clash on the field was only capable of symbolizing matters far less weighty than an Indian-versus-Pakistani clash.

Once as I umpired, the square-leg fielder asked where I was from. I was wearing a South African team cricket cap purchased while visiting Pretoria and an All-Blacks shirt purchased in North Launceston on a trip to New Zealand. He could not place my mongrel accent, Indian with a dash of the U.S. East Coast. He did not associate brown skin with South Africans, and he did not understand why I wore an All-Blacks shirt. I was an Indian with a U.S. passport playing cricket in Australia.

Watching India from Australia

As the 2001 International Cricket Council knockout tournament in Nairobi began, I walked up to Bondi Junction from my apartment in Bondi Beach, and settled down at the Billy the Pigs pub to watch the India-Australia game on a large screen. Tendulkar was on fire early, hitting six after six. I reveled in the new verbal aggression shown by Tendulkar as I lip-read a "Fuck off" directed at Glenn McGrath. It made for an interesting reversal of the usual roles occupied by the two. As Yuvraj Singh, a feisty new breed of Indian player, debuted, I was struck by his scowling demeanor, his bristling batting. I found myself entertaining the unthinkable thought: Did he impress me so because he seemed, er, Pakistani?

India, resurgent with a new captain Saurav Ganguly, and a crop of younger players, played New Zealand in the final. I walked over to Billy the Pigs again on a Sunday night. Thanks to Sydney's idiosyncratic licensing rules, the pub shut down early at 10:00 P.M. A man sitting next to me asked if I knew of another viewing venue for the cricket. I did. We walked over to the Easts Leagues Club, which would remain open through the night. My New Zealander friend, shy but still garrulous, generous in his appreciation of his team's opponents, was an ideal companion for watching cricket. We bought each other beers and talked about the trials and travails of our respective teams. As the match wore on and as the game got closer, my friend was beside himself, preparing for a devastating letdown should New Zealand lose. I did not think I would have been as devastated had India lost; I was not when they did. For I was ready to "let" New Zealand win so that this man would not go away disconsolate. When I found a safe space with another cricket fan, I was sufficiently relieved to let my allegiance to the Indian team weaken. Much as I enjoyed cheering for India, I was happy to cheer on other teams if their fans were as catholic in their tastes as my newfound friend was.

The spunky new Indian side, led by Ganguly, gave me cause for hope. There was Zaheer Khan, a young fast bowler and left-handed at that, and the perennially grimacing Yuvraj Singh, batting and fielding with élan and zest. But I was not prepared for Ganguly's behavior; it was a stunning change in an Indian captain. I was moved to send the following e-mail to an Indian news website:

> Ganguly is an embarrassment for India as a captain. He needs to grow up, and someone needs to talk to him about the responsibility that goes with being captain of the Indian cricket team. Watching him on the ground is all too often like watching a child throw tantrums. What's more, he comes across as a bully. He squabbles with umpires about no-balls, gesticulates loudly and angrily at ground staff, yells at his batting partners, and pouts and sulks aplenty. When it comes to taking on fast bowlers and their aggro, he has no answer. Why doesn't he try his antics against Donald, Akhtar, Lee or McGrath? His comments after yesterday's awards ceremony were in extremely poor taste. He ran out two of India's best batsmen and had nothing to say about this. I dare say it was the most appalling display of running that I've seen from a test batsman in years. In Dravid's case, Ganguly changed his mind after Dravid was almost at the batter's end. Ganguly is a fine, but limited batsman, and he needs to stop behaving like he is God's gift to mankind. At the moment, he is a bit of a liability.

And there was still the falling at the last hurdle business. Victory had stared India in the face and the team had contrived to lose. The new Indian aggression, the new captain's spikiness, now on display, would have gone down better had it resulted in a Cup win. It would have retrospectively justified Ganguly's behavior. I was starting to learn how the victorious thought.

The White Raven

THE AUSTRALIAN CRICKET TEAM'S aspirational final frontier—a series win in India—lay just ahead: the 2001 Test series. Australian papers dutifully printed the usual columns on India's cricket-crazy crowds; the sheer masses of colorful, adoring humanity that would transform the Australian cricketers into demigods; the hero-worship of Tendulkar; the deafening, cacophonous stadiums; and the dusty, spinning, and yet batsman-friendly tracks. India could be both paradise and purgatory. I thought India would lose 0–2; I did not see how they could win a Test. This Australian side was too strong; they had won fifteen Tests in a row.

The Tests would begin during work hours and go into the night. I scouted pubs—potential cricket-viewing venues—around the university campus and settled on the Royal Hotel on Anzac Parade. It featured several large televisions and was strategically proximal to the university for convenient hooky-playing. On the first day, postdoctoral fellows and doctoral students alike made a beeline to the Royal. As we watched the game, one Australian colleague told me—hearkening back to Cardus's relationship with Victor Trumper—that he hoped Australia would win even as Tendulkar scored a hundred. A drunken lout nearby offered a radically different sample of Australian fandom: rare was the image of something Indian on the screen that did not provoke a comment featuring the word *curry*. Australia's relationship to the Indian presence in its midst—its large immigrant communities in Melbourne and Sydney, for instance—was considerably different from the American one. The Indian was simultaneously more familiar—due to geographical proximity, cricket, the long-standing field hockey rivalry in the Olympics, common membership in the Commonwealth, and familiarity with Tintin and Asterix, which both Australian and Indian children had grown up on—and yet more worthy of a genial contempt. I wondered how much of it was due to the weakness of the cricket team: Would a land and a people with a stronger, more visibly assertive cricket team provoke such dismissive reactions? My university colleagues were aggravated sufficiently by this unreconstructed witless buffoon to want to leave en masse in search of greener pastures for cricket viewing—an act of solidarity I thanked them for. There was little India-Australia friendship on the ground as my predictions began to come true: Australia ran out easy winners by ten wickets.

I staked out another pub—the Crown Hotel in Surry Hills—to watch the first day of the second Test at Kolkata. I watched Australia's batsmen dominate before Harbhajan Singh's hat trick—marred by a ghastly LBW decision against Adam Gilchrist—brought India back into contention. On the second day, as Steve Waugh and Jason Gillespie took the game and the series away from India, I sat despairing in my office, unable to go to the pub to offer my virtual support to the Indian bowlers. India's innings was in tatters by day's end. Tendulkar had gone for ten.

The next day, I took a train to Wollongong—an hour away from Sydney—for a research group meeting. Formal models of human reasoning competed for attention with cricket scores. Late in the day, on a break, my colleagues and I visited the university pub. On the television news the lead line was, "In the second Test, India on its knees." That image of subjugation and defeat stung—my worst fears were coming true. We were to be eviscerated, going down to defeat to the accompaniment of jeers and jibes. The Indian team had been unworthy guardians of the final frontier. My day's work done, I found a bar close to the train station where I could watch the Test while I waited for the late train to Sydney. As I walked in, a replay on the television showed Tendulkar's dismissal, out again for ten. Laxman stood at the other end. Scattered around me were a few crestfallen Indian undergraduates, staring hard at their Cokes and fries.

Few Indian cricket fans remember that between the dismissal of Tendulkar and the epic Laxman-Dravid partnership, Laxman and Ganguly started the Indian fight-back with a partnership of 117. It was easily overshadowed by the gigantic stand that followed. As Ganguly was dismissed, thus bringing to an end an irritating innings that threatened to roadblock the Australian juggernaut, a bar patron who had been entertaining the Indian youngsters with a patronizing "Don't worry, your lot will get better over time" routine, jumped up, punched the air and yelled, "Off with you, cunt! Fuck off!" When Laxman got to his century, I stood up, pointedly cheered, and then left for the one-and-a-half-hour train ride back to Sydney.

On the fourth day I left work at 3:00 P.M., walked down to the Royal, and watched the Laxman-Dravid partnership blossom. If India saved the innings defeat and put some runs on the board, a last-day chase could make the game entertaining; we would have made a fight of it and held our heads high (as at Leeds in 1967). Australia would not underestimate India again. India would have resisted. I could remain unafraid to converse about cricket; my opponents in recreational cricket—and even my teammates— would not send sledges my way, skeptical about my ability to defy Indian tradition and play competitive cricket. I had long defended Laxman—in online forums—as the right man to make India's fortunes come right. He had seemed, even more than Rahul Dravid and Sachin Tendulkar, best equipped to handle pace attacks, the kind that exposed Indian batsmen and forced uncomfortable thoughts to the fore about Indian insufficiency in the face of cricketing examination. And he did so in the right way, with not just obdurate defense but also sparkling stroke play.

As the day wore on, news of the partnership sent Indian students from the university to the pub; they came flocking to see if their standing in local hierarchies would receive such unlikely support. Australian fans stopped in at the Regent, expecting to see the Australians knocking off the winning runs, to receive confirmation of a coronation and to cheer at a victory parade. They were brought to a puzzled halt by the Indian score flashed up on the screen, by this evidence of usurpers at the banquet. Their bemused exclamations suggested I was not mistaken in my assessment of the significance of the changes being wrought on a cricket pitch far away; a premonition of revolution had stolen over me. As a sneering voice called out, "The curry munchers have come out of the woodwork tonight," I chortled. There was no need to rise to this crudely dangled bait. Frustration was setting in—a sign of the crumbling resistance in the face of the scoreboard's implacable evidence. The cricket thousands of miles away could always act across the intervening distance to resolve cultural conflict. The doings of cricketers intervened directly in personal interactions far removed from their immediate impress.

The Dravid-Laxman partnership went on. There was no end to the runs made. No one could have played Shane Warne better than Laxman and Dravid did that day. Laxman's driving through the leg side is a sight that will live with me forever. As will that feeling of sitting in an Australian bar with the doors and windows open, a cool Sydney breeze blowing through, as the runs came cascading down. The stage was perfect. A huge crowd was in attendance, like the one that had disgraced me in the riots during the 1996 World Cup in the semifinal and in 1999 against Pakistan at this very ground; they had come to make amends. It was the second Test of the series with India one down against the all-conquering Aussies, and my hero, V.V.S. Laxman—the only batsman after Zaheer, Hughes, and Gower to attract my emotional investment in his success—was leading the charge.

On the final day of the Test, after my sprint to the Crown Hotel with eight Australian wickets down, as I watched Australia's run chase on the final day splutter and die, I wondered whether this improbable fantasy— one I had not even dared to dream—would come true. India won. I had seen the white raven. That day in Sydney, I experienced cricketing perfection. No sporting fan could have dreamed of more, asked for more, received more. Paradigms and conceptual frames of reference were rewritten. I struggled to shoehorn these new reams of observational data into the theoretical structures that had thus far enabled me to make sense of cricket and the Indian presence in it. I was disoriented.

In the last Test of the series, played at Chennai, as India chased 155 to win the series and complete its astonishing narrative arc, I left early and took a cab to my now-favored viewing venue for cricketing miracles: the Crown Hotel in Surry Hills. My cabbie, a Lebanese Australian, would have failed one version of Norman Tebbit's test: he wanted the Indian team to "kick Aussie arses." As India crept closer to its target, an older Australian man got up to leave and turned at the door to yell out "Aussie, Aussie, Aussie!" There was no "Oi, oi, oi" in response. A dozen curious brown faces turned to look at him. He flashed a toothy grin and shrugging his shoulders, walked off into the night. The turn was complete. There *we* were, in the heart of Surry Hills, cheering for India taking on and beating, the mighty Australians. The sun had set outside. It would soon follow suit in Chennai, casting darkness over Australian hopes of marching on and over their final frontier.

The day after the Chennai Test, I wrote to Indian friends scattered all over the world:

I know not everyone on the list above is a cricket fan, but you've got to be one now, after this amazing test series we had against Australia. We beat the world champions, and we did it in style, and we did it by creating one of the greatest fight backs in the history of test cricket. What India did at Calcutta has been done only 3 times in 125 years of tests. And to come back from the defeat at Bombay and clinch the series at Chennai. Such music to the ears, these names: Mumbai, Kolkata and Chennai. All these new names, shrugging off our colonial past, and perhaps this cricket win means a new start for a team of players that carries so much of the country's hopes on its shoulders. Indian fans have supported the team for so long and got so little in return that we had stopped believing in this team, but now it's been paid back and in style. I'm glad I was here in Australia to see it.

Last night, when it looked like India was going to pull it off, I ran out of the university, and tried to catch a bus to go to Surry Hills and watch it at this pub (the rest of the crowd is quite a mix, a few derelicts, some hard-core Aussie fans—the bathroom has a blue light in it so that heroin addicts can't find their veins!). I could not get a bus, so I jumped in a cab. The driver, a Lebanese-Australian, said to me, "Mate, I hope you kick the Aussies' arses—those guys are way too cocky." I replied, "Yup, we'll do it." I got there and the Indian collapse started right after I got there. My friends, a French and Swiss couple, can you believe it, I managed to get them interested in cricket, joined me in the raucous cheering. I had to have a whisky to calm my nerves toward the end. For a change, I was not the pessimist. It was perhaps appropriate a guy with the same first name as me [Samir Dighe] kept his cool and took India through to the end. And, Harbhajan Singh, the Pride of Punjab, got the winning runs.

Afterward, we bought champagne and celebrated back at my apartment, looking out over the Sydney skyline. What a feeling. In the papers the headlines said it all: "You beauties!" "India Singhs a tune of triumph" "The man who broke Australia's heart" (for Harbhajan). One letter writer wrote last week, in a letter titled "Dravid and Goliath": "If it was not bad enough that we had to deal with the tax-man, now we have to deal with the Laxman." One guy wrote: "I woke up today feeling happy, and realized it was the vibes from a billion happy Indians."

Cheers all, think about making a trip here someday. The beer is cold, the weather is fantastic, and Indians get a lot of fucking respect now.

I was happy to get some of that fucking respect.

Cricket was still inserting itself into the contours of relationships; it was still altering power structures, capable of rewriting the terms and arrangements of a symbolic order; it was still capable of radically transforming the self and other- conceptions of groups and individuals. Australians would not see Indians in the same light again; Indians would not see themselves in the same way. Every Australian-Indian interaction from here on, indeed every encounter between an Indian cricket fan and the rest of the cricket world, would take place in the shadow of this series, that Test at Kolkata.

After I sent the e-mail, I decided I would write this book.

Back in the USSA

As 2002 BEGAN, I interviewed in New York for a tenure-track position as assistant professor in a computer science department and was offered the job. A and I separated on the same trip. With that tie cut loose, I had to decide whether I wanted to return to New York. I agonized, reconsidering my options and decisions several times during the course of a single day.

On one such day, when I thought I had made up my mind about moving back to New York to take on the security of a possibly permanent academic position in a terrible job market, I took four wickets in an innings for the first and only time in my Sydney cricketing career. After the game, I sat on a park bench, tired and sweaty, drinking a cold beer, soaking up the praise for my bowling performance, dissecting the four dismissals—one batsman caught at mid-on, two clean bowled, one caught at deep fine-leg. I knew I would not experience this in New York. I was to leave a land whose cricket-laden ambience I would not be able to replicate in the United States. My teammates and I could play, listen to, and watch cricket together. I could participate in childhood rituals and cultural rites I had grown up with. My teammates loved my recall of cricket statistics, my knowledge of cricket history, my appreciation of Australian cricket, and my plucky representation of Indian cricket.

There was little value attached to these attributes in the United States. There, I would not find the acceptance I had found here. My mates in Sydney were more accepting of me than those on any softball team I had played for in the United States. Then, I had been supposedly a novice in the game, someone to whom the rules had to be explained. My protestations that I was aware of them had no effect. No matter how much I had learned about baseball and American football and their history and statistics—the books by Roger Angell and David Halberstam, the subscriptions to *Sports Illustrated*, the endless hours watching and listening to baseball and football games, the immersion in the rituals of trips to Yankees Stadium, the football dates on Thanksgiving, getting caught up in the fortunes of the perennially falling-short New York Knicks of the 1990s—my relationship with American sport was up for contestation. My participation in a conversation about American sports, in an Indian accent, was always fraught. Perhaps my interlocutors expected embarrassing displays of ignorance and steeled themselves to explain an elementary distinction. My participation in their conversations was an intrusion of sorts. I was always to be a tourist, one who would always need directions to Yankee Stadium. But when I played and talked about cricket, my knowledge and proficiency was assumed. My teammates acknowledged my embedding in cricketing culture.

There was a larger rejection in the United States. In the thirteen years I had lived there, I had not been invited home by an American friend for Thanksgiving or Christmas. In sharp contrast, both Christmases I had spent in Australia had seen me invited to several homes. That failure to be called in out of the cold had rankled. When I was offered homes, even nominal ones, I gladly accepted. I longed to be taken in.

I was not going back to India. And neither would any other place ever become home for me. I knew enough about being an immigrant to sense that. But if something could approach that exalted state of being, it would be a place that, besides playing host to me, also entertained cricket. And in Australia, there was cricket aplenty. In both Sydney and Melbourne I had made a coterie of cricket fan friends who would and could turn Test watching at their historic grounds into new, secular, profane rituals: a visit to the MCG for a Boxing Day Test, the day after a Christmas Day barbecue; the New Year's Test at the SCG. From my apartment in Surry Hill in Sydney's center city, I could walk to the SCG; my home was within a figurative stone's throw of a field of dreams. I could attend Tests at Brisbane and Adelaide and Perth; I still held on to their status as exalted places on my mental cricketing maps. And then there was this acute sensation of sitting on the sidelines after a victorious game, sipping on a cold beer, cracking jokes only Australians, fellow cricket fans, could understand.

One way to put my personal accomplishments in Australia into perspective is that at the age of thirty-four, in the space of two years, I had formed three new friendships likely to endure. This, as any thirtysomething will tell you, is a remarkable feat at an age seemingly intended only for consolidating older friendships. I had put down firmer roots in Sydney than I had in the United States. What made them so was the recognition of fundamental aspects of my being in its climes. Conversations about cricket had helped; cricket had enabled me to reveal a great deal, to make myself vulnerable, to let others in.

In two brief years, Australia had become the place where my cricketing fantasies as player and spectator had come true. When I thought of the 2001 series, I thought of my place in Australia—my relationship to those games had been what it was because I had watched them *in* Australia. It represented the neatest inversion of my childhood cricket-watching experiences. In 1985, while watching from India, I had watched India earn its greatest triumphs in Australia. Then, Australia had been the perfect stage for Indian glory. Now, it was possible for India to provide that same stage while I viewed it from Australia. Living in Australia entailed a perfect reversal. When India toured, I could watch them as the proud diasporic. I was keen to watch them do well, to represent me, and to enable me to hold my head with pride. When Australia toured India, I would cheer again for India, from my location as overseas patriot. The best way to make sure I would stay a fan of the Indian cricket team was to not live in India.

I felt a primal, existential anxiety at the thought of returning to New York City. I would not be true to myself; I would negate an essential part of myself for mere professional gain. Returning to New York did not feel like a return home. It felt like a return to a place of employment, a victory for pragmatism and hard-headedness. A tenure-track position not in my chosen field, philosophy, but instead in one that had jobs, computer science, seemed like a terrible compromise. An inauthentic life was a steep price to pay for a career. But living in Sydney could mean a departure from academia altogether, a fate I could not then bear to contemplate. A job back in New York City meant a chance to follow my not inconsiderable intellectual ambitions. I had not put down adequate roots in Sydney, and

I did not have a job here. Because I had spent so much time trying to rescue a failed long-distance relationship, I had failed to make adequate emotional connections, and I had failed to find romance. I had stranded myself with a foot in both camps, belonging in neither. That sounded familiar.

I turned down the New York job offer, writing a careful letter to my genial department chair. Two days later, I panicked. There is no dignified way to describe the fear that possessed me as I thought of a jobless future, desperately seeking work, once again going through the grind of the immigration process, this time in Australia. I was exhausted; the never-ending stream of bad news about the academic job market had worn me down. An older anxiety about destitution, of abandonment, one that reared its head as I suffered the cognitive dissonance of rejecting secure employment, trumped my eloquent justifications of why Australia was the right place to make home. I asked for the job back; it had not been offered to anyone else. Miraculously, I did not have to leave my chosen field of study. I was assured I could teach both philosophy and computer science; I could straddle departments and disciplines. I was reassured. I signed the offer letter. The die was cast. I was headed back to New York—a land free of cricket but a place that might enable intellectual satisfaction in writing and teaching. It was a part of me that jostled for space with cricket, and I could not leave it unacknowledged. I spent the rest of my time in Sydney wrapping up my academic responsibilities and sampling the pleasures of Sydney's hedonistic nightlife.

My cricket team gave me a fond farewell. They poured beers over my head after the last game of the season, a narrow loss in the Grand Final. They took me out for drinks and dinner and asked for reassurances I would never cheer for England. I supplied them. On the night I returned to the United States after a mind-numbingly long flight from Seoul, I met an old girlfriend for drinks. Late at night, I left her apartment for my temporary digs in Harlem. As I stumbled through Manhattan's Lower East Side at four in the morning, a drunken young man said I sounded Australian.

The Great Miss

I SPENT A FEW MONTHS living out of suitcases in Harlem. I dreamed of Australia, made many phone calls to Sydney and Melbourne, and traveled back in the southern summer of 2002 and the northern summer of 2003 to watch cricket and meet old friends. I was in a familiar nether region: one home left behind, another adopted and abandoned, this time in the Antipodes. I was willfully making myself homeless again. My old friends in New York City had moved on with family and children, and the ones in Australia, too. When I visited Sydney, I played cricket with my old team-mates; they were glad to welcome me back and slot me in for a game. There too, the playing eleven featured new faces I did not know. Everyone settled down, put down roots. I kept on moving. I was an indistinct blur, even to myself.

During the southern summer of 2003–2004, I would be performing yet another long-distance pilgrimage to see the Indian team. I would watch Test cricket at my old haunts, the MCG and the SCG. An Indian online acquaintance invited me to join a large Indian contingent traveling to the MCG on Boxing Day. I declined; I wanted to watch the cricket with my Australian friends in Melbourne. Cricket in their company felt more organic, a more appropriate binding to the game. I associated this city, this home away from home, with these companions, not those with whom I had once shared nationality and now shared cricketing allegiances.

At Adelaide, Dravid and Laxman had done it again, forming yet another massive partnership, this time in Australia, to set up a win. I now dared dream of a series win in Australia. On Boxing Day, as I waited in line to enter the MCG, roars from its cavernous interior made me wonder whether Indian wickets were down. I prepared for a collapse, for a ribbing from my friends. But the roars had been from Indian fans—out in large numbers—cheering on Virender Sehwag en route to a coruscating 195. I was in Australia, watching a Boxing Day Test as a Delhi boy scored a an aggressive, initiative-seizing hundred. The next day India collapsed. Australia did not.

On the fourth day, I traveled to the MCG by myself, and as India engineered a fight-back, I went looking for an Indian crowd. I found a group of young Punjabi lads—students at a local university—getting rambunctious as Indian partnerships flourished. Their cheering was electrifying; I enjoyed the quick-fire Punjabi quips and racy repartee. When some Australian fans tried shushing them, the Punjabi lads yelled back just as loudly. The stands in the stadium were more than spectator spaces; they bore witness to a conflict of another sort. I could imagine what it had been like at university for these Indian youngsters: endless jokes about curry, turbans, comical accents, the embarrassing Bollywood movies, the skinny Gandhi who looked like "he needed a feed," the bumbling Indian batsmen on the 2000 tour, the friendly medium-paced bowling. When these lads spoke Punjabi in public spaces they might have dealt with graffiti or verbal instructions to "fuck off back to where you came from." They might have been accused of being cliquish for daring to choose who they associated with. Now the Indian team was here, threatening to secure them bragging rights in those exchanges.

Sitting in their midst, I felt it was possible—just as it had been back on that Kirti Azad night in Delhi—to lift the game up and to take it with you, to change on-field fortunes with off-field endeavor. But just as that seemed possible, India collapsed again. The Punjabi contingents fell silent, their shoulders slumping as the wickets fell. Their disappointment spoke of a chance lost to rise higher in their local pecking orders. They would not walk out of the MCG with their heads held high; they would slink away. They would not bring up the game at the university pub. They would resolutely change the subject and dream about the next time Australia would tour India, envisioning spinning tracks and close-in fielders hounding bumbling Australian batsmen to their doom. They would—now and later, here and elsewhere, online and off-line—curse the Indian team for not having done right by them with bat and ball.

At Sydney on the second day came glory as Tendulkar and Laxman ground the Aussie attack into the dust. I walked around the stands, meeting old friends from my cricket team, drinking multiple beers, and as the scoreboard inexorably mounted, I felt if I closed my eyes, I could be transported back to the Bradman days of the 1930s—the ruthless, methodical taking apart of an attack. Only this time the Sydney scoreboard, the new electronic version of the beautiful entity Bradman had so admired in *Farewell to Cricket*, it would speak of Indian glory.

On the last day, as India failed to clinch the series thanks to Ganguly's timidity in setting attacking fields for his bowlers, his failure to trust the young debutant Irfan Pathan's ability to swing the old ball, his over-bowling of Anil Kumble, I sat crestfallen in the stands, aware a golden moment was passing me by. A series win over Australia in Australia—so near and yet so far. A deeper sadness was created by the vitriol directed at all things Indian from the stands. Australian cricketing crowds had not been this ugly while I was watching Australia play England or the West Indies. I wondered whether, during those years in the 1980s when the West Indies had done them cricketing and bodily harm, the Australians had reacted in the same way to the token Caribbean fans in the crowd. But then there were not so many easy targets around: the clueless taxi driver, the shopkeeper with the funny accent, the prickly international student. It was not the team in the middle that was sledged. The ones being sledged were the fans—now instructed to shut up, go home, and not make too much noise. Yet again, the police cracked down on Indian drumming, quickly hustling the offending fans and their instruments of musical destruction away, accompanied by cheers from the stands.

My honeymoon with Australia was over. Rejection at a cricket ground did it. Australia was the country that had elected John Howard, whose minister of immigration and multicultural affairs was Phil Ruddock, a man whose offensive pronouncements on the new "boat people"—Afghani and Iraqi refugees seeking shelter and asylum in Australia—I had never forgotten. I considered Australian cricketing crowds the most knowledgeable fans of all, but that summer they were decidedly unfriendly; they painted my mood a distinct shade of black. There was good reason for this hostility. Australia had expected a walk-over during Steve Waugh's farewell tour. Instead, they had spent the last day of the series fighting for survival. There was little historical precedent for India's performance. Indian teams were expected to provide a bit of stylish batting and some quirky spin bowling and then fade away, providing grist for the mill that turned out gallant losers. India had done more than that.

I was angry enough to write to an Australian friend: "Your fellow Aussie fans distinguished themselves with plenty of racist heckling in the stands and the cops cracked down pretty hard as well. Good on you Oz. You might have to be dragged, kicking and screaming into the next century, but when you get there, you'll find Indians ready to hire your kids for janitorial work." That last sentence, unhinged in its anger and immoderation, showed I had retreated to the deployment of stereotypes of my own: the industrious Asian immigrant would rescue the lazy Anglo-Saxon. I was thirty-seven years old, but juvenilia still came easily to me, and it was always provoked when those two forces—cricket and nationalism—came together. I wondered whether cricket was an edifying presence in my life.

As Steve Waugh's final stand wound down to a draw, I stood up and applauded for Waugh's valedictory parade around the ground. But the failure of nerve at Sydney, and thus the failure to win the 2003–2004 series, ranked right up there with the Oval Test of 1979. India's win would have ranked as one of the greatest ever had they pulled it off. Praise for the Indian team was rich and fulsome—richer than it had been when Australia had toured India in 2001. Then, India had not cooperated in Waugh's "final frontier" campaign. Now India had ensured a great send-off for Waugh. Rather than raining on his parade, they had helped him go out in style. We had been good sports; we had done the right thing and not won the series.

I remembered another series India had played in Australia. In 1977–1978, India played against a team severely depleted by the absence of its Packer stars, bursting with rookies like Tony Mann, Wayne Clark, Alan Hurst, Peter Toohey, Kim Hughes, and Graham Yallop and led by a recalled retiree, Bobby Simpson. In the first Test, six Australians made their debuts; India lost by sixteen runs. In the second Test, two more Australians made their debuts. India batted first, took an eight-run lead, and set Australia a victory target of 339. India lost by two wickets. After Australia lost the third and fourth Tests by margins of 222 runs and an innings and two runs, in the fifth Test, another four Australians made their debut, and India lost by forty-five runs. In three Tests in which twelve Australians made debuts, India lost three narrow encounters.

Long after I have made the appropriate concessions for the talent of the Australians, and for the unfamiliarity of Indians with Australian pitches, I am left confounded. Even a generous cricket fan would be hard pressed to find solace in those results. The narratives of that series speak of the Indian brand of attacking batsmanship, clever spin bowling, and sportsmanship that rescued cricket in Australia. None of this would have been true if India had simply played to its potential and given the Australians a 5–0 thrashing. Instead, India was a good loser that returned with a 2–3 loss. For a country and a cricket board recovering from the shock of the Packer and World Series Cricket crisis, India was the perfect answer. We would lose, we would not complain about the umpiring, and we would be good enough to keep the matches close. Indian cricketing history was richly replete with brave fights, narrow losses, and wins turned into draws. India did what it was good at back then, and apparently still was: coming tantalizingly close, falling short, and having those encounters hailed as great ones. Coulda-woulda-shoulda.

"Only Net Pakistanis Are Like This"

INDIA'S 2004 TOUR TO PAKISTAN was in some doubt thanks to concerns about security in Pakistan, a situation that was made especially dire by a bomb attack during the 2002 New Zealand tour.* Pakistani journalists lectured India on the need to tour; some suggested the Indian team was more scared of Shoaib Akhtar's pace than the terrorists' bombs. While I liked the idea of India touring just to silence this chorus—which reminded me of no one quite as much as those Pakistani fans online years ago—I remained apprehensive of attacks on the Indian team.

I found the argument—advanced by that intellectual and political lightweight, Imran Khan—that terrorists would not attack a cricket team because they would lose support among the local Pakistani populace—asinine. It was a reckoning wildly at odds with the nihilistic political phi-

---

* Guardian Staff and Agencies, "Bomb Ends New Zealand Tour of Pakistan," *The Guardian*, 8 May 2002, available at http://www.theguardian.com/sport/2002/may/08/cricket, last accessed 14 April 2015.

losophy that underwrote the activities of the militant groups operating in Pakistan. That argument committed the singular fallacy of imagining that those who could attack cricket teams had some stake in winning the hearts and minds of the Pakistani populace. But the actual ideology at play was far more committed to destabilizing the Pakistani polity, damaging its economy, and demonstrating the Pakistani state incapable of protecting the lives of its citizens. A mere cricket team—especially one made up of Indians—meant little. Pakistan's militant groups were killing hundreds of innocent Pakistani men, women, and children every year—that was alienating the Pakistani populace quite effectively. Sparing international cricketers because of concern for their public relations profile was not part of the tactical arsenal of a group used to generating photo opportunities of women and children grieving for their dead; the radical groups operating in Pakistan were not cricket fans who fired off a few AK-47s in their spare time. Indeed, given the focus on the international cricket scene and its security hassles, it was eminently plausible that the groups in Pakistan, who did not lack a deadly single-minded nous, would step up their efforts to attack a cricket team to discredit the Pakistani government and set back international cricket in Pakistan. I would be proved tragically right five years later when Sri Lankan cricketers were attacked in Lahore.*

But just like it did in 1999, cricket went ahead. India toured. In the first Test, a Delhi boy, Sehwag, scored a triple ton in Pakistan. Sweet dreams are made of these. I expected a draw, but India kept taking wickets. When Kumble spun India into control on the fourth day, I spent the afternoon anxiously checking the weather forecast in Multan for the fifth day. But Multan was always dry. The next day, India won in Pakistan. It had finally happened. It had never seemed possible in the past; I had never wanted it to happen. Now it was the sweetest cricketing result of all.

For the third Test, I paid my dues and spent sleepless nights in Brooklyn watching the action away in Pakistan. The games began at one in the morning and went on till eight. I watched the pre-lunch sessions and sometimes a bit of the post-lunch, and then slept for a couple of hours before waking to watch the end of the post-tea session. On the first day, India ran through Pakistan, and then Dravid, Parthiv Patel, Laxman, and Ganguly took the game away from Pakistan. Pakistani spinners and pacers wheeled away as the score mounted. Now I enjoyed watching Pakistan

---

* ESPNcricinfo Staff, "Sri Lankan Cricketers Injured in Terror Attack," 3 March 2009, available at http://www.espncricinfo.com/pakvsl/content/story/393212.html, last accessed 26 January 2015.

getting ground into the dust. This was a sweet dual to the 1982–1983 series; an Indian batsman was scoring double centuries against Pakistan, and India was racking up more than six hundred runs.

When India won, I could not get enough of the post-match celebrations. I could not hear enough grudging praise from the Pakistani commentators for the Indian team. But I was not interested in hearing how John Wright, the Indian team's New Zealander coach, had had an overwhelming role to play in this win over the Pakistanis. I did not need to be informed that the firm hand of non-Indian control had been needed to guide the Indian ship into this pleasurable harbor. Indian players were perennially cast as those in need of coaching, a smoothing out of rough edges, a disciplining, a talking-to, a taming of wild, indiscreet impulses, a setting along the right path in the right groove. The best placed to provide such edification were invariably English, Australian, or South African coaches, whose guidance brought their callow wards success. They introduced the unruly and undisciplined to the intricate technical crafts of cricket, otherwise incomprehensible to the woolly, restless, Eastern mind. I was not feeling generous; I wanted only a nominal share of this win to be placed on the plate of the non-Indian coach.

During India's tour, I read many reports about Indians visiting Pakistan, impressed by Pakistani hospitality. (Indeed, a cousin traveled to Pakistan and came back having made friends good enough to invite back to India.) These descriptions of the friendly reception Indian fans and cricketers received were gratifying. Perhaps it was true what that Indian friend of mine had said to me on IRC back in 1997—that "only net Pakistanis are like this." The Indian tourists' experience in Pakistan was an acute reminder that the world of online encounters, anonymous vituperation, and endless, futile flame wars could often be a far cry from that of face-to-face interaction in the right circumstances and settings. I wondered what encounters I would have had had I traveled to Pakistan. I wondered if my Punjabi would have earned me extra mileage and whether I could have met and talked cricket with those who remembered the 1978 series. The Indians who visited Pakistan in 2004 were Johnny-come-latelies. I had known Pakistan for much longer than they had, but they were the ones touring Pakistan and enjoying Pakistani hospitality. Perhaps here in the diaspora, such relationships were not possible. But I had been told they were; here was another failure of mine.

Even so, I wondered how Pakistani reactions to their defeat—which described Pakistan's performance as "spineless," "gutless," and "cowardly," thus using adjectives used to describe soldiers who run away on the field of battle, or that noted a "black day for Pakistani cricket" and a "a day of shame," the language of mourning—would build bridges between India and Pakistan. Conspiracy theories made the rounds; the Pakistani cricket—the inconsistent pace attack, the poor batting and fielding, and the usual internecine disputes—could not be the reason Pakistan lost to India. The attitudes I had seen online were apparently still present in Pakistani sensibilities, but now they could be swamped by the visible, manifest evidence of Pakistani and Indian relationships formed on the streets and in the stands.

Later that year, I married a Muslim American woman of Indian origin. We had met in New York City; we were social justice activists, and appropriately enough, we met at one of those interminable planning meetings that are the hallmark of progressive activism. We dated; we fell in love. I proposed; she accepted. My in-laws, hailing from Lucknow in Central India, had not been happy about her choice of husband—an older "Hindu" man—but after a few conversations during a visit to their home in Cincinnati, they came around to it. I spoke Urdu, I understood their jokes, I shared my father-in-law's interest in history, and I made appreciative remarks about my mother-in-law's fabulous cooking. Those were not inconsiderable blessings in this land. I was preferable to a Muslim—a young black Somali perhaps?—who could not do any of those things. We went to Brooklyn's city hall, carrying our New York State marriage license, and signed the legal documents. We were resolutely skeptical in our religious beliefs: there was no *nikaah*, no seven circles of the fire, just a nod to a bureaucratic functionary, an acknowledgment of the state's power to regulate the personal lives of its citizens.

My father-in-law's sisters lived in Pakistan and were married to Pakistani men. My wife had Pakistani cousins, and she had grown up with Pakistani friends in Cincinnati's tiny Muslim community. Among them was a Pakistani professor of computer science whose name sounded familiar when I was first introduced to him at a party. With a start, I realized he had been a frequent user of rec.sport.cricket, a rare Pakistani fan whose writings had struck me as measured, coherent, and generous. It was a signal from the gods. We talked about cricket. He remembered my posts, noting I had been "prolific" online. I blushed. Surely he remembered the intemperate arguments I had gotten into with his countrymen? Mercifully, he did not.

My brother brought many gifts to my wedding. Included in them were two DVDs: one of India beating England in 2002 in the NatWest Trophy final at Lord's and the other of India beating Pakistan in the 2003 World Cup. As India won at Lord's, as a young Punjabi and Muslim pair took India to victory after their team had been confronted with almost certain defeat, as our Bengali captain took his shirt off and danced on the balcony, daring to be indecorous at the home of cricket in full sight of those who kept their jackets and ties on, thumbing his nose at England's India-born Muslim captain, Nasser Hussain, I realized I would not get tired of those images.

My descriptions of India's players should tell you I had started to internalize Indian claims about the syncretic, secular space the cricket team provided for the nation's sportsmen. I wanted the cricketing success of an Indian Muslim to provide cricketing proof that the two-nation theory was incoherent, in the same year that the ghastly massacres of Muslims in Gujarat made Jinnah's case for a separate nation for the subcontinent's Muslims all over again.* The Indian team was still making statements about the nature of the Indian nation, the success of its nationalist project, and the distance it had traveled along the road to self-realization.

I watched that DVD again and again, and just like those videos that alleviated my homesickness in New York, it would restore my mood on a bad day in this city far away from home. Along with my writing military history, my family in India, and the memories of my parents, the Indian cricket team made me feel Indian. It was the most concrete expression of my Indian identity, vigorously jostling for space with my American one.

---

* Wikipedia, "2002 Gujarat Riots," available at http://en.wikipedia.org/wiki/2002_Gujarat_riots, last accessed 26 January 2015.

Part V

Brave New Pitch

I RETURNED TO TALKING ABOUT CRICKET ONLINE: after years of hesitation and vacillation, I started a blog, Eye on Cricket. I wrote one post in December 2004 and then did not write again till December 2005. My first foray into writing about cricket online scared me back into the shadows quickly. But I began writing regularly, committing myself to the discipline of a daily post, no matter how short. I did not know if anyone read my posts; occasionally, I would find a comment or two. Two years later, having found my online lair, ESPNcricinfo invited me to start blogging for them.

My blogging exposed me again to residents of virtual spaces. The comments flowed in, often angry and querulous. Pakistani readers thought I was "anti-Pakistani" and bigoted. English and Australian readers thought I dwelled too much on postcolonial resentment, that I needed "cheese to go with my whine." I infuriated Indians: I criticized the Indian team's tactics and Indian cricketing administration. I must have been doing something right. Returning to blogging exposed me to the emotions I had sought to keep under check by stepping away from cricket's Internet forums. I noticed old emotions recur; I sought to distance myself from this sphere in which I could bring Hyde alive and keep Jekyll dormant.

Soon, my enthusiasm flagged. There was too much writing on cricket. It had all been said; the same discussions repeated time and again. Worst of all, blogging on cricket distanced me from America. My return to the United States had immersed me in a different American life, one in which I felt a greater investment in being American. I was a citizen, I voted in American elections. I spoke more often of "us" and "we" in American contexts; I took greater ownership in the nation and its supposed dreams and idealizations. I cheered for the U.S. soccer team in the soccer World Cup. It was perverse to live in New York City and write on cricket, marginalizing myself in American life. It was a ball and chain dragging me under, not letting me come up for American air.

I noticed a new breed of Indian fans online. They were irate and edgy; they were obtuse and blind to subtlety; they were defensive about the Indian team—and, more problematically, about Indian administration of world cricket. They initiated and conducted flame wars. Many were the blogs—Indian, Australian, Pakistani, and English—that felt the ire of the irate Indian patriot protesting the bias of the author against all things Indian, or the BCCI, or the refusal to acknowledge Indian players as the best. I often found I could not support my supposed cohort in contestation against those they disputed. But Indian fans were responding to clear provocations similar to the kinds that had lit my fuse many times in the past, now morphed into a review of the cricket world's ills and how they were to be blamed on the BCCI and its "overpaid" team of "stars." The single biggest reason for this outpouring of often unbalanced and misdirected critique was growing Indian cricketing power of the financial and administrative kind and three words: Indian Premier League.

Twenty20: A New View

TWENTY20—the impossible compression of cricketing action into twenty hectic overs per side, a three-hour, sticky-sweet confection dreamed up to bring crowds back to domestic cricket in England—sneaked up on me and everyone else. When the first ICC World Twenty20 kicked off, I paid little attention. I failed to understand Twenty20's attractions and regarded it as a form best suited for benefit games and lighthearted festivals. Besides, the Indian team being sent to do national duty was a second-string outfit—its superstars had chosen this opportunity to put their feet up. As the tournament wore on, my inattention continued apace. When the India-Pakistan match ended in a bowl-out, my impression of Twenty20 as ersatz cricket was confirmed. But by the time of the India-England game, I was paying enough attention to the World Cup to have a tab open on the ESPNcricinfo scorecard as I worked on my desktop machine at home. The crucial moment came in the nineteenth over, bowled by Stuart Broad to Yuvraj Singh. Six sixes in an over off an unrepentant spoiled pouter and sulker who thoroughly deserved such a public drubbing—provoked by Yuvraj's angry verbal on-field encounter with Andrew Flintoff, England's new Botham, the man whose shirtless sprint around an Indian cricket ground had inspired Ganguly's matching striptease at Lord's after the 2002 NatWest Final—was enough inducement to start paying attention to the format. It did not matter what the cricketing format was if it allowed for a settling of scores; it was an entirely irrelevant consideration to the sight of the bullying Australian opener Matthew Hayden getting his comeuppance from India's hotheaded Sreesanth in the semifinal. The cricket ground would still provide a zone for channeling emotions and sentiments; it would still allow for a parade of politics.

The final was an India-Pakistan game—the wet dream of Indian and Pakistan fans. My attention to it was involuntary. I went hunting online for bootleg video streams, found one, and paid up. The final was on the same day as a departmental faculty meeting; I would have to hope the final ended on time and then briskly walk the thirty minutes to campus to make the meeting. On the day of the final I settled down with a cup of tea, linked to the URL provided by the bootleggers, and began watching. The Indian score of 157 was inadequate but would have to be chased in a final, the kind of situation that induces palpitations in the best batsmen. Early Pakistani wickets fell, giving me hope even as Pakistan stayed abreast of the run rate. And then, unbelievably in the year 2007 in New York City, the lights went out. A power failure rendered my computer monitor quiet and dark. I stared at the screen in disbelief: the combined dysfunctional Third Worldness of India and Pakistan brought together in a cricket World Cup and attended to by millions of their fans the world over had overpowered New York City's power supply. The curse of the outage, which had invariably fallen on me during big games back home, had followed me here and left me, as always, incoherent with frustration.

I had but one way out. I lived just off Coney Island Avenue in Brooklyn, site of one of New York City's biggest Pakistani neighborhoods. One of the umpteen restaurants on that street would be showing the game. I headed out of my apartment, walking briskly down Coney Island Avenue, my eyes scanning the street ahead of me, my ears cocked for the sound of a cricket telecast. I saw a gaggle of Pakistani men standing on the sidewalk, peering inside a storefront. As I approached the group, my pace slowed. I was heading into a Pakistani stronghold to fly solo during a World Cup final. The last time I had seen an India-Pakistan game in New York City had been the 2003 quarterfinal in a Bangladeshi establishment in Manhattan, which had featured Indian and Pakistani fans watching together. The demographics of zip code 11218 were different; I would be on my own here. The prospect was daunting.

I would have to go undercover. I sidled up to the crowd and asked solicitously about Pakistan's progress—in Punjabi. My disguise worked; I had slipped over the Wagah border. I was one of the crowd, hoping for a Pakistani win. The nineteenth over had just begun, twenty runs were still needed, and Pakistan had two wickets in hand. A few balls later, I almost blew my cover as R. P. Singh bowled Umar Gul; I had to restrain my desire to holler. When the final over began, I did my best to join in the jubilation as Misbah clobbered Joginder Sharma for a six after a first-ball wide. One ball later, it was all over as Sreesanth held on to a failed over-the-head paddle. I was circumspect; my jubilation would have been in terribly poor taste and smacked of schadenfreude. I left quickly; I had a meeting to attend. As I walked toward campus, the jubilant text messages came in from London, Bangalore, and New Delhi. An hour later, as I sat in the faculty seminar room discussing curricular changes, I was still smiling. Format be damned: India had beaten Pakistan in a World Cup final.

The 1983 World Cup changed cricket because it turned India into a financial superpower; the 2007 World Cup transformed cricket all over again because it introduced India to Twenty20 cricket and paved the way for the Indian Premier League.

The Indian Mutiny

I HAD BEEN HEARING about Indian cricketing power since 1987, when India had been awarded the World Cup, wresting it away from Lord's and transporting it to Eden Gardens. It had been the first sign that the home of cricket could be elsewhere than England. The original locus had spoken of an archaic history; this one would supply a new version, one composed in a novel idiom. I had read many tales of Indian cricketing wealth, such as the gigantic television deals the BCCI signed that made world cricket solvent, the Indian assumption of the presidency of the ICC, and the coalitions with ICC members that produced voting patterns in India's favor. But I had understood the pro–South Asian World Cup votes over the years as mere influence of a color bloc in the ICC and not as Indian financial influence. I had paid little attention to stories of cricketing governance and television deals; the finance and administration of cricket was of no interest to me. Discussions online had resolutely centered on current games, nostalgic recollections, and player hagiography; there had been little discussion of the business side of our beloved game. During my trips to India, I had witnessed the satellite television explosion of cricket, the endless proliferation of cricket telecasts, talk shows, and players hawking everything from cricket equipment to shoes and soap. I had understood the greater visibility of cricket on Indian television as merely the latest expression of the cricket craze India always had—one manifest in the emotional longings of fans like me. The emerging television rights–based cricketing economy—the player salaries, the increased prize money, and the income inequality in cricket worldwide, which favored the BCCI—had not been visible to me.

I had become immune to stories of Indian success. When I traveled to India, I saw signs of the changes wrought in an older socioeconomic order by the new liberalized economy, but many Indian realities remained unchanged. For every gleaming new mall, there were many potholed, traffic-choked roads. For every gleaming new mansion, there was a new slum or a new rubbish dump festering in the open. For every story of social advancement, there was a tale of persistent social atavism and of unhinged violence against women, Dalits, and Muslims. If the middle-class seemed resurgent, so did nationalist, chauvinist, xenophobic sentiments that infected the nation's politics with an intolerant streak. (Pogroms had not ended either. When I had lived in India, there had been the 1984 killings of Sikhs, and when I had not, in 2002, the massacres of Muslims in Gujarat.) There were many, many tales of Indian wealth, Indian billionaires, burgeoning stock markets, and drunken nouveau riche excess in Indian cities, but much of the Indian landscape remained depressingly familiar. A veneer of luxury covered an old story of poor human development indexes and political primitivism.

Indian cricket's story was similar. Indian cricketing wealth had not translated into cricketing power on the field. India's track record remained dismal in the one dimension that every Indian fan knew to be crucial: away from the subcontinent. So long as most Indian wins came at home and followed familiar templates of competence and incompetence, its cricketing wealth meant little. We could not be considered a cricketing powerhouse if we did not have nets in every school, a stable of fast bowlers, batsmen who hooked and pulled, and consistent victories in South Africa, Australia, and England. That old longing had not gone away. I could easily parrot the level-headed analysis that suggested marking all Indian victories at home with an asterisk was unfair, but I could not stop craving series wins overseas. What was the use of multi-million-dollar television deals, with all the talk of "billions" of fans, if the images on television were the same old ones—batting collapses overseas, long days in the field, and polite speeches in defeat?

The first time I became aware of Indian administrative cricketing muscle came during the so-called Pretoria crisis in 2001, La Affaire Mike Denness.[*] When I first heard of the suspension of Indian players on a litany of disciplinary charges, including ball tampering and overly aggressive appealing during the Port Elizabeth Test against South Africa, my reaction was blasé indifference. But my reactions soon took on a sharper tone in an e-mail I exchanged with an Australian friend:

> Charge [of ball tampering] against Tendulkar: Looks bad. But the ground was wet, and there was a fair amount of mud, so I can believe his claim that he was cleaning the seam. Still, perhaps that is tampering, so, fine. The rest is just horseshit. Sehwag has been suspended for a test for excessive appealing and charging the umpire. I saw the incident and there is nothing in it that has not been done a million times worse by lots of other players. As for the business against Ganguly, well, I think cricket admins are out to discipline him. Kallis screamed abuse at Dravid the other day. Nothing happened. Old habits die hard in the white man's empire.

An old prejudice, one that underwrote a selective dispensation of justice, had been enforced again. I was used to the notion of the unhinged, irrational, excitable subcontinental, frenetic and frantic, appealing like a whirling dervish. As Alan Ross described Abdul Qadir's response to a denied appeal against Ian Botham during the 1982 tour of England: "Qadir, incensed, begins the kind of aggressive mating dance with accompanying cries that small animals produce in intense frustration."[†] These subcontinentals were drawn from the same stock as those that came to cheer them, whose support Ross described as "childishly shrill."[‡] It was in these descriptions of non-Anglo-Saxon passion, incomprehensible to older sensibilities, that I had found solidarity with Pakistan.

---

[*] Martin Williamson, "The Denness Affair," ESPNcricinfo, 15 January 2011, available at http://www.espncricinfo.com/magazine/content/story/496743.html, last accessed 26 January 2015.

[†] Patrick Eagar and Alan Ross, *Summer of the All-Rounder* (London: HarperCollins, 1982), 85.

[‡] Ibid., 92.

The contrast, the set of images that accompanied English or Australian bowlers denied an appeal versus those that accompanied the subcontinental bowler denied one, was irresistible. The Anglo-Australian confronted in an Asian or Caribbean umpire a curious, inexplicable, baffling resistance to reason. When the subcontinental confronted an Anglo-Australian umpire, the roles were neatly reversed; now blind, undirected passion ran aground on the implacable fount of that same cricketing reason. Reason and rationality were not to be found in the cricketing roles of player or umpire but in the nationality that went with them. In these circumstances, a brown man charging a white umpire—excitability meeting imperturbability—was never going to look good. I had learned as much in the racial politics of the United States, where a black man walking down the street in the evening conveyed threat to white neighborhood watchers and police officers, but the deadly threat posed by armed white police officers in a black neighborhood was never reckoned with, even as they shot a black man dead every twenty-eight hours.

I thought of the fast bowlers and fielders who over the years had sledged and abused Indian batsmen and intimidated Indian umpires without fear of retaliation or punishment. (Alan Donald's foul-mouthed tirade against Rahul Dravid in 1996 was a notable instance of this kind of unpunished behavior.) For as long as I could remember, the Indian on the field had adopted one demeanor: the batsman staring back at the bowler, perturbed and bemused by a fast bowler's snarl; as the verbals were sent his way, the batsman answered with an uneasy smile or a turning away. The constant television replays of the Australian or English fast bowler's aggressive stare, the thinly concealed, one-step-away-from-fisticuffs verbals, and the send-offs with the arm pointing to the pavilion had been visible for a very long time on Indian television. They had been talked about and written about; they were now part of the adornments of the modern game. The aggressive appeal, the rush toward the umpire, and the standing around in dismay and disbelief—all part and parcel of the arsenal for subjecting umpires and batsmen to pressure—were now visible on screens everywhere. They had long been part of the armory with which many teams had successfully battered down the gates to the raised finger.

Those Indian kids who had been brought up on a diet of satellite television had seen these gestures and mannerisms for a long time. They had also seen—more uncomfortably, thanks to the close-up and the slow-motion replay—that their cricketers did not seem to want to fight back or to talk back. Instead, the players took refuge in codes of conduct that were not operative around them and were content with gold stars for good behavior. Their fans had come to sense the manners and the rituals of an ostensibly genteel society, violated with expediency and impunity, did little for them. Exhortations to behave were repeated like chants with magical powers, but Indian youngsters had seen that the victors' other principles—a willingness to cut corners defended in the name of gamesmanship, sharp practice, and playing the game "hard but fair"—worked everywhere. The Indian fan and the Indian player had seen the system, and the system did not work.

I had often cursed the lack of Indian aggressiveness and welcomed signs of it in the new-look Indian team. These penalties and reprimands, the responses of match referees and umpires, and the efforts to enforce a disciplinary code indicated a young, aggressive team being taken down a peg. Indian volatility in the field stood out as a novelty: sledging and bristling aggressiveness was associated with Australian and South African teams. They would not be penalized for displaying commonplace behavior, but those that did not do it often enough would be. When the Indian player did talk back, he was warned for having crossed a line, one drawn up somewhere in a planning salon unknown, its boundaries mysteriously unspecified.

Match referees knew of the existence and location of this line and were able to view the behavior of the Anglo-Australian–South African combine through a lens that cast a suitable interpretive light over their actions and fitted them into categories more amenable to a forgiving understanding. When, during India's 1999–2000 tour of Australia, Venkatesh Prasad was hauled up for aggressive celebrations following the fall of a wicket,* he might have considered himself to be merely exultant, but to those on the outside it spoke of something else: a set of gestures out of place on a stage suited to displays of body language cast from historical molds fashioned over the years. Match referees had added a layer of judgment over and above the umpires; they were jolted out of their dogmatic slumbers when they saw behavior they could not or would understand. Often, it was the dancer that was the problem, not the dance itself.

There were many who egged on the Indian team and who wanted to see more aggressiveness on the field. One of the most satisfying aspects of the 2001 series win against Australia had been the revelation that the Indian team under Ganguly had sledged the Australians, that the close-in fielders had chattered away like magpies, setting up a chorus that "mentally disintegrated" the Australian batsmen. The Indian captain, Ganguly, had led the choir. Indeed, even the normally gentlemanly, shy, and reticent Tendulkar had sledged Steve Waugh, setting up his "handled the ball"

---

* ESPNcricinfo Staff, "Venkatesh Prasad Fined for Pumped-Up Celebration," 27 December 1999, available at http://www.espncricinfo.com/ci/content/story/79190 .html, last accessed 26 January 2015.

dismissal at Chennai. The great Australian captain was hoisted on his own petard, mentally disintegrated by the same strategies he had championed.

Most telling were the reactions to it all. Now India was the despoiler of cricketing traditions and Australia the upholder. Ganguly managed to induce in all of Australia a collective conniption, an outpouring of enraged emotion that used to be reserved for the archetypal Pommy. But a Pommy was still recognizable, still familiar; your Australian friend might have had a pair of Pommy parents in Sydney or Melbourne. With the Indian player, with the Indian captain, there was no such familiarity. And, too, with the English fan and the English journalist, who were brought up on a diet of cricket writing that spoke of Indians in much the same language as those intrepid travelers of the nineteenth century in the Indian subcontinent did, who regarded Indians as exotic—as in Alan Ross's invocation of "fakir" in referring to Viswanath*—or mild-mannered and vaguely obsequious. It was never going to be easy to let go of such archaic stereotypes.

The Indian team's on-field demeanor—and its fans' support of it—could be understood as a protest. It was thus subject to the usual strictures that it be cast in forms most amenable to those subject to the protest. But the anger of the Indian fan was underwritten too, by the disappointment that the on-field contretemps were not backed up by cricketing performance. No matter how much you egged on the in-your-face tactics, what you really wanted was the West Indies' 5–0 score line with its opponents and its location. That contributed to Indian fans' increasing frustration: Here was financial power, here was the right aggression. Where were the results?

The tampering charge too—a slur leveled by an Englishman in South Africa, a representative of the ICC, an administrative body headed by an Australian—touched a raw nerve. I was sick and tired of the wily subcontinental tag that was extended even to those Indian managers of cricket who had made cricket financially solvent in the 1980s after years of bumbling, amateurish management by those paragons of cricketing spirit, the Anglo-Australian cabal. Thanks to the Pakistani fast bowlers' escapades on the 1992 tour† and Mutthiah Muralitharan's throwing controversy,‡ messing with the cricket ball was now reckoned a "South Asian thing." We

* Eagar and Ross, *Summer of the All-Rounder*, 51.

† Martin Williamson, "An Establishment Fudge," ESPNcricinfo, 25 September 2010, available at http://www.espncricinfo.com/magazine/content/story/478574 .html, last accessed 26 January 2015.

‡ Chloe Saltau and Andrew Wu, "The Day a Throw Changed the Game," *Sydney Morning Herald*, 26 December 2012, available at http://www.smh.com.au/sport /cricket/the-day-a-throw-changed-the-game-20121225-2bvab.html, last accessed 26 January 2015.

were always a bit devious, a bit underhanded. The modern ball-tampering and throwing South Asian was the latest instance of the shifty corner shop owner, the greasy convenience store manager who stocked expired milk, the dishonest coolie who overcharged for carrying a few heavy bags a hundred meters or so, the lazy native that sought underhand methods to do a hard day's work. The difference in the initial treatment of Michael Atherton in his ball-tampering case by Peter Burge was instructive: for Burge, Atherton's word as English captain was good enough.* Tendulkar's personal statement that he had done nothing illegal was not for Denness. The word of the "native" never would be; face-value understandings of his pronouncements were always to be accused of bad faith.

Because I was unaware of BCCI influence, I saw its reaction to Denness's charges as colonials standing up to the imperial ICC; it was the interpretive framework I deployed. I had read many stories of how ICC voting patterns had changed in response to the presence of the BCCI, how the old guard was suitably resentful of the new guard, how cricket's "colored folk"—the West Indies, Pakistan, Sri Lanka—were part of a new color divide in cricket. This was the time for the colored folks to speak up. Even as the BCCI protested the charges and demanded Denness's replacement as match referee for the next Test in Pretoria, I was ready for a split to take place in the ICC, for the Asian countries to break away. I wanted them to go all the way, to take the ICC on, to defy them till the end of the affair. Every bit of pent-up resentment—a bilious mix generated by those early years in the United States and the endless suggestions we were emasculated perennial ninety-seven-pounders—rose up in me, and urged the BCCI to take on the fight. It did, but the resolution was deeply unsatisfying; the Pretoria Test was declared unofficial and the BCCI compromised. I had been ready to scuttle the ship, but the BCCI preferred its own brand of brinksmanship.

The next time I was exposed to BCCI power was during "Monkeygate," when Harbhajan Singh—India's hotheaded and foul-mouthed off-spinner, a card-carrying member of the new brigade—had run afoul of Australia's equally hotheaded and foul-mouthed all-rounder Andrew Symonds, never shy of a word or two on the field. Singh had supposedly subjected the mixed-race Symonds to racial abuse, calling him a monkey, and had been hauled up for disciplinary action, including possibly a ban. The Australians had however not abided by their own self-professed principles that

---

* Andrew Miller, "The Dirt in the Pocket Affair," ESPNcricinfo, 11 September 2004, available at http://www.espncricinfo.com/magazine/content/story/143193.html, last accessed 26 January 2015.

what happened on the ground stayed right there, to "Leave it out on the paddock, mate." They had chosen to find a line in the sand, one not drawn up in consultation with the Indian team. With an inner moral conscience no one else had access to, they had decided Harbhajan Singh needed to be taught a lesson, to be turned in, reported, punished. No one should be under any illusion that Australian sledging was of the lighthearted bantering variety, and Symonds was no angel himself, having chosen to instigate the confrontation with Singh.

I constructed the following analogy at Eye on Cricket:

A women's basketball game in the WNBA is underway. One player on a team is a lesbian and is out of the closet. It's a public, well-known fact. This same player, let's call her Lauren, is playing defense. A player from the opposing team goes up for a shot. Lauren jumps up, blocks it, and yells in the other player's face "Get out of my goal, you bitch!" The opponent yells back, "Fuck you, you dyke." At this, Lauren goes over to the referee, and complains. The referee reports this to WNBA officials, who bring disciplinary proceedings under the WNBA's code of conduct and suspend the opponent player for three matches.

I then ask my audience, has justice been served? To render the analogy more exact, I say that the same pair of players was involved in a spat a few games before, that Lauren was called a "dyke" then as well (once again, in a situation which she might have provoked), that Lauren instigated at least two other clashes with other players on the same team, and that at various away games, Lauren was subsequently heckled as a "dyke" by the home team's fans (the home team in this case being the banned player's). I then ask, does the three-match ban make sense? Interestingly enough, no one who has heard this story thinks the three-match ban is justified, and everyone thinks that "if Lauren wants to do a whole lot of trash-talking on the court, she should just deal with it."*

But I refused to consider the Harbhajan-Symonds fiasco, and the associated Indian complaints about umpiring, as the reason for India's loss in the controversial, infamous 2008 Sydney Test, one that soured Indian-

---

* Samir Chopra, "Just a Small Analogy," Eye on Cricket, 29 January 2008, available at http://eye-on-cricket.blogspot.com/2008/01/just-small-analogy.html, last accessed 26 January 2015.

Australian cricketing relations. Even as I knew the umpiring by neutral umpires was incompetent, I also knew why India had lost at Sydney. It had batted poorly, and it had lost three wickets in four balls on the last day. India had never, ever, by going on the front foot, put Australia on the back foot. Umpiring decisions should not have derailed the Indian cricketers; they had to be bloody-minded enough to get over them, to resist stubbornly. Yet again, my desire for off-field resistance was brought up short by the realization that the resistance that mattered, the one I truly craved, was with bat and ball. If those would be wielded better, then here would be little need for these off-field battles. I did not think the ICC and its match referees and umpires were the ones holding up Indian cricketing progress. That lack of competency with bat and ball was an Indian failing.

The story of the Indian Cricket League (ICL) made clear to me what power the BCCI could command; till then the complaints from other sources—Anglo-Australian ones—had fallen on deaf ears. It was only then that I began, finally, as a forty-year-old cricket fan, to understand a dimension of cricket I had never understood before. That change came about because of the Indian cricket player.

The Indian Cricket League

IN *BRAVE NEW PITCH*: *The Evolution of Modern Cricket*, analyzing a cricket world rapidly changing in response to the Indian Premier League (IPL), I noted:

> While the BCCI now gives Indian players, international and domestic, 26 per cent of its gross annual revenues, it has done little to promote player autonomy or ownership of the game. The Indian player, cognizant of the fickleness of the BCCI, is predisposed to make the most of his possibly truncated relationship with riches and fame. He understands the BCCI, whether in dealing with temperamental talent or with professional ambition, has not been afraid to be ruthlessly autocratic. There is ample historical precedent in the tales of Lala Amarnath's return from England after the 1936 tour, Vinoo Mankad's troubles in playing for Haslingden in the Lancashire Leagues in 1952, the various difficulties Indian players have faced in representing English county sides, the banning of half-a-dozen Test cricketers for playing unauthorized cricket in the US in 1989, the denial of permission to players to

participate in the Sri Lankan Premier League in 2011, and of course, the ICL.*

The Indian Premier League was formed as a reaction—I use that word advisedly, with its attendant political connotations of counterrevolution—to the Indian Cricket League, a renegade cricket league that dared to encroach on the BCCI's turf, that gate-crashed "official" cricket's party by signing up Indian and overseas cricket players to play in a Twenty20 tournament. As the BCCI cracked the whip on the ICL with a series of bans and retaliatory measures—such as preventing ICL games from being staged in stadiums managed by cricket associations affiliated with the BCCI and declaring past champions like Kapil Dev persona non grata for their involvement with the league—behaving like the worst monopolists, protecting their "brand" (Indian cricket) and their "property" and "investments" (Indian players), my pendulum swung the other way. I had never, and have never since, felt such unhinged anger at cricket administrators. The immediate target of this ire was Lalit Modi, the BCCI's new enfant terrible, a hustler and dealer nonpareil.

As I wrote in Eye on Cricket, "I've always detested this loathsome, greasy-mannered corporate type, but with the latest set of pronouncements on how counties shouldn't sign ICL players, he's outdone himself, and put a few standard deviations between himself and the average person on my shitlist. Because Modi sounds and acts like a real old-fashioned *zamindar*, and that type of creature needs a good old booting around the park from all and sundry."† In a later post, I continued:

> Modi is a *zamindar* incarnate. If he didn't have to wear a suit, and be bound by law, he'd be running around flogging peasants and repossessing their homes. He doesn't give a rat's arse about Test cricket. He doesn't give a rat's arse about developing cricket at the grassroots level in India. Why doesn't he, rather than concentrating all his energies on the IPL, put up a cricket net in every single residential neighborhood in all major metropolitan centers in India? Modi is a corporate suit, who happens to be running a game. He'll make money. Good for him. . . . If he happens to shit all over

---

* Chopra, *Brave New Pitch*, 69–70.

† Samir Chopra, "Return of the Feudal Lord," Eye on Cricket, 1 March 2008, available at http://eye-on-cricket.blogspot.com/2008/03/return-of-feudal-lord.html, last accessed 26 January 2015.

the game that matters the most to me, he wouldn't give a damn. Don't expect me to like someone who sounds like a prick, talks like a prick, walks like a prick. Even if he happens to be a rich one.*

India occupied the position the old boards had in the past; now they were the ones full of the swagger, the bluster, the money, the big mouths, and the greasy talk. While I had not been paying attention, preferring to keep my eye on bat and ball, the Indian board, and Indian cricket, had gone from being supplicants to supremos. They could now tell other boards of cricket control where their players could play, and they could draw on the inequities always implicit in the international labor cartel the world of international cricket was and exploit them to their advantage. ICL players could not play in BCCI tournaments; nor could they play elsewhere in the world of official cricket, because to do so required the permission of the BCCI. They were lepers: no one could play against them or with them for fear of offending the BCCI. Persona non grata did not begin to describe this expulsion, this banishment to Coventry. It was a treatment that would not have been permitted by employment or labor law in any self-respecting legal jurisdiction, but in the world of international cricket, it was business as usual.

The treatment of the ICL players was unmistakably feudal: they were the serfs, and the BCCI was the landowner. Even if the ICL's owners could take care of themselves, Indian players could not. I had seen Indian players—on college teams—touch the feet of their coaches; this classic Indian expression of respect for the teacher was the banner gesture of the inegalitarianism that was the hallmark of Indian life. The BCCI's office bearers were the ones who would get their feet touched by the players; they would demand such fealty as their right. I could just imagine, as in a tableau from a Shyam Benegal movie, which sought to capture the unique Indian dysfunction of unequal power in its hinterlands, a cricket player being brought to meet a BCCI official and being told by his handler to touch his feet; the humble lungi-wearing peasant would comply. I knew enough of the inegalitarianism of Indian society that this was no idle fantasy. In a land where first names were not common, where everyone said "Sir" and was made to bow and scrape in the face of a superior, there would be little fighting back.

The ICL was where I parted ways with the Indian fan online. We might have been fans of the same cricket team and thus ostensibly of the same

____

* Samir Chopra, "How Many Ways Do I Dislike Thee, Lalit Modi?" Eye on Cricket, 20 April 2009, available at http://eye-on-cricket.blogspot.com/2009/04/how-many-ways-do-i-dislike-thee-lalit.html, last accessed 26 January 2015.

nation, but I could not abide the BCCI. Over and above every story of its corruption—as it turned a blind eye to match-fixing and failed to support women's cricket—this heavy-handed treatment of the Indian player became the proverbial straw. I had steadfastly remained oblivious to critiques of the BCCI. I would glower with resentment if the ICC's Malcolm Speed were to castigate the BCCI.* I could throw in my lot behind the BCCI's financial muscle, and I enjoyed the spectacle of making the ICC's members squirm for BCCI approval. I had reveled in this new power, this expression of old resentments. I had made much of the old veto power of the Anglo-Australian guard and how it had used it, and how the shoe was on the other foot. I considered the Anglo-Australian guard hypocritical and self-satisfied, and in *Brave New Pitch*, I pointed out how the journalistic rhetoric directed at the Indian team and the BCCI—even though the BCCI had done a great deal to provoke that reaction—was bound to raise Indian hackles like mine.† Our antennae finely tuned, we could always detect patronizing tones in external critiques of the BCCI. When Indians—like those magisterial worthies Ramachandra Guha and Mukul Kesavan—wrote searching critiques of Indian power in cricket, they came to rest within me. Others, written elsewhere, I could not abide. All because I had never put a face to the BCCI's muscle, to the face being stomped on by the BCCI's boot. It was that of the Indian player.

The history of cricket had produced an insurrection led by the BCCI that was underwritten by the wrong lessons learned. That revolt enlisted many to its cause who felt solidarity with the BCCI for purely nationalistic reasons—because the BCCI had succeeded in conflating itself with India and Indian cricket. But much in the way the modern model of consumption of the East aped the worst aspects of the West's technical and material advancement—relentless consumerism and rapacious, selfish, and shortsighted commercial instincts—and threatened to destroy this world's environment, the BCCI had only learned how to bully and boss and jeopardize world cricket. Cricket was the latest instance of the golden goose with its head on the chopping block, facing the axe of its greedy, myopic executioners. Because money came to cricket via the television deal, everything was subservient to it: the relentlessly scheduled calendar, the commercials, and the slow pitches that guaranteed five days of cricket. The famed veto power of the Anglo-Australian cabal in the ICC was re-

---

* Siddarth Vaidyanathan, "Money Alone Can't Buy Success," ESPNcricinfo, 1 November 2006, available at http://www.espncricinfo.com/ci/content/story/266507 .html, last accessed 26 January 2015.

† Chopra, *Brave New Pitch*, 162–166.

placed by the BCCI's moneyed power; what it wanted, it got. The IPL's season was not in sync with international cricket's calendar; the BCCI did not care. The BCCI wanted only to play against the Big Three—England, Australia, and South Africa; it did not care for associate members of the ICC; it did not care to nurture the game that had made it rich by taking care of it elsewhere. In starting up the endlessly scandal-ridden IPL, it made clear it regarded cricket as a cash cow to be milked, a property to be rented out. No wonder the politicians and businesspeople who ran the BCCI wanted in; they wanted a piece of the action. They knew they could draw on the new fervor of the India Shining crowd; they could conflate the Indian team with the BCCI playing eleven. Few noticed that the Indian team did not wear the Indian tricolor when they played but rather the logo of the BCCI.

I cared little for the IPL's balance sheets; I took little pride in the numbers thrown at me about how it was the world's richest league. I wanted away wins; I wanted fast bowlers; I wanted a good fielding side. I felt a curious hollowness as Indian cricket successes remained hard to come by. Even as I defended franchise cricket's promise in *Brave New Pitch* and argued that it could lead to a welcome displacement of the power of national cricket boards, a more open labor market in cricket, and better labor relations, I knew that for someone like me, raised on a diet of international cricket, the only successes that would matter would be in a distinctive domain. I was fuming again at the Indian cricket team: Why could it not win in old venues of defeat and disaster? Australia could; it came to India and won in 2004–2005. Most gallingly of all, England refused to go under easily and kept on drawing blood, time and again refusing to fall apart obligingly like the tourists of old. Indeed, after handing out a 4–0 thumping to India at home in 2011, England came to India and won 2–1 in 2012, including a win delivered by its spinners on a turning track made for Indian ones. Test series wins overseas and World Cup wins—these were the currencies I wanted to trade in. The BCCI's monies, the IPL's wealth, did little to realize these aspirations.

Indeed, matters were now worse. When India had been resource-strapped and mediocre overseas, its players could have been reckoned plucky fighters, overcoming adversity to stand bravely on the world stage. But the narrative of wealth attached to the BCCI had changed the rhetorical pitch in describing Indian cricket. Now it was the home of cricketing millionaires, of Bollywood-connected stars hobnobbing with the rich and famous, dancing with Bollywood stars on television, arriving at cricket stadiums like English Premier League stars with headphones on. (Some had glamorous girlfriends and wives too.) Somehow, we had become the Americans of the cricket world without the medal tally to show for it. I could have put up with this material excess if it had had the stamp of cricketing success. I wished the story of Indian cricketing success would be rounded out with a denouement that would deliver fans like me from our prolonged vigils. But the Godot of Indian cricket refused to play ball.

India, we were told, is the world's richest cricketing nation. But after many years of the financial domination of the BCCI, India was still not rich in cricketing terms. The BCCI's fortunes had not flowed back into local development schemes for cricket; there were no BCCI-subsidized cricket nets at schools and colleges. The BCCI had not upgraded cricket facilities across the country so that the next generation of cricketers could grow up with ready access to the game. Instead, it dispensed largesse to incompetently administered state cricket associations in India and asked for no financial accounting, no assessment of cricketing outcomes. Cricket was a cash cow, and the devotion of the Indian cricket fan was an easily exploited quantity. In the new India, infected by the neoliberal, globalizing spirit, it was the perfect target.

I found myself unable to support the BCCI—a clumsy and cynical manipulator of power—because I could not identify with its officials. I could not support the BCCI even if it was a symbol of India, because it stood for the wrong kind of India: corporate and corrupt. I had seen behind the veil of the Indian team; the "national team" was a conventional arrangement, propped up by historical contingency. Sometime in Indian cricket's hoary past, an organization had placed itself in charge of Indian cricket and retained its first-mover status to ensure no competitors would emerge. The BCCI's officials were like those bureaucrats who had blocked my Indian dreams; they had blocked my father's and my mother's dreams too. Those who ran the BCCI resembled those neighbors of ours who had once harassed my mother and brother when our presence in the street we lived on had irked them; they resembled those cliché-spouting corporate types I disliked intensely. They might have been Indian, but I felt no solidarity with them.

Patriotism had become a much more contested notion for me. I did not feel unambiguously Indian. (I did not feel unambiguously American either.) Like those who had resisted that label because of their ethnicities and languages and cultures in the Indian nation that claimed them, I resisted it because of other affiliations I felt. I was an "American progressive" now. It was scarcely credible to me that I was a nationalist sports fan online. I was a hypocrite, railing against the tacky nationalism in the Republican Party and in conservative political animals but dipping into it myself when it came to sport. More than ever, I felt the discordance between what I wrote online in non-cricketing forums and the way I pungently expressed myself when I spoke to other cricket fans.

Now too, I consciously sought to distance myself from any such straightforward nationalist orientation, because, quite bluntly, it was not as sophisticated a political and intellectual stance as others I could take on. Not for the first time, I found myself regretting the older intemperate self who had left traces of his immaturity online. Thin-skinned Indian patriots, resident online or abroad, were ubiquitous; they were younger versions of myself. Their response to critiques of the BCCI's operations or the influence of Indian cricket on world cricket was like my older, defensive pronouncements online. They possessed, like me, sensitive, finely tuned radar that easily detected colonial stereotypes and archaic prejudices. I often agreed with them, but I could not join in their reflexive defenses of the BCCI, not because I did not smart as they did but because I could not defend the men who were the face of Indian cricket. I could defend the Indian player but not those who supervised him.

Coda

THERE ARE MANY PRISMS through which to view cricket: as a game, a national encounter, a pastime, an opportunity to view the human body in action. No cricket fan has a simple following of the game. No sport fan ever does. It's never just wood on leather or hitting little balls into the ground. Our appreciation is never an unmediated take on the game. There are always interpretive filters through which our sporting experience passes and finally comes to rest. We might crave unmediated experience in a wishful dream for an unattainable innocence, but there is none. The emotional coloring the spectator supplies is a vital and essential part of the game; it lends meaning to a meaningless activity.

I began this book with how cricketing fantasies can be revealing of much more. My own cricketing fantasies revealed the diminished sense of myself and my country as I grew up in India. Years later, I have found cricketing fantasies centered on India. The fantasies are different, the feats slightly altered, and the aspects of my heroes I choose to emphasize are different. They sledge their opponents, speak articulately and honestly to the press, take on the BCCI, fight for player's rights, and seek to become owners and managers of cricket—the game that nurtured them and offered them a means of livelihood. As my cricketing fantasies changed to those of an Indian fan, I stopped living in India, moved to another country, and then another, and much changed along the way. My place in life changed and in response, so did my reactions to Indian cricket.

Cricket might not retain its place in the Indian imagination. This displacement will be accelerated if Indians succeed in other international sports and siphon attention and sponsor monies away from cricket. It might accelerate too, if Indians come to expect more Indian success and find it elsewhere, on other domains. Cricket itself will shrivel up if the BCCI draws all nourishment to itself and refuses to water cricket's roots. But it will not be alone in the dock; cricket's abiding colonial legacies will have played an equally pernicious role.

The Indian team remained, in many ways, the same. There were some high points and plenty of low ones. The general confusion, disarray, and flashes of brilliance that mark Indian cricket still manifest themselves. Other disillusionments and new love affairs happened over the years. The English team I thought represented glamour came to represent a reactionary cricket body, and the English press I thought represented the fount of cricketing wisdom became associated with patronizing self-centeredness. The Australian team that supplied my childhood heroes of fantasy became associated with the slogan, "We can dish it out, but we can't take it." The West Indies team—so powerful that reading the word *West Indies* produced awe—became associated with mediocrity. And the South Africans, whose return from an exile I thought was an event on par with the fall of the Berlin Wall, became new rivals, worthy of vanquishing in their own lair. I do not adore teams or cricketers with the fervor of my childhood days. Now they are human, flawed in all their varied ways. Some of these changes are the inevitable result of childhood hero worship being tempered by reality. And some are because I left home and encountered the cricket world through the unique medium of the Internet.

I have, with deliberateness, made much of my encounters online. I grew up in a world of print media, then live television, and then cricket on the Internet. First, I encountered the distant wisdom of the former masters of cricket, then I encountered less exalted representatives. The endless flame wars, the nationalist disputes online, and the discursive space the Internet provided often made me view cricket in a light that unrelentingly emphasized the often-ugly conflict among its fans. The Internet was that uniquely human creation, that immediately ambiguous medium; if I encountered wisdom online, I also encountered great prejudice. Once I could only watch cricket on television and then discuss it in person with my friends. Now I can only watch and discuss cricket online. Unless I stop talking about cricket, I'm stuck encountering the best and the worst of online cricket.

The story of my relationship with Pakistan and its team is one of disappointment, of a kid unable to hold on to his childhood heroes. In my encounters with Pakistanis online, I desperately wanted to read words of conciliation, words that would acknowledge the humanity Pakistanis must have known existed across the border. That Pakistanis liked Indian movies was no consolation. I wanted more evidence of a conciliatory spirit than being able to joke in Urdu or Punjabi about harmless topics. But because they and I, approached our virtual encounters with the baggage of times and ages gone by, we found its barriers insuperable. Such a story about naivete should be worth telling. I wonder how such a story would be told by a Pakistani fan, what its twists and turns would be, who its heroes and villains would be, and what the author would reveal about him- or herself in doing so. For my part, I brought to my cricket watching too many unresolved internal battles; too many feuds, psychological and political, were to be settled for me on a cricket field. But cricket has afforded me a lens with which to think about colonialism, globalization, labor relations, and media. To leave cricket would be to impoverish my life. What would I of cricket know, if only cricket I knew?

I never intended this book to be the record of a reasonable man, but someone who was always aware he was not watching a mere game when he saw cricket being played. I have a Ph.D. in philosophy, but reason and argumentation are easily subverted by emotion. I never intended this book to be academic. That would take me too far from the immediacy of the emotions I try to relate. I purposely chose not to research the sociological details of the time period I wrote about. I do not want to indicate a depth to my knowledge I did not possess then. I have sought to report my responses as they occurred to me. Telling me I'm naive or that I only have access to a very partial picture is missing the point. Still, in making these confessions here, in offering what might pompously be called honesty, I wonder if they are self-serving, made in the expectations of forgiveness. If I express the opinions I held in the past, or whose traces survive now, but do so only to psychologize or sociologize them into bland inoffensiveness, then I have not done much except assure like-minded folks we have comfortable consensus. So I plead guilty to all those baser emotions I have often put on display in my writings online and to all the dangerous flirtations with intolerance I have indulged over the years.

I'm Indian by birth but have not lived in India for thirty-three years now. I hold a U.S. passport. I came from a socioeconomic milieu common to millions of urbanized Indians, and I followed a path common to many Indians: I emigrated. I chose to live abroad, and I chose to not return. I'm a cliché: the immigrant, romanticizing his homeland, taking his resentments at the loss of his imagined dream and the insults he suffered overseas and channeling them into a hoped-for expression on the sporting field. I plead guilty to that charge. My relationship with cricket and the rest of the world was mediated by my distance from my imagined homeland. My reactions might indicate responses that would not have occurred had I continued to stay in India. But, given the histories of the two countries since 1987, my reactions might have been modified in roughly the same trajectory as the one that I describe here. My living outside India meant I would be exposed to utterances emitted by people like me, defending a land that has moved on without them.

The Indian win in Kolkata in 2001 forced me to start writing this book, and the changes in the management of world cricket that might produce a new colonial fiefdom provided the appropriate coda.* I will continue to change; cricket will too. My cricketing life is not yet over.

---

* Sharda Ugra, "Big Three Could Control Revamped ICC," ESPNcricinfo, 17 January 2014, available at http://www.espncricinfo.com/ci-icc/content/story/710723.html, last accessed 26 January 2015.

Postscript

ALL SPORTS FANS ARE SUSTAINED by white ravens, the sights we imagine are ruled out by improbabilities but which bring us back to the "action" again and again, hoping against hope and empirical plausibility, letting their associated dreams and wonderings live and flower within us, because it is they and not anything else, that grant meaning to otherwise absurd activity. Over the years, as the preceding pages have hopefully shown, my cricketing fantasies, created and sustained over decades of cricket spectatorship and its interactions with the events in my inner and outer lives, morphed and grew new forms reflecting my changing self and my most deeply felt inclinations and desires. For this aggrieved, "homesick" postcolonial, it was not enough to beat old foes—England and Australia especially—in facile fashion at home. Cricketing adversity—match situations, ground conditions, injuries, hostile opponents—had to be overcome; ideally, away from home. Resistance had to be enacted, figuratively and literally, in the right venues.

India won in Australia in 2018/2019, marching across a figurative "final frontier" and affording another sighting of the white raven first glimpsed at Kolkata in 2001, but without adequately satisfying my daydreaming impulses. The Australian team was crucially weakened; the Indians lost at Perth, supposedly the fastest wicket in Australia; Virat Kohli lost the battle of the big mouths to Tim Paine, the Australian captain. But India's series win over Australia in January 2021 did it all. India won on the last day of the last Test of a series that began with them collapsing to their lowest score in Test cricket. They came back in the second Test to win; they drew the third Test after batting out the final day; they won the fourth Test by three wickets with a feisty youngster leading the way. They lost their captain and their first eleven; they mastered a three-pronged barrage of witless player sledging, press sniping, and racial fan abuse. No other team in cricket's history has overcome so many adversities away from home to win in a former domain of subjugation—reams will soon be written in an attempt to understand just what transpired on Australian cricket grounds in the antipodean summer of 2021. My fantasy did not come to fruition in one day; instead, improbabilities built and simmered over the course of a series, finally coming to a head on a glorious afternoon in Brisbane, delivering a result that will reconfigure the writing of future cricketing histories.

The white ravens my cricketing fandom will now seek will be of an entirely different plumage. I look forward to their sightings.

Index

Samir Chopra is a Professor in the Department of Philosophy at Brooklyn College of the City University of New York. He is the author of *Eye on Cricket: Reflections on the Great Game*, and coauthor of *Decoding Liberation: The Promise of Free and Open Source Software* and *A Legal Theory for Autonomous Artificial Agents*.